44⁹⁵

ROYAL DRESS

The Image and the Reality 1580 to the present day

ROYAL DRESS

The Image and the Reality 1580 to the present day

Valerie Cumming

HM

Holmes & Meier
New York

Published in the United States of America 1989 by
Holmes & Meier Publishers, Inc.
30 Irving Place
New York, NY 10003

Library of Congress Cataloging-in-Publication Data

Cumming, Valerie.
Royal Dress
Bibliography: p.
1. Costume — England — History.
2. England — Courts and courtiers — Costume — History.
I. Title.
GT733.C77 1989   391′.22′0941   88-34741

ISBN 0-8419-1267-X

Typeset by Lasertext Ltd.,
Stretford, Manchester, England
and printed in Great Britain by
The Bath Press, Avon

CONTENTS

ACKNOWLEDGEMENTS

I am particularly grateful to my editors at Batsford – firstly Belinda Baker, and then Rachel Wright – for their considerable patience and support as this book metamorphosed from a picture book on royal and court dress into something more substantial. The responsibility for its idiosyncratic approach is mine, but I would like to offer my thanks to the many colleagues and friends who have discussed the subject with me, and have contributed ideas for reading and illustration: most notably, Olivia Bland, Celina Fox and Aileen Ribeiro. My colleagues at the Museum of London have, with their customary good humour and efficiency, assisted in a variety of ways, and I would like to record my appreciation of the help I received from Davina Fennemore; the staff of the library; the paintings, prints and drawings department; and photographic services.

As always, my especial gratitude is reserved for my husband, who was both encouraging and remarkably good-humoured about a project which lasted for more than four years.

Lastly, I must acknowledge my gratitude to the many authors, listed in the footnotes and select bibliography, whose analyses of royalty and 'the upper ten thousand' have helped to enrich and clarify my ideas about royal dress and English court life.

LIST OF ILLUSTRATIONS

PROLOGUE

Princes know themselves to be princes, and are not snobs; besides they believe themselves to be so far above everything that is not of their blood royal that great nobles and 'business men' appear, in the depths beneath them, to be practically on a level.

Proust's description of the attitude of royalty differs little from Machiavelli's recommendations to his prince regarding princely behaviour, although four centuries divide these two views of this select minority. In Chapter 21 of *The Prince* there are a number of observations on the subject of how an intelligent prince should conduct himself in order to gain the respect of his subjects. Amongst these courses of action the outward manifestations which play such an important part in princely propaganda are described: the prince 'ought to entertain the people with festivals and spectacles at convenient seasons of the year... show himself an example of courtesy and liberality; nevertheless, always maintaining the majesty of his rank, for this he must never consent to abate in anything.'[1] The English monarchy has, over many more than four centuries, proved itself erratically capable of producing rulers who have combined princely condescension with showmanship and undoubted power. The purpose of this book is to examine one of these elements: the appearance of royalty and their courtiers, engaged, primarily, in those 'festivals and spectacles' which Machiavelli recommended.

The competitive visual propaganda of Renaissance and later European courts thrived upon memorable set-pieces of princely magnificence – ceremonies of exclusive orders of knighthood, accession day feasts, the reception of foreign envoys at courts thronged with powerful and noble courtiers, and other similar festivities. By considering the reasons why such effects were thought necessary, how they developed and were maintained, it is possible to conjure up a world in which illusion and harsh reality were woven inextricably together to form an exclusive circle within which privileges were guarded jealously, but not closed to the ambitious and talented who were prepared to accept its rules.

As, until the second half of the nineteenth century, a sovereign's court (in England) was the fount of all substantial patronage, it was frequented by powerful subjects who 'courted' royal favour. The ritual and seasonal activities of a royal court created a momentum and a mythology which sickness, warfare, abdication, and less violent death might disrupt temporarily, but never wholly change. The survival of princes became dependent upon their aptitude for stressing historical continuity, the dignity of their role and their separateness from the vagaries of policies undertaken in their name. It was in the interests of sovereigns and their courtiers to present a situation of untroubled harmony if effective government was to flourish, and it became apparent that, from the late fifteenth century onwards, a country's major asset was a sovereign who in addition to his ability to govern ably, relished personal finery, insisted upon respectful and dignified courtiers, enjoyed antiquarian ritual and symbolism, and wished, wholeheartedly, to impress others with the splendour of his person and his court.

In writing principally, but not solely, about dress, I may be seen to be addressing a frivolous and ephemeral aspect of royal life. This would be to underestimate the import-ance of the personal and collective images of royalty to contemporary observers over four centuries. Clothing was a potent visual symbol of power and authority; in the Middle Ages kings and princes, throughout Europe, enacted laws about it – sumptuary legislation – in order to classify society. Types of material, jewellery, furs and decorative accessories were restricted according to rank, with the king and royal family enjoying the distinction of wearing the rarest, mostly costly and luxurious items. Kings and princes created exclusive orders of chivalry, with carefully designed dress and insignia as a potential reward for exceptional endeavour on behalf of the state (that is, the monarch), regardless of rank. They required their courtiers to be expensively dressed, to demonstrate national prosperity and strength; and they used artists to create images of their likeness for internal and inter-national propaganda. The royal household was the most spend-thrift and most costly employer of labour and distributor of goods in the country – open to abuse, replete with opportunities for corruption, instantly recog-nisable through its liveried servants and the patronage wielded by its greatest officials, supposedly on behalf of the sovereign.

An examination of the dress of royalty will only make sense if it takes place within its natural context – the palaces with their cour-tiers and ceremonies. Until comparatively recently, royalty lived constantly in a semi-public domain, surrounded by the extended 'family' of their large households, and regu-larly accessible to those members of society who were eligible to attend court. A hundred years ago, it would have been thought incred-ible that a royal house could thrive and prosper without the necessary foil or counter-balance of an extensive court. There was a healthy tension between royalty and their greatest subjects, with both parties given to rage and reconciliation; gracious interest and frank boredom; exploitation and cynical fas-cination. This tension was seen as a necessary element in the maintenance of a social accord, and many of those closely involved in the process of serving royalty will be examined in this book. By concentrating upon the outward and public display of royalty and the court, and the relationship between these two groups, it is possible to introduce a wide range of evidence – wardrobe accounts, diaries, letters, memoirs, contemporary journalism; illustrations ranging from formal portraits to cartoons, and surviving items of dress. It is not, however, my intention to offer more than an introduction to a subject which is voluminous and subject to partisan and anec-dotal information. In choosing, intentionally, to develop certain strands of the story – the royal partiality for uniforms and uniformity, rigorous etiquette, and patronage of British goods – I have omitted areas which other commentators on dress are better qualified to analyse in detail.

The core of this book deals with the views of participants in and observers of court life, and the relationship between the perfection which is implicit in the paintings of royalty and their courtiers, and the rivalries, disorder and confusion which such formal images dis-guised. It is a story which provides heroes and heroines, misfits and unexpected successes; it is akin to a series of theatrical set pieces, for it has much in common with theatre. It is a story which is often unintentionally absurd and occasionally tragic, but because it is about illusion and sleight-of-hand and, at the same time, about historical continuity, the dignity of a hierarchical society, and the grandeur of the state, it illuminates attitudes towards and aspects of the more obscure areas of dress.

Dress is the most fluid and ephemeral of

the minor decorative arts, constantly shifting like quick-silver, but, in this area, often preserved like a fly in amber. It can act as a disguise, armour, projection of joy or misery, flaunting of riches, uniform of exclusivity and much more. It records the translation of royalty from a context in which royal clothing was married to that of a well-trained supporting cast, to splendid, glamorous isolation. Uniforms once spelt active command; they now equate to a 'chocolate soldier' Ruritania. Diminished political power but much increased wealth and privilege has maintained the fiction of the superiority of traditional forms, but there is no apparent understanding of the historical process which ensured the incorporation of change in order to ensure continued survival. In royal terms, the medium of dress has become the message of fossilized grandeur.

I. Elizabeth I c.1592; M Gheeraerts the Younger

This portrait is related to an entertainment given in honour of the Queen in September 1592. She was on progress and stayed briefly at Ditchley, marked on the globe beneath her feet. The elongated and spikily fortress-like quality of the dress and the bejewelled magnificence of the queen's appearance convey the image of a 'pagan goddess'.

ONE

'Pompous Ceremonies' and 'Costly Apparell' 1580–1649

In 1561 the Imperial agent Coloredo had written, in a despatch to his masters, that Elizabeth I,

lives a life of magnificence and festivity such as can hardly be imagined, and occupies a great portion of her time with balls, banquets, hunting and similar amusements with the utmost possible display; but nevertheless, she insists upon far greater respect being shown to her than was exacted by the late Queen Mary...[1]

Coloredo had identified the highly developed strand of exhibitionism in Elizabeth's personality which she had inherited from her father Henry VIII and great-grandfather, Edward IV. All three were fascinated by the relationship between the exercise of power and the external manifestations of royal status. It became an essential ingredient in Tudor royal policy to attract and retain the loyalty of powerful nobles. Desire for office, favours and royal goodwill was made more attractive

2. Elizabeth I

These two engravings of the Great Seal of Elizabeth I are taken from Speed's *History of Greate Britaine*, c.1650. They depict the Queen in state on her throne, and on horseback; the latter was a tra-ditional pose for male monarchs, but the Queen carries the symbols of her office, not those of warfare. Her dress is the bulky but still relatively balanced fashion of the mid- to late 1580s.

by the knowledge that the royal court was the instigator of and arena for the most significant ceremonial and festive occasions. No ambitious individual or family wished, voluntarily, to exclude themselves from the excitement, pleasure and promise of advancement to be gained from attendance on the queen as she perambulated between her various palaces of Whitehall, Windsor, Richmond and Hampton Court.

Elizabeth expected to be:

most Royally furnished both for her person and for her train, knowing right well that in pompous ceremonies a secret of government doth much consist, for that people are naturally both taken and held with exterior shows.[2]

This emphasis upon both public and private grandeur meant that by the 1580s when Elizabeth was losing those inestimable assets for a female ruler – youth and good looks – her personal popularity, the brilliance of her court and her remarkable and diverse talents were at their height. Wholly British in parentage, without personal knowledge of foreign countries, she thrived upon self-imposed isolation, and fostered an idiosyncratically English court life in which she provided a secular focus for awe and admiration. She became that 'pagan goddess surrounded by her priests and worshippers' of whom her nineteenth-century biographer, Agnes Strickland, so disapproved.[3] A crucial adjunct to her role was an orderly, obedient but magnificent court at which household officials, courtiers and visiting embassies conformed to their allotted roles. The royal household and court were regulated by ordinances which gave precise instructions about every aspect of daily life – allowances of food and wine, liveries, furnishings – and details of behaviour expected of household officials in the exercise of their duties, and courtiers in the royal presence. Royal portraiture was similarly regulated, at the Queen's command, for she wanted no permanent reminders of the passage of time.

In the 1580s a great number of portraits, in every medium, were produced, but they presented a stylized version of the 'goddess', what Roy Strong describes as 'the creation of a legend'.[4]

At much the same time, during the last 20 years or so of Elizabeth's reign, the clothing worn at the English court became more idiosyncratic, mirroring the increasingly ornate and artificial world of the Queen and her courtiers. The English court's revival of interest in the chivalry of the mediaeval period, explored in verse, masking, tournaments such as the Accession Day tilts, and the splendid public processions and rituals of the Garter ceremony at Windsor led to curious changes in the appearance of both women and men.

Women's dress, which in the early 1580s had a full-blown but relatively balanced appearance, gradually stiffened, elongated and acquired a fragmented quality in the 1590s. Alongside such unnaturally long-waisted bodices, wide farthingales and huge, decorated sleeves, the men, whose clothing in the early 1580s suggested a complementary bulky, swaggering bravado, became slender, insubstantial, top-heavy ciphers, wearing narrow, padded doublets, shallow trunk-hose and short capes. Fashionable women had evolved into spikily-caged fortresses to which none of the apparently emasculated, dandified men would consider laying siege. It was an uncanny physical reflection of the contemporary literary descriptions of the quasi-mediaeval world of *amor courtois*, as if daily life had become 'the continual masque of outlandish habiliments' of which Thomas Nashe had written in 1593.[5]

Criticism of unusual, expensive or foreign elements in fashionable dress, epitomized by the appearance of courtiers, was a feature of English social comment throughout the centuries. There was no specified form of court dress; some of the Queen's household servants wore livery, allotted on an annual or half-

3. **James I and VI c.1610; J de Critz**
Although not dressed in the height of fashion, the King's white doublet and trunk-hose do not give the impression of carelessness or timidity, the attributes usually ascribed to him by commentators, but neither is he especially prepossessing.

yearly basis, but the majority of courtiers had to acquire and pay for their own finery. As luxury goods were all imported – silks, velvets and satins from Italy and Spain; linen from Germany and the Low Countries; lace from Italy; leather from Spain; embroidery silks, braids and ribbons from various near-Eastern and European centres; and ideas from many sources for cut and construction – there were constant criticisms. England was 'the ape of all nations' and 'there is nothing in Englande more constant, than the inconstancie of attire'.[6]

Neither courtier, such as the Earl of Leicester writing to his agent in the Low Countries to order velvets, satins, silks, cloth of gold 'or

such pretty stuff' to the value of several hundred pounds, nor Queen was deterred by this xenophobia.[7] Her wardrobe accounts are full of items made in the French, Spanish and Italian manner and her chief minister, Lord Burleigh, wrote to her ambassador in Paris enquiring about finding the Queen 'a tailor that has skill to make her apparel after the French and Italian manner'.[8] Courtiers were actively encouraged to dress fashionably, but within the limits of sumptuary legislation, for the Queen 'often chid those that bought more finery than became their state', but when everything was to her liking, 'The Queen was much in commendation of our appearances'[9].

The Queen's interest in clothing was highly developed, and she demonstrated an almost theatrical sense of dress which courtiers and visitors would expect of an attractive and powerful female ruler. Her preferred colours were black and white, the former for constancy, the latter for purity; colours and emblems–jewels or embroidery–such as the crescent moon, the pelican in its piety, the phoenix and eglantine provided subtle messages for those educated to understand such matters. She liked wit and novelty–a realistic black spider pin attached to the veil of her head-dress; a gown embroidered with flies, worms and snails; another with 'leaves, pomegranats, and men'.

Above all, however, she liked to add to her wardrobe and stock of jewellery without incurring personal expense.[10] During progresses around the country, or in the traditional presentation of New Year gifts to the monarch she expected to receive valuable gifts. These varied in value according to the donor's circumstances, from a pair of gloves to complete garments. In 1584 the Earl of Hertford and Lord Rich gave her, separately, but obviously after prior consultation, a petticoat and a doublet of 'pechecollored satten' embroidered with designs in gold and silk.[11] She took pleasure in rich gifts, but she was not extravagant, demonstrating a prudent attitude towards her clothing. A gift of a gown to a servant in 1584 was made only after the sable fur was removed, and in 1585 the remains of an old kirtle of cloth of silver was only given away after 'beinge part cut out to enlardge a paire of sleives...'.[12] Royal grandeur did not, in her mind, equal royal prodigality, but whenever it mattered she was still able to astonish visitors with the splendour of her appearance. In February 1603, shortly before her death, a Venetian envoy was confronted by a frail, but magnificent old woman covered in jewellery and wearing a dress of silver and white taffeta embroidered with gold–the living personification of one of her official portraits.[13]

The contrast between Elizabeth and her successor, James I and VI, was much more than the obvious one of an old, unmarried woman and a younger man with a wife and children. The house of Stuart was different in manner, methods and style to the inherently English Tudor dynasty. Scotland had, traditionally, looked to Europe for allies, particularly to France. James was one quarter French and his wife, Queen Anne, was wholly Danish; their alliance, and those of the next three generations of the House of Stuart, placed English royalty into a European context which was often at odds with the xenophobia of their English subjects.

In James this foreignness was unleavened by a kingly appearance. He was:

of middle stature, more corpulant through his clothes than in his body, yet fat enough, his cloathes ever being made large and easie, the doublets quilted for steletto proofe, his breeches in great pleits and full stuffed, hee was naturally of a timorous disposition, which was the reason of his quilted doublets...

James's early years in Scotland when his personal safety was often threatened and, later, the assassination of Henry IV of France in 1610 may have suggested that wariness was the better part of valour. Men's fashions in his reign used considerable amounts of padding in doublets and fullness in trunk-hose and breeches, so there is no definite evidence to support allegations of timidity.

The same commentator defined James as a creature of habit, preferring familiarity in matters of diet, travel and 'in his apparrell so constant, as by his good will he would never change his cloathes untill worn out to very ragges; his fashion never....'[14] The King's physique, with overly large head, nondescript features and ungainly limbs did not inspire awe or affection, and he made no attempt to disguise his appearance. In 1603 the observant Venetians recorded that,

from his dress (the king)... would have been taken for the meanest among the courtiers, had it not been for a chain of diamonds round his neck and a great diamond in his hat.[15]

He shared, with his subjects, a diplomatic but impractical aversion to foreign fashions, for clothing was international in both design and materials. When presented with 'a hat of Spanish block', however, 'he cast [it] from him, swearing he neither loved them nor their fashions.'[16] He was at his happiest in pursuit of good hunting, away from the circle which surrounded his wife and elder son, Henry, Prince of Wales, which emphasized cultural pursuits – painting, architecture and masking.

Criticism of clothing for its foreign aspects, its indication of political allegiance or its sheer extravagance, was, under the early Stuarts, extended to encompass moral degeneracy. The court was 'a nursery of lust an intemperance' of which courtiers 'were entertained with masks, stage playes and sorts of ruder sports' and 'wantonnesse in things belonging to the bodie is shewed in costly apparell.'[17] The King's male courtiers vied with each other to meet his requirement for 'good fashion in cloathes... good looks and handsome accoutrements', knowing that he, 'laugheth at the long grown fashion of our young courtiers and wisheth for change every day'.[18]

4. **Anne of Denmark, consort of James I & VI**

This engraving, published after the Queen's death in 1619, depicts her in her preferred, but unfashionable court style which retained a wide farthingale beneath the skirt. The Queen's fine bosom, of which she was justifiably proud, is displayed to advantage.

Perversely, the Prince of Wales, at much the same time, abandoned the frequently changing, costly French fashions for the simpler, 'more convenient' Italian styles, and was promptly congratulated by the Spanish ambassador for favouring Spanish styles![19]

It was a time of regulated confusion, with courtiers uncertain about whether to demonstrate allegiance to the King or his eldest son, Prince Henry, whether to favour the bucolic, drunken revels and corrupt political practices which characterized James's circle or the aloof, almost Puritanical chivalry and connoisseurship of the Prince's court. Henry's death in 1612, closely followed by the marriage of his beautiful sister, Princess Elizabeth to the German Prince Palatine, deprived the English court within six months of its two most lively, attractive and intelligent younger royals, creating a vacuum only partly filled by the King's favourites and the lazy frivolity of the Queen.

Queen Anne was an extravagant blonde whose good looks ran to plumpness. She had 'the finest neck that could be seen, which she took care it should by the fashions of dress which she from time to time brought up'.[20] Her preference was for low oval necklines, stiff bodices and full skirts worn over wide, tiptilted farthingales – the style favoured by Elizabeth I at the end of her life – which emphasized Anne's best features whilst disguising her ample waist and hips. The theatricality of the farthingale provided a formal grandeur unmatched by softer, less statuesque styles of dress such as night-gowns (unstructured gowns worn without a hooped petticoat), bodices, skirts, shawls and sleeveless overgowns, and it was worn, somewhat reluctantly by court ladies until the Queen's death in 1619, although by 1618 the ladies attending a court masque wore dresses 'of such variety in cut and colour as to be indescribable'.[21] These included loose gowns and the newly fashionable rising waistline.

Anne's traditional approach to formal dress did not deter her from being an active patron and participant in court masques, of which there were many between 1603 and 1619. After raiding Queen Elizabeth's wardrobe in 1604 for suitable garments for the Christmas masque, she progressed to more expensive, specially created garments; but money meant little to her in pursuit of royal splendour. By the time of her death her jewellery was supposed to be worth £400,000, and her estate included '124 whole peaces of cloth of gold and silver, besides other silkes, linnen for quantitie and qualitie beyond any Prince in Europe' and a grant of £8000 per year for clothes.[22]

As queen consort she was a glamorous, albeit extravagant arbiter of taste but rarely criticized; it was her delight in entertainment and clothing which were remembered, 'The Court being a continued masquerade, where the Queen and her ladies like so many sea nymphs or Nereids, often appeared in various dresses to the ravishment of the beholders.'[23] She was also influential in her patronage of artists and architects; Paul van Somer's portrait of 1617, depicting the Queen as a gracious but purposeful huntress, heralded a new era in English portraiture, and Inigo Jones designed not only masques for her, but began the Queen's House at Greenwich at her instigation.

James was not interested in the subtleties of visual propaganda until late in his reign when his taste was influenced by his favourite, the Duke of Buckingham, and his son Charles, Prince of Wales. The flat, controlled images of his Sergeant-Painters Robert Peake and John de Critz dwelt upon details of dress and jewellery, summarizing the wealth and dignity of sitters rather than experimenting with context or interpretation of personality. Yet it would be incorrect to view the English court during the first half of the seventeenth century in terms of the division between the tastes and temperament of James I and Charles I, which so neatly occurred in 1625.

When he became king, Charles I inherited a partly developed cultural revolution. Queen Anne and Prince Henry's tastes for masquing, ceremonial displays of martial prowess, patronage of foreign artists and acquisitions of paintings and *objets d'art* formed and influenced his life-long pursuit of connoisseurship. His more practical father also contributed to this change in emphasis. Although unsuccessful at introducing silk production into England, James had established a native tapestry weaving workshop at Mortlake, commissioned Inigo Jones to design the Banqueting House at Whitehall and received both Rubens and Van Dyck at the English court. His last years were a prologue to many of the developments which reached fruition in Charles's reign, introducing the idea that a wealthy country at peace with its neighbours might use both native and foreign talent in the creation of a more civilized, pan-European state.

Charles I had a vision of an ideal royal family and court, and his patronage of artists,

5. **Charles I and his Family c.1632; R Van Leemput after Sir Anthony Van Dyck**

The King's patronage of Van Dyck resulted in a series of individual and group portraits of the royal family which disguised their physical disadvantages and produced an idealized vision of a handsome, gracious and exquisitely dressed group. No artist since has provided quite such a persuasive view of British royalty.

most notably Van Dyck, provided a persuasive visual presentation of elegance, harmony and tranquillity which glossed over the dissension and discord endemic in court life and English society in the period c.1625–42. The rich, decorative but often ungainly fashions of the Jacobean period were apparently replaced by the flattering, simpler styles in lustrous plain satins with discreet embroidery and lace. The vulgarity and uncertainty of the early years of the century, still apparent in the late teens and early 1620s when waist-lines rose for both men and women, creating an unflattering bottom-heavy bulk of skirt or breeches, seemed to disappear with the change of monarch. This is the illusion, at variance with the reality, which old-fashioned painters, working in the manner of Gheeraerts and Peake, painstakingly recorded throughout the 1630s, demonstrating that fashionable dress was as susceptible to disproportion and vulgarity in Charles I's reign as it had been in his father's. It is ironical that the stiff, assured and wary courtiers depicted in such excessive finery in the first quarter of the century convey those mental attributes required for survival in the upper echelons of Stuart society more vividly than the relaxed, charming sitters in portraits by later artists patronized in court circles.

As a child, Charles I had been a late developer, taking longer to master his lessons and to establish physical authority over his puny body; he even wore boots specially strengthened with metal to assist his walking, a pair of which survive in the Museum of London collections. As an adult he was a shy, private and humourless man, excessively preoccupied by the dignity of his office. Sir Philip Warwick described his manner:

His deportment was very majestic, for he would not let fall his dignity, no, not to the greatest foreigner that came to visit him at his court; for though he was far from pride, yet he was careful of his majesty and would be approached with respect and reverence.[24]

In the first weeks of his reign it was noticed that 'the court is kept more strait and privat than in the former time', and this emphasis on correct behaviour was accelerated after the arrival of his wife, the French princess Henrietta Maria, who was accustomed to the most formal etiquette.[25] Royal palaces were rearranged to create private apartments for the King and Queen and access to them was regulated; protocol required courtiers to 'use great distance and respect to the royal persons, as also civility to one another'; no-one below royal rank could sit in the Queen's presence; no courtier might enter the royal presence in boots and spurs; and all who attended court were required to wear 'gowns or fit habits answerable to their degree'.[26]

Such minor restrictions did little to rebut the Venetian ambassador's criticism that Charles's court was 'extravagant with super-fluity'.[27] No reforms of the corrupt practices endemic in a royal household, which was both court and government were undertaken, and favourites were lavishly rewarded. The Duke of Buckingham could well afford the extravagant apparel taken to France in May 1627, which included amongst the 27 outfits a

rich white satin uncut velvet suit, set all over, both suit and cloak, with diamonds, the value whereof is thought to be worth fourscore thousand pounds, besides a feather made with great diamonds; with sword, girdle, hatband and spurs [set] with diamonds. . . .[28]

The court might be better behaved, more respectful of the royal family, encouraged to favour the finest forms of cultural and social activity rather than the crasser variety, but it was oblivious to many of the problems which exercised thoughtful members of society, and open to criticism for its extravagance in regard to dress, entertainments and preference for Catholic artists and cultural developments. The King's major personal expenditure was on additions to his great collections of art; his expenditure on clothing was approximately

£5000 per year in the period 1633–35. He was supplied with clothes for daily wear and for special occasions and there were garments for his gentlemanly pursuits of hunting, riding, tennis and masques. Items were altered and re-trimmed, indicating some measure of economy, and an innovation of the King's is noted in the accounts: the embroidery of 'rich orders set upon clokes and coates'.[29] In 1627 Charles had decreed that all Garter knights must wear on the left side of their outer garments 'at all times when they shall not wear their robes, and in all places and Assemblies, an Escotcheon of the Arms of St George'.[30] This regulation provides an early example of uniformity enforced by royal decree upon the fashionable clothing of an identifiable group of courtiers, and can be observed in portraits.

Portraiture is the key to posterity's view of Charles I, particularly the portraits of Anthony Van Dyck. These record the King's vision of the royal role – cool, contained grandeur which emphasized kingly attributes and domestic harmony. In Van Dyck's studio the royal family were transformed (as were many of their courtiers) into graceful, assured and elegant sitters – a perfect family. Good-looking, exquisitely dressed, happy and healthy, they personified the stability and continuity which the English crown was supposed to have acquired along with its Stuart monarchy.

The propaganda was so convincing that even members of the King's family were startled by the reality when they encountered it for the first time. Charles's niece, Princess Sophia, had seen the beautiful Queen Henrietta Maria of Van Dyck's portraits and was disconcerted to meet 'a little woman with long lean arms, crooked shoulders and teeth protruding from her mouth like guns from a fort.'[31]

Both King and Queen were short, and Henrietta Maria lacked the buxom curves which characterized English beauties, but the French fashions of the late 1620s and 1630s

flattered her. The low necklines, high waists and plain or lightly patterned silks gave an illusion of height; and the fine Italian lace of collars and cuffs, and the sheen of pearl jewellery provided a discreet magnificence. Van Dyck's portraits of the Queen imply impeccable elegance, but studies by Mytens demonstrate that she and the King were often awkward and unbalanced in the more formal court styles, which were over-decorated with rows of applied braid, heavy embroidery, fussy paned sleeves, ribbons and ill-considered accessories. Other, less prominent, sitters allowed Van Dyck to experiment by reducing the fashionable elements in dress to a minimum, arranging shawls or cloaks to soften awkward lines. He did not attempt this with the King and Queen; all the details of lace and jewellery were as they would have appeared, but he seems to have cajoled his royal sitters into the plainest of satins with minimal decoration, presenting an image of refined simplicity which was flattering, and suggested, quite literally, that they were larger than life.

Along with portraiture, the performance of masques in which the King and Queen took leading parts throughout the late 1620s and 1630s, dressed in appropriately fantastic costumes, created the illusion of a glorious monarchy that was the equal of any in Europe. The last masque was performed in 1640 and Van Dyck died in 1641; both events pre-dated the upheaval and tragic consequences of the Civil War but spelt the end of the King's idyllic vision of the perfect monarchy. Later portraits of the King are purposeful, work-manlike studies of the sturdily dressed military commander, or elegiac depictions of the ageing captive. The last portrait of Charles was painted by Edward Bower and represented the King at his trial in January 1649. This uninspired study became a symbol of martyrdom to royalists, joining other souvenirs which were cherished by Cavalier families after the King's execution. The royal jewels had been

LE CERCLE DE LEVRS MAGESTES DANS LA CHAMBRE DE
PRESENCE A S. IAMES

sold in Holland in 1642, leaving few objects to be presented by the King to his remaining servants and none of more than sentimental value. Lace collars, cuffs, nightcaps; pairs of richly embroidered gauntlet-gloves, handkerchiefs, shirts – including the exquisitely knitted, pale blue silk Italian 'vest' which the King wore beneath his other garments in order not to shiver (and be thought afraid) at his execution – all assumed the status of holy relics. They are, after more than three centuries, faded reminders that even if the artistic vision is timeless, the uninhabited personal mementoes are little more than a prosaic footnote to a transitory vision of an ideal monarch.

6. The Royal Family, St James's Palace 1639
This anonymous French etching was produced as part of a series commemorating the visit of Queen Marie de Medicis to see her daughter Queen Henrietta Maria in 1637. As etiquette required, everyone except the King, Queen and French Queen Dowager are standing. No women are present with the exception of the Queen's household and the French Queen; such gatherings were for male courtiers only.

TWO

'The pageantry and splendour, the badges and trappings of royalty'

The state entry of Charles II into London on 29 May 1660, the day of his 30th birthday, seemed to signal a restoration of not just the monarchy, but of all those other elements of ceremonial splendour and cultural and social life that the Commonwealth had swept away. John Evelyn observed the festivities:

> the bells ringing, the streetes hung with tapissary, fountaines running with wine; the Maior, Aldermen, and all the companies in their liveries, chaines of gold, and banners; Lords and Nobles clad in cloth of silver gold and velvet.[1]

Amongst the last group was the Earl of Bedford, his son William, his master of the horse, a coachman, a postillion, three grooms and six footmen, all equipped with new clothing and caparisons. The years 1660 and 1661 were expensive for the Earl, who provided the necessary finery for himself, his family and his household on the occasions of the King's return and coronation. In 1660 he spent £245 2s on liveries, £538 17s 9d on his own wardrobe and £255 on diamonds and rubies for his wife to wear at court.[2] It was a welcome fillip for London merchants and tradesmen, and a demonstrable sign of the British nobility's expectations of the style required at a restored royal court.

Few people knew quite what to expect of their new King. Samuel Pepys, who had travelled with the royal party from Holland, was impressed by the monarch's down-to-earth affability. There was little indication that he had inherited the distant, controlled regality of his parents. In both temperament and physique, he seemed to resemble his French Bourbon and Italian Medici grandparents. He was intelligent, pragmatic, lazy and charming, with a tall, spare frame and a face 'composed of harsh features, difficult to be traced with pencil; yet in the main it was agreeable, and he had a noble majestic mien.' The same commentator opined, with the vision of hindsight, that 'Never prince loved ceremony less, or despised the pageantry of a crown more; yet he was master of something in his person and aspect that commanded both love and reveration at once.'[3] It was quickly apparent to all but the most prejudiced observers that Charles II had innate physical and temperamental advantages which set him apart from both of his predecessors on the English throne, presenting him with the opportunity, had he chosen to take it, of reforming and remodelling the image of royalty and the style of the English court.

He did not, however, have the singular advantage of his more recent predecessor, Oliver Cromwell, in being able to sweep away all of the expensive, inessential nonsense and then to reinstate only the elements of monar-

AVDIANCE QVE DONNE LE ROI D'ANGLETERRE
A SON ALTESSE MONSEIGNEVR
LE PRINCE DE LIGNE
EN QVALITÉ D'AMBASSADEVR EXTRAORDINAIRE

chy and court life which suited him. He was accompanied to England by his mother, with her memories of the formal, orchestrated idyll of Charles I's court and her obsession with the minutiae of court etiquette, reinforced by her years of indigent exile at the rigorously formal French court of Louis XIV; by his sister Princess Mary, widow of the Stadtholder of Holland and a life-long advocate of the superiority of the English royal house and court over the Dutch; by his two brothers, James, Duke of York and Henry, Duke of Gloucester; and by his cousin Prince Rupert. This ready-made royal family had expectations which, when combined with the hopes of reward by loyal royalists and the wishes of the nation as a whole, made economy and change unrealistic.

The King's advisers felt that it was wise to present him as a man of moderate tastes in

7. **The Reception of the Prince de Ligne 1660; G van Tilborch**

The Prince de Ligne was conveying good wishes to Charles II from his master Philip IV of Spain. The fashionable elegance of the visiting entourage was suited to the splendour of the Banqueting House, but inappropriate for the circumstances. The King's brother had just died and he was in royal purple mourning, the court in black.

everything from recreations to clothing, but the nation was in exuberant mood and wanted the reinstatement of 'the bells and the tinsel, the outward pomp and gilding' which they traditionally associated with successful, popular monarchs such as Henry VIII and Elizabeth I.[4] Charles, himself, had been much influenced by his years as a penniless, dispossessed embarrassment to his European cousins. His memories of his parents' court were those of a child; his adult views of what a monarchy might be were refined during his exiled years in France and Holland, but it was the French model that he most admired. Fortunately, neither his temperament nor his financial circumstances inclined him towards the stultifying etiquette of Louis XIV's court, the pursuit of extravagant building schemes or the egomaniacal wish to be the glorious, central figure around whom every activity must revolve. Pomposity and self-regard were not amongst Charles' faults. However, much of the general style of the French court life – its fashions, its entertainments and its frivolity – were mirrored in England. Thus, a combi-

8. The King's Procession from the Tower to Westminster 1661

This engraving, taken from a contemporary painting, records Charles II's journey from the Tower of London to Westminster on 22 April 1661, the traditional procession which preceded coronation day. Such processions allowed the wider population, not just the courtiers and officials, to participate in great state occasions. Pepys thought, 'The King, in a most rich imbroidered suit and cloak, looked most nobly'.

nation of circumstances, hinging upon the King's strong wish to stress the unbroken continuity of the monarchy, his need to reward loyal followers, and the enthusiasm of the nation for the 'outward pomp', led to the reintroduction of the traditional posts for officials and servants in the royal household, and led inevitably to all of the old corrupt practices.

Pepys recounts, at some length, a trivial incident concerning the King's shortage of personal linen, the reason being that the grooms of the bedchamber '(took) away the King's linen at the Quarter's end, as their fees'.[5] In fact the grooms received lodgings, board and an annual salary, but custom and usage decreed that such personal linen was their prerequisite. Such customs continued without regard for the King's financial circumstances. In 1667 the royal linen draper was owed £5000, which suggests that the bill had not been settled since the restoration in 1660. Certainly, by 1670, the King's bills for linen and lace, for a period of eleven months, had sunk to a modest £385 9s 2d.[6]

Charles was unable to live within his income, for the Stuart family had no independent fortune to bolster their allowance from Parliament. As early as August 1660, the King told the politicians, 'I am not richer, that is, I have not so much money in my purse as when I came to you.' Parliament had agreed that the King should receive £1,200,000 per annum to cover all expenses, excluding warfare, but he rarely received much more than three-quarters of this sum each year.[7] For part of the reign the shortfall was covered by a secret pension from Louis XIV, but the deficit between what Parliament was prepared to pay for a traditional monarchy with all of its complicated and costly rituals spread throughout a range of ramshackle palaces, and what the process actually did cost, was an intermittent cause of embarrassment to the English monarchy until Queen Victoria's reign. This did little to inhibit Charles or his courtiers, and he encouraged splendour and personal display, conscious of the comparisons drawn between the French and English courts.

In temperament, Charles was like his grandfather James I, relaxed about behaviour at court and wholly lacking in personal vanity. This casual attitude did not please everyone; Pepys' bourgeois soul was shocked by reports of Dutch cartoons which 'pictured our King with reproach. One way is with his pockets turned the wrong side outward, hanging out empty – another, with two courtiers picking of his pocket – and a third, leading of two ladies while others abuse him – which amounts to great contempt.'[8] In fact, the sober, upright Dutch were merely recording what they had observed at first-hand during Charles' exile in Holland. His character, behaviour and personal tastes did not change when he became King of England.

Although Pepys might be shocked by the *lèse majesté* which the King's behaviour prompted, he understood the need for close observation of the court and its habits, and, if it was appropriate, for regular attendance

9. **Catherine of Braganza, consort to Charles II c.1660–61; D Stoop**
Catherine is depicted in the fashion of her native Portugal the 'monstrous fardingals or guard-infantas' of Evelyn's description. She quickly abandoned this style and wore French fashions at the English court.

upon the King.[9] His diaries are full of sightings of, and occasional conversation with the royal family, and with influential courtiers of both sexes. He made the best possible use of his connexions through Lord Sandwich and by his own efforts as an increasingly important 'civil servant' (at the Navy Board) to watch the Queen Dowager, the Princess Royal and Princess Henriette dine in public in November 1660; to view the coronation in Westminster Abbey in April 1661; to see royal portraits in Lely's studio (June 1662); to have a private tour of Queen Catharine's bedchamber and closet in June 1664; and to wait upon the King and Queen when they dined in public at Whitehall in May 1669. Unlike his contemporary, John Evelyn, he did not have the entrée to formal court occasions, such as

10. Charles II
This wood carving attributed to Grinling Gibbons
is an example of how royal images could be
reproduced in every medium – seals, coins, medals,
on pottery – and still capture a considerable
likeness. This carving depicts the fashions of the
late 1660s and early 1670s and is obviously the
work of someone who had seen fine lace at close
quarters.

birthday balls and drawing-rooms, but, like
Evelyn, he was both fascinated and repelled
by the extravagant and luxurious arrangements at court, and by the dress of the leading
participants.

Evelyn affected to despise the expensive
and constantly changing French fashions, even
writing a pamphlet on the subject, *Tyrranus,
or the Mode*, a copy of which he presented to
the King. Pepys, however, took an exuberant
enthusiasm in acquiring new clothes and
accessories, spending more each year as his
circumstances improved. The nine years of his
diary (1660–69) chart the changes in men's
fashionable dress from the loose, short jackets,

evolved from doublets, and worn with wide-
legged petticoat breeches, generously trimmed
with loops of ribbon, billowing linen shirts,
lace-edged bands and cuffs, wide-brimmed
hats and full cloaks, to the narrower lines of
the knee-length vest (coat) worn over longer
breeches – a style which, in the late 1670s
and early 1680s, became an unsophisticated
version of the coat, waistcoat and breeches
which formed the basic elements in the male
wardrobe for over a century. Women's dress,
at this period, consisted of a low-cut, tightly
fitted, boned bodice with a full trained skirt
worn over a contrasting petticoat for formal
occasions, and, less formally, a looser,
unstructured robe, which in the late 1670s
developed into a mantua – a style of dress
in which bodice and skirt were constructed
together and worn over a petticoat. The
last, with variations according to fashion,
dominated the female wardrobe for much of
the eighteenth century.

Expenditure upon fashionable clothing still
meant importing foreign luxury goods. The
finest linen and lace came from Europe, as
did the costly silks, but increasingly from
France, where Louis XIV's finance minister
Colbert, invested in lace-making and silk-
weaving industries. Both of these industries
quickly overtook the long-established centres
in Italy in terms of quality and ingenuity of
design. The constant criticism of costly and
extravagant French fashions refers, from the
late seventeenth century onwards, to materials
as well as to styles of dress. Fashion seemed
to be on the verge of becoming a wholly French
monopoly. Naturally, this caused alarm to
the traditionally important English woollen
cloth industry and also to the emergent linen,
cotton, lace and silk industries. The need to
support English textile manufacturing industries began to signify with the government of
the country, not just momentarily to assuage
a temporary bout of xenophobia, but as a
constant factor in the national economy. Dress
worn by royalty and by their courtiers began

to present opportunities for promoting the national interest.

Charles II's interest in dress seems insignificant when compared to the amount of time and energy that his cousin Louis XIV invested in perfecting his appearance and that of his courtiers. All European courts, however, looked with increasing admiration at Louis's achievements. By laying emphasis on 'the tinsel, the outward pomp and gilding', Louis gradually tamed a wayward and embattled French nobility, presenting them with forms of etiquette and dress for every type of occasion which were so convoluted that even experienced courtiers could be reduced to childish shame at committing a minor solecism. Stressing outward forms and appearances was a crucial facet in Louis's pursuit of glory, and it undoubtedly dazzled and influenced other European courts. Its strength lay in its unrelentingly high standards and its use of Versailles and the French court as a glossy advertisement for the superiority of French goods, French crafts, French ingenuity and French taste.[10]

When Charles prepared for his return to England he ordered a new range of appropriate clothing from the Parisian tailor Claude Sourceau, and eventually persuaded him to settle in London.[11] A French influence can also be detected in the style of under-dress which the King decreed should be worn beneath the robes of the newly reconstituted Order of the Garter. He was obviously aiming at a solemn uniformity, in keeping with the dignity of the Order, but invested it with a self-consciously quasi-historical appearance by reverting to 'the old trunk-hose or round breeches, whereof the Stuff or Material shall be some such Cloth of Silver, as we shall chuse and appoint, wherein as we shall be to them an example, so do we expect they will follow us in using the same and no other.'[12] In fact, this style seems to have been based upon the under-dress devised for the Order of the St Esprit (which drew upon historical precedents

and the quasi-historical formulas of masque dress), and worn to such good effect by Louis XIV. That it was a most effective, flattering and lavish form of official dress is confirmed by the formal portraits of the King. The majority of official portraits depict him in Garter robes; there are full-length versions by Lely, c.1675, Lauron, 1684, and Hawker c.1683–85 which impress with their baroque curves and billows of satin, cloth of silver, linen and lace. A variant of the trunkhose also appear in Wright's mid-1670s portrait of the King, painted wearing state robes and enthroned with the attributes of kingship and placed before a canopy of state. This portrait is an affirmation of the continuity of sovereignty (even if crown, orb and sceptre were all new, acquired in 1661 for £30,000) and is traditional in pose, although contemporary in the excessive use of looped ribbon on the King's garments and in the artfully arranged curls of the full, dark wig.[13]

Festive occasions, such as the King's and Queen's birthdays, balls and entertainments for visiting embassies and foreign royalties, were appropriately formal in their dress. There are enough descriptions by Pepys, Evelyn and others to attest to the importance of 'exceeding splendid ... clothes and jewells' and 'rich ... apparell' on formal occasions.[14] It was, however, a period of experimentation and change, in dress as in many other aspects of life, and the King, always interested in new ideas, was closely involved in changes to men's dress. Initially this was for the sound, economic reasons mentioned earlier; Pepys recorded, in late October 1665, that 'The King and Court ... have now finally resolved to spend nothing upon clothes but what is of the growth of England – which if observed, will be very pleasing to the people and very good for them.' This resolution, coming as it did after the appalling plague of that year, was rendered even more essential after the costly disaster of the Great Fire, which consumed much of the City of London in the late summer of 1666. By early October, 'The King hath ... in council declared his resolution of setting a fashion for clothes, which he will never alter. It will be a vest, I know not how. But it is to teach the nobility thrift, and will do good.' Thus began the experiment of the so-called 'Persian vest', with which Charles II attempted to achieve three, fairly irreconcilable objectives: the encouragement of English textiles, the establishment of a standardized

11. Charles II and Queen Catherine 1682

This engraving illustrates the King and Queen and their courtiers in formal dress. The comfort and the new style of man's coat is not matched by the boned court bodice and looped petticoat worn by the women. Variants of this 'stiff-bodied' gown continued to be court wear for royal ladies well into the eighteenth century.

English male fashion and the introduction of a simpler style of masculine court dress. Pepys had a preview of the new fashion on 13 October when he waited upon the Duke of York whilst the latter tried on 'the king's new fashion'. Two days later the King wore the new style for the first time, surrounded by similarly attired members of the Lords and Commons and other notables. The garment in question was 'a long cassocke close to the body, of black cloth and pinked with white silk under it, and a coat over it, and the legs ruffled with black riband like a pigeon's leg.' By 17 October, 'The Court [was] all full of vests', but already there was an element of dissatisfaction with the prototype and a potential leader of fashion emerging; Lord St Albans had a plain black vest, and the King

decided that black pinked over white made his courtiers 'look too much like magpyes', and ordered a plain velvet vest for himself.[15]

At this juncture John Evelyn's observations and opinions on the new style of clothing are introduced. His diary entry for 18 October conflicts with Pepys's evidence,

> *To Court. It being ye first time his Maty. put himself solemnly into the Eastern fashion of vest, changeing doublet, stiff collar, bands and cloake into a comely dress, after ye Persian mode, with girdle or straps, and shoe strings and garters into bouckles, of which some were set with precious stones, resolving never to alter it, and to leave the French mode, which had hitherto obtain'd to our great expence and reproach. Upon which divers courtiers and gentlemen gave his Maty. gold by way of wager that he would not persist in this resolution.*

Evelyn went on, somewhat coyly, to suggest that he might have influenced the King by praising the 'usefulness of the Persian clothing' in *Tyrannus, or the Mode*, a copy of which he had presented to Charles. By 30 October he was wearing the new fashion, but observing cynically, 'It was a comely and manly habit, too good to hold, it being impossible for us in good earnest to leave ye Monsieurs vanities long.'[16] On 15 November, Pepys observed the ball at court which celebrated the Queen's birthday, and saw 'the King in his rich vest of some rich silk and silver trimming, as the Duke of York and all the dancers were, some cloth of silver, and others of other sorts, exceeding rich'.[17] The novelty endured, despite Louis XIV making fun of the fashion by dressing his footmen in vests, and in February 1667 Evelyn was at a court entertainment at which the men were dressed 'in their richly embrodred most becoming vests.'[18]

The King's excursion into the world of fashion innovation was a partial success. His introduction of an English style of men's dress which was simpler in construction and which could be made from native wool cloth was a skilful piece of propaganda, seeming to pacify English xenophobia by breaking the tyranny of French fashions and goods. By requiring his courtiers to wear a specific type of garment (in effect establishing English court dress), the King demonstrated that it was not merely a personal whim, but being a pragmatic man he soon realized that uniformity of style would only succeed if accompanied by choice of colour, material and detail. Inevitably, the most brilliant court occasions required luxurious (imported) materials, but he set an example at less formal times by wearing, from preference, a plain cloth coat. He was a humorous propagandist for all types of English wool, telling Courtin, the French ambassador that he could stay warm in England by wearing sensible underclothes made from 'a plain sort of woollen stuff woven in the cottages of Wales.'[19]

The King led his life within relatively unrestricted circles. With the exception of the rituals of the levee and couchee at which ministers, officials and favoured courtiers might attend him during his ceremonial preparations for rising and retiring, he was remarkably unfussed about whom he met at court. Unlike his father or, more relevantly, his cousin Louis XIV, he had no interest in constructing elaborate circles of accessibility to the royal family. The King's withdrawing room (or drawing room, as it was more usually described), which marked the area between the private and public apartments in royal residences, was open to every 'Person of Quality as well as our servants and others who come to wait on us.'[20] It was a self-limiting regulation which relied upon the good sense, knowledge, connexions and appearance of the individual.

Similar rules applied to the Queen's apartments, which consisted of the same arrangement of private, semi-public and public rooms, but with one important difference. When the monarch was a man both custom and etiquette forbade women to be received in his apartments (with notable private exceptions); consequently, the King's levee and couchee were strictly male occasions. Inevitably the rules and arrangements for a queen-consort's household were different. The most private times in her day – rising, dressing, preparing to retire – were strictly female events, with the Queen surrounded by the ladies of her household, both officials (mistress of the robes, ladies of the bedchamber, maids of honour) and servants, but as her household also included men holding official posts, they would also be received in her closet or withdrawing room. When the King joined the Queen in her 'drawing room' such occasions provided opportunities for male courtiers not attached to her household and distinguished foreign visitors to wait upon the Queen. The 'drawing room' evolved from a place into a formal gathering, which, unlike the king's levee and couchee, was more social than business-like and also offered a meeting place for courtiers of both sexes. John Evelyn attended such gatherings; in January 1671 'The King came to me in the Queen's withdrawing roome from the circle of ladies...' and in May 1671 'grandees' from Louis XIV's army encamped at Dunkirk, 'in fantastical habites' arrived to visit the English court and 'were conducted into the Queenes withdrawing roome...'.[21] In May 1669 Pepys had 'waited upon the King and Queen all dinner-time in the Queen's lodgings', a sign that he, like Evelyn, was now a 'person of quality'.[22]

If Charles II was an unlikely leader of men's fashions, his Queen, Catherine of Braganza, was even less well-equipped to influence female tastes in dress. A short, rather plain and pious princess of the Portuguese royal house, she had been brought up in a conservative court at which formal dress still included the old-fashioned farthingales which are familiar to us through Velasquez's portraits of Spanish infantas of this period. As a courtesy to the man who had chosen her to be his

Queen, she was dressed in the English manner on her arrival at Portsmouth in May 1662, but to please the Duke of York she changed into a Portugese style. John Evelyn recorded her wearing similar attire, 'with a traine of Portugese ladies in their monstrous fardingals or guard-infantas' when she reached London.[23] After some initial and understandable difficulties in adjusting to her new role, country and English customs she became a model wife to the King, loyal, docile and compliant. She was not, however, successful at providing the King with an heir to the throne, neither was she witty and intelligent like her sister-in-law, the Duchess of York, nor beautiful and influential like the King's mistresses. It was the celebrated beauties like Barbara Villiers, Frances Stuart and Elizabeth Hamilton, 'A model copied by all other women in the matters of clothes and hair-dressing,' who were admired for their looks and fashionable appearance; they vied with each other to introduce new styles of dress, hair-dressing and jewellery, often, as in February 1668, 'far outshining ye Queene'.[24]

Pepys thought Catherine unsuited to the French fashions worn at court; observing her 'in her white pinner and apern;' he decided that 'she seemed handsomer, plain so, then dressed.'[25] She tried to compete, using the services of a French dress-maker, Desborde, and wearing the fashionable quasi-masculine style of 'cavalier riding habite, hat and feather, and horseman's coate' in September 1666, but some three months after Pepys had recorded his disapproval of seeing her ladies-of-honour dressed 'for all the world like men' in riding habits 'with perriwigs and with hats.'[26] This fashion continued for some years and was even worn at a court ball in February 1671, at which Lady Bertie saw Barbara Villiers, 'very fine in a rich petticoat and halfe shirte and a short man's coat very richly laced, a periwig, cravate and hat.'[27]

The portraits and engravings of Queen Catherine in which she is depicted wearing fashionable dress as opposed to the artistic undress which was such a feature of English female portraiture in the late seventeenth century, support the literary evidence that the Queen followed fashion rather than changed it. There is no suggestion that she, like the King, tried to devise an English style of female court dress to complement the Persian vest experiment of 1666–67. French fashions for women, particularly after the visit of the King's sister Henriette (wife of Louis XIV's brother) in 1670, and the arrival, in the Princess's entourage of Louise de Kéroualle who became Charles II's mistress, were firmly in the ascendant. Despite his persistent infidelities, the King was fond of Catherine and insisted upon the greatest possible respect being paid to her as his wife and queen-consort. The celebrations at court on her birthday, 15 November, often exceeded the festivities held on Charles' birthday. In 1668 Evelyn commented on the 'very fine fireworks' and 'greate... gallantry,' and in 1674 he considered the splendour of clothing and jewellery worn was 'the height of excesse'; by 1684 the occasion merited 'fireworks on the Thames before White-hall' and a ball at which the court 'had not ben seene so brave and riche in apparell since his Matys Restauration'.[28]

It was not only sober-minded Englishmen like Evelyn who disapproved of the lavish expenditure on outward show which became such a feature of Charles II's court. Prince William of Orange Nassau visited his uncle, the King, in 1670 and found the informality and raffishness of the English court difficult to tolerate. In his plain, dark clothes, worn without a wig, he looked out of place, but the ladies of the City of London thought him 'a nice young gentleman... not like those popinjays (at court)'.[29] William's clothes were, in fact, ordered in Paris, but made in the sombre tones and discreet styles which would not offend his fellow Dutchmen, many of whom, unlike their Prince, did not admire French culture and goods. On his return to England in 1677 to negotiate a marriage contract with his cousin Mary, daughter of the Duke of York, the court ladies considered him, 'the plainest man ever seen and of no fashion at all'; in marked contrast to his tall, lovely bride-to-be who attracted attention and compliments in her Parisian trousseau.[30] As was the custom for royal weddings, this one took place privately, on the evening of the Prince's birthday, 4 November, and the couple left London two weeks later for the quiet, dignified Dutch court.

Charles II's court was complemented by that of the Duke and Duchess of York. The duke's first wife, Anne Hyde, was a commoner but, in the words of her husband, 'what she wanted in birth was so well made up by other endowments, that her carriage afterwards did not misbecome her acquired dignity.'[31] This opinion was not shared by Prince William of Orange Nassau who always considered his wife – Princess Mary, daughter of the Duke of York and his first duchess – of inferior rank to himself because of her Hyde blood.[32] The duchess was a shrewd and capable manager of financial and business matters, she was witty and intelligent, attracting people to her court who avoided Queen Catherine's because of its dullness. Her only surviving children were her two daughters Mary and Anne, both of whom inherited her propensity to corpulence. As his second wife James chose the Italian princess, Mary of Modena. She was tall, dark and graceful, but reserved and pious. At their apartments in St James's Palace she and the duke presided over a miniature court, with levees and drawing rooms held,

as regularly as the King and Queen held theirs at Whitehall, but on different days. There was not however, the slightest rivalry either intended or suspected. King Charles always said that the most loyal and virtuous portion of his courtiers were to be found in his brother's circle at St James's Palace.[33]

James, Duke of York was very different in

personality and ability to his brother Charles II. He was tough, humourless, lacking the Stuart charm and grace; 'his outward carriage was a little stiff and constrained,' similar in manner to the autocratic, self-regarding Louis XIV. Neither this, nor his professed conversion to Roman Catholicism made him a welcome heir to the throne, and he spent several periods in temporary exile. One of these was spent in Edinburgh in 1679–80. He and the Duchess were welcomed by the Scottish nobility, and the local tradesmen and merchants had a brief but profitable time benefitting from the increased expenditure which a royal visit ensured.[34] During his short reign as King, James II revived and reconstituted the Order of the Thistle in 1687, re-establishing and strengthening the link between the house of Stuart and the Scottish nobility which was to prove so troublesome to the first two Hanoverian kings. In statutes and forms of dress the Order of the Thistle was modelled on the reconstitution of the Garter by Charles II, but with 12 knights rather than 24.

In the awkward, unstable period of his reign James found time to emphasize the outward symbols of autocratic monarchy. He and his Queen were treated with greater deference, there were attempts at introducing a higher moral tone into court circles, and a flurry of portrait painting took place. Kneller, who had become principal court painter on the death of Lely in 1680, the Dutch artist Willem Wissing and the Frenchman Nicolas de Largillière, all produced images of James and Mary. It must have been a particularly unhappy time for the Queen, constantly

12. James II 1685; Sir Godfrey Kneller
The King as military commander was a recurrent theme in royal portraiture. James's military and naval prowess is indicated in this formal depiction. The absurdity of mixing armour with the fine lace, silk stockings and soft leather shoes does not seem to have worried either artist or sitter.

watched and discussed by courtiers who feared that she might produce a healthy, male Roman Catholic heir to the throne. Much later, in impoverished exile in France, she recalled the luxuries which she had taken for granted, remembering the smallest details– the one or two new pairs of shoes she wore each week, and the new gloves changed nearly every day.[35] Perhaps the memory of such harmless fripperies prevented recollection of less happy events.

When James followed his wife into exile he was replaced on the English throne by its only joint-rulers, his daughter Mary and her husband Prince William of Orange Nassau. It was a dramatic and unwelcome elevation for both of them. In Holland their court had been modest, almost domestic in scale, the equivalent in size to that of a powerful member of the English nobility. William's sobriety of dress and reserved nature, so remarked upon by the English court, was appreciated by the Dutch, who were suspicious of flamboyance and extravagance. They admired Mary's youthful beauty and charm, treating her with great deference, for at William's insistence, etiquette was very formal at the Hague. The Dutch responded to her natural dignity, pleased that, 'Her manners, beautiful though they were, never failed to inspire respect'. Mary, conscious of her role as an arbiter of fashion, often ordered materials and accessories from London or Paris, but she did not adopt every new style, telling a correspondent, 'I would not bring up such a fashion heer which the pursses could not bear.'[36] This admirable sense of responsibility was vitiated by Mary's taste for diamonds; by the 1680s she was in debt to her jeweller Adam Loofs, or borrowing money to pay him for new stones.[37] William did not discourage his wife's fashionable indulgences, for he relied on her to be the focus of court life, a role which he found tedious. Formal occasions – balls, entertainments on the Prince's birthday, dining in public – were limited, and the

The INTHRONIZATION of Their MAJESTIES King IAMES the Second and Queen MARY.

13. The Coronation of James II and Queen Mary 1685

Francis Sandford's lavishly illustrated history of this coronation provided a detailed record of the ritual and etiquette of the occasion. A number of important revisions included the standardization of coronation robes for all participants, and this, in turn, influenced the formal depiction of royalty and peers for over one hundred years.

royal couple lived simply and privately by contemporary royal standards.[38]

When William reached London on 18 December 1688, the population greeted him enthusiastically, sporting orange ribbons on their hats and head-dresses, and that evening John Evelyn scurried to St James's Palace, to join 'All the world (who) go to see the Prince at St James's, where there is a greate Court', which included the Princess Anne, William's sister-in-law, who dressed herself and her ladies in orange to indicate her loyalty to England's new rulers.[39] The enthusiasm waned when William 'shew'd little countenance to the noblemen and others who expected a more gracious and cheerful reception when they made their court.'[40] The English propensity for criticism found another target when Mary joined her husband in February 1689; she was chastised for being unfeelingly high-spirited and cheerful as she took possession of her father's throne and palace, but Lady Cavendish thought her 'altogether very handsome. Her face is very agreeable and her shape and motions extremely graceful and

fine. She is tall, but not so tall as the last Queen.'[41]

Such praise was rare. The court and country, having decided upon radical change, were not sure that they could live with the consequences of their actions. The new rulers were criticized for spending time at Hampton Court rather than Whitehall, the presence in London of 'ill-looking and ill-habited Dutch and other strangers', and the King's obvious preference for and reward with office of his Dutch nobles. It was similar to the xenophobia which had confronted James I and his Scottish entourage at the beginning of the century, but since then the English had 'beheaded one king and thrown out another and we know how to deal with the third.'[42] Gradually, the King and Queen became more accessible, visiting the City of London, celebrating royal birthdays, holding courts and paying visits between the necessary work of state, reforming the royal household and embarking upon ambitious building programmes at Hampton Court and Kensington Palace. It was, however, increasingly obvious that the court was becoming a centre of political life with the ceremonies and

14. James II's Arrival at the French Court 1689

This detail from a larger souvenir of the triumph of William of Orange depicts James II's reception by the French King Louis XIV at St Germain-en-Laye. Although probably not the work of an eye-witness, it indicates the formal dress and etiquette which characterized the French court.

festivities associated with the royal year fitted around the hours of business. Court etiquette became more ritualized, in the French manner. The Queen's sister, Princess Anne, was particularly sensitive about such matters, on one occasion refusing to be seated on a tabouret 'until it was removed to a correct distance from the state-chair of the Queen her sister.'[43] This understandable foible in a poorly educated, under-occupied Princess was to become a life-long obsession.

Queen Mary had more natural intelligence, and had made use of her years in Holland to read and develop many interests, including a taste for the visual arts. During William's absences she conducted affairs of state with a group of advisers appointed by the King, but

15. **The Prince and Princess of Orange 1688**
The proliferation of engravings and etchings which recorded the triumph of William and Mary over James II convey the importance of visual propaganda. The lavish dress and deferential etiquette of the previous illustration (14) contrasts tellingly with the apparent simplicity of William and Mary's Dutch entourage. Ironically, all the figures in the latter are taken directly from contemporary French fashion plates.

retained a handsome woman's interest in fashion. The King's birthday celebrations in November were marked in the traditional manner. Preparations for the 1691 festivities, at which 'The court was all in their splendour, the Queen very rich in jewells...', provided London tailors and suppliers with their greatest increase in trade since the Restoration. There are few portraits of the Queen which record her tastes in dress in the short period before her death in 1694, but there is evidence,

in an account book of the last year of her life, of some of her preferences. Like Mary of Modena, she required a great many pairs of shoes and gloves; seven pairs of the former and two dozen of the latter each month. Italian silks, lace, ribbons, painted fans; fur-lined petticoats and sable muffs for the winter; and jewellery of diamonds, pearls and emeralds add substance to the black and white engravings which delineate the few depictions of her fashionable wardrobe.[44] Even these must be treated with caution, for they are sometimes based on French fashion plates and not necessarily taken from life.

The portraits of Mary show no attempt to re-work or re-present the image of a female monarch who was also, uniquely, a queen-consort. The dress follows the pattern established by Lely in the 1660s and continued by other court painters. The emphasis was on 'court beauties'—a display of languorous women with rounded shoulders and arms and voluptuous uncorseted bosoms loosely clad in linen shifts and lightly-clasped robes. In English royal portraits authority and power were hinted at by the inclusion of a velvet mantle deeply edged with ermine and a discreet crown, but were rarely expressed overtly in the manner of European royal portraiture. The latter confirmed the exclusivity of rank and privilege by a careful depiction of formal dress, richly patterned silk brocades, velvets, lace and fine jewellery. In pursuing a so-called 'timeless' informality of dress, artists working at the English court suggested a relaxed, informal society. In reality this type of portraiture coincided with a period in which the details of etiquette and dress were being refined and strengthened more purposefully than before.

Princess Anne embodied this emphasis on traditional forms, drawing upon her formidable knowledge of court etiquette. After Mary's death in 1694, she and William, never friendly, managed to reach an accommodation, sweetened by the gifts of Mary's jewels and the royal apartments at St James's Palace. In 1696 the King considered re-marriage and inspected a daughter of the Elector of Brandenburg. The Brandenburg court dispirited both William and his entourage; the women were thought plain and 'all ill-dressed, in old-fashioned stiff-bodie gowns, too big for them, with their breasts and shoulders naked.' William rejected the alliance and reconciled himself to a life in which his sister-in-law acted as his hostess on formal occasions. He was too reserved for English taste, banning triumphal arches from a ceremonial entry which marked his return from Europe in 1697; it smacked too much of the vanity which characterized his greatest rival, Louis XIV. Matthew Prior visited Paris in 1698 with William's first ambassador to the French court and thought Louis, 'the vainest creature alive even as to the least things'; Versailles attracted equal condemnation, with its King 'strutting in

16. **William III; attributed to T Murray**
Formal portraiture for English kings usually included depictions in Garter robes, parliamentary robes, armour and, on occasion, coronation robes. William III is almost swamped by his red velvet and ermine parliamentary robes and his long curled wig, but his formidable determination and lack of vanity are evident in his face.

every panel and galloping over one's head in every ceiling'[45] Temperamentally, William was akin to the next 'foreign' ruler of England, George I; both of them preferred the country of their birth, felt out of step with the frivolity and intrigue of English court life, and believed that sound government required application rather than vanity and extravagance.

Louis XIV had angered William by refusing to put his court into mourning after the death

17. Louis XIV 1701; Studio of H Rigaud
Matthew Prior thought Louis 'the vainest creature alive even as to the least things'. Some of this vanity is conveyed by this state portrait. His insistence upon etiquette and correct dress influenced many of the other European courts during his long reign. Cousin to all of the post-Restoration Stuart monarchs, he reigned longer and outlived all of them.

of Mary in 1694 – at the instigation of Mary's father, the exiled James II. When James died in 1701 William ordered secondary mourning 'as for a relation: persons of quality not to put their liveries into mourning', only Princess Anne, belatedly conscience-stricken, had ordered full mourning, and then had to retract at the King's order. Vengeance was not long delayed. On William's death, early in 1702, Anne made a point of indicating that her black mourning was in memory of her father; only secondary trimmings of purple were for William, and all mourning ceased after the coronation, six weeks later. She emphasized the difference between her and her predecessor by proclaiming, 'I know my heart to be

entirely English', and went on to state that she would do anything required 'for the happiness and prosperity of England.' This zeal for English prosperity took curious forms; it was recorded that:

> *For the encouragement of our English silk, called a-la-modes, his Royal Highness the Prince of Denmark (the Queen's husband) and the nobility appear in mourning hat-bands made of that silk, to bring the same in fashion in the place of crapes which are made in the pope's country, whither we send our money for them.*[46]

This play upon English sentiments, combining support for indigenous industries with a reminder of the religious bigotry from which the nation had escaped, indicated the style of the new reign. Anne saw herself as a wholly English symbol of national aspiration and unity, upholder of Protestant ideals and the traditional 'middle way' of her great predecessor as Queen of England, Elizabeth I. It was a natural analogy. She, like Elizabeth, had a royal father and a mother who was a commoner; she had been distanced by events from an older sister who was a queen with a foreign husband, and she knew, from early in her reign that she would be the last of her line to rule the country. It is not surprising that she quickly adopted Elizabeth's motto *semper eadem*, and chose to wear, for her first speech to Parliament in 1702, a dress which took as its exempla Elizabeth's gold brocade coronation dress of 1558.[47] This degree of propagandizing is not associated with Queen Anne; in the popular mind she is the prematurely infirm, overweight, pathetic monarch who was dominated by her mistress of the robes, the Duchess of Marlborough.

This is a view of the Queen that the Duchess spent the last years of her life discussing in her memoirs and correspondence. When describing the Queen's memory she wrote,

> *she chose to retain in it very little besides ceremonies and customs of court and such like insignificant*

18. The Royal Family c.1700

This idealized engraving of the widowed William III, his sister and brother-in-law, Princess Anne and Prince George of Denmark and his only surviving nephew, Prince William, is heavily reliant on French fashion plates. Only William's face is accurately depicted, and no member of this group was renowned for such a developed fashion sense.

19. **Queen Anne c.1702; Studio of J Closterman**

This formal portrait is reminiscent in pose and certain aspects of dress, allowing for changes over nearly 150 years, of the coronation portrait of Elizabeth I painted in 1559. It was perhaps inevitable that Anne should take Elizabeth, the last Tudor monarch, as her exempla.

trifles, so that her conversation . . . was only made the more empty and trifling by its chiefly turning upon fashions and rules of precedence, or observations upon the weather or some such poor topics . . . Upon which account it was a sort of unhappiness to her that she naturally loved to have a great crowd about her, for when they were come to Court she never cared to have them come in to her, nor to go out herself to them, having little to say to them but that it was either hot or cold, and little to inquire of them but how long they had been in town, or the like weighty matters.[48]

The Duchess, a self-assured, bombastic woman, did not make allowances for Anne's acknowledged shyness or for a natural regal reserve. The Queen was conscious of her great

responsibility, a particularly onerous one at a time when the country was engaged in a major European war, and when emergent political parties were causing dissension in government. Neither circumstances nor intellectual ability allowed Anne to emulate Elizabeth I, but, ever-conscious of her dignity, she laid considerable emphasis upon correct behaviour at her court, providing a model for a female monarch's role which still had some relevance at the beginning of Queen Victoria's reign. Her conversational banality is more charitably interpreted as discretion, and has been a royal habit well into this century.

The actual location of the court could play a part in its apparent dullness. In 1711 Dean Swift described a Drawing Room which was so thinly attended that the Queen invited everyone into her bedchamber,

where we made our bows, and stood about twenty of us round the room, while she looked at us round with her fan in her mouth, and once a minute said about three words to some that were nearest her, and then she was told dinner was ready and went out.

This was at Windsor Castle, which with Kensington Palace were Anne's preferred residences. However, Windsor was inconvenient for many courtiers, so Swift's other much-quoted remark that, 'the Court serves me for a coffee-house once a week I meet acquaintances there that I should not otherwise see in a quarter,' is a more accurate description of the bustle and purpose of these events at which intrigue and gossip could enliven the dutiful paying of respects to the monarch.[49]

Royalty was also capable of criticism of its courtiers. Anne, whose poor eye-sight might have overlooked minor solecisms, was quick to observe and comment upon incorrect dress. Prince Eugene of Savoy arrived at St James's Palace for his presentation to the Queen in 1711 'without a Court wig, which at last was dispensed with only on account of the particular celebrity of his character and which the Queen said 'should not be drawn into precedent'.[50] The Prince had been poorly advised, for he had queried whether he might wear his shorter campaign wig rather than the usual 'full-bottomed' variety, and was told that 'it was a thing of no consequence, and only observed by gentlemen ushers'; his adviser was either intentionally malicious or unfamiliar with the fact that the Queen's preferences were interpreted by the gentlemen ushers who monitored access to the inner rooms of the court.[51] Prince Eugene was more fortunate (being rewarded on the Queen's birthday in 1712 with 'a sword sett with diamonds') than the young officer who appeared at court in a campaign wig: 'the Queen, who was quick to spot these irregularities, immediately asked who he was, and how he presumed to appear before her in undress?' Explanations about him not being familiar with royal etiquette met with royal

disdain, the Queen's view being that 'if she suffered this indignity, she supposed she must soon expect to see all her officers come to court in boots and spurs.'[52]

Cocooned within the royal rituals connected with the dressing of a monarch, with bed-chamber women assisting bedchamber ladies with the putting on of the royal shift, the pulling on of royal gloves, even the presentation of a fan, it is hardly surprising that the Queen expected others to be careful of their appearance. When she was in reasonable

20. Queen Anne and the Knights of the Garter c.1713; P Angelis

Queen Anne fulfilled all of the ceremonial duties required of the monarch even when unwell. She instituted the female royal's convention of wearing the garter on her left arm. By this date, the flamboyant, 'Tudorbethan' style of garter underdress introduced by Charles II, looked uncomfortably anachronistic.

health she made an effort to appear in appropriate grandeur, having a preference for gold thread brocades and silks. At her coronation she wore, 'gold tissue, very rich embroydery of jewells about it,' and four years later, for a thanksgiving service at St Paul's Cathedral, she chose 'a riche gowne and Petty Coat of Cloth of Gold brocade' with a Garter collar and 'a rich diamond garter on her left arm.'[53] *In extremis*, during bouts of poor health, she could be a pathetic sight, with a blotched face, 'rendered something frightful by her negligent dress'. Whenever possible she tried to maintain a brave facade in an attempt to assist, amongst others, those London merchants and tradesmen who dealt in rich materials and clothing and had petitioned for festivities on her birthday and 'other public occasions' as 'the greatest support to ours and almost all other trades.' The Queen ordered new clothes annually, and every January, as was her custom, she took 'all her cloaths, and devided them herself in six several heaps, and stood by whilst the bedchamber Women chose as they were eldest'[54] A good many of these garments must have found their way into the Duchess of Marlborough's hands. In 1760 Horace Walpole went to Blenheim and was not impressed by 'all the old flock chairs, wainscot tables, and gowns and petticoats of Queen Anne, that old Sarah could crowd amongst blocks of marble.'[55]

After the death of Anne's husband Prince George in 1708, she, like her exemplar Elizabeth I, was a solitary figure. There was, however, no repetition of the dandified emasculation of the fashions of her male courtiers. She had no interest in becoming an idiosyncratic but memorable focus for female fashions, although she seems, consciously, to have avoided adopting the archaically formal style of court dress worn by female royalty in France which was gradually spreading to other European courts. The men of power and influence who ran Anne's government were determined and self-confident, and they

dressed accordingly. The three main components of men's dress – coat, waistcoat and breeches – which had evolved in the late seventeenth century underwent various changes in the eighteenth century. Side pleats in the skirts, stiffening and lining transformed coats from loose, almost shapeless garments into substantial (in size, weight and breadth) formal wear complemented by waistcoats, often sleeved, of matching or contrasting material. Reserving the finest clothes, usually new and acquired at great cost, for court festivities became more noticeable in the eighteenth century, and within the male wardrobe the waistcoat lent itself to virtuoso displays of colour, rich embroidery and bejewelled and metallic decoration. Such waistcoats were often interlined to bear the weight of the heavy brocaded silk and the embroidery which adorned the fronts and edges. On one occasion an attempt to kill the Earl of Oxford, one of the Queen's ministers, was prevented because the assassin's knife could not pierce the solid gold brocade waistcoat which he was wearing for the court held on the anniversary of the Queen's accession.[56]

It was fortunate for Lord Oxford that Anne was a traditional ruler who promoted the idea that respect for the monarchy could be measured in outward forms. Although she did not have the time, and was often not well enough to be an active leader of a fashionable circle, she conscientiously performed all of the expected ceremonial duties: speaking to parliament, presiding over Garter day ceremonies (and initiating the queenly manner of wearing the actual garter around the left, upper arm), receiving ambassadors, and holding the drawing rooms which she so obviously disliked. Her strong sense of duty triumphed constantly over her wish for privacy, and her belief in national unity and harmony led her naturally to a view that a well-ordered, respectful court could only be achieved by guidance on matters of etiquette and dress. This explains her reliance upon precedents and her encouragement of formal, agreed rules of ceremony and behaviour. She was helped in this by her favourites – courtiers who by attaching themselves to the royal mistress acted as a conduit for her cherished aims, and, in the process, rose effortlessly to the highest offices in the land. Both the Duke and Duchess of Marlborough benefitted from their association with the Stuart monarchy, especially under Anne; but whereas the Duchess was far from an ideal courtier – jealous, quick-tempered and opinionated – her husband provided a model for others to emulate. He was thought, 'consummate in all the arts of a courtier, supple, affable, sedate; reserved, both with friends and enemies; sober, averse to luxury... ambitious, but free from haughtiness and ostentation.'[57]

Such courtly arts were all-important when Anne died and was succeeded by a relative stranger in 1714. Her death provided the country with an enlarged royal family, none of whom, with the exception of the new King, George I, had ever set foot in England. The King was over 50, spoke little English (not an insuperable barrier as most of his new courtiers like their King, spoke excellent French), and was settled in his ways, preferring relative privacy and informality. There was no Queen, the King being divorced; consequently the first lady in the land was the Princess of Wales, the handsome, intelligent blonde, Caroline of Anspach. This ready-made, albeit German royal family – the House of Hanover – inherited a way of life and a system of political and social patronage which was evolving quickly in the political sphere, but more slowly in matters concerning the royal household and court ceremonial.

Financially the new King was somewhat better placed than either of his predecessors. Arrangements made in 1715 guaranteed him £700,000 p.a. with the possibility of an extra £120,000 p.a. (of this total amount £100,000 was for the use of the Prince of Wales and his family), but he generally received about

21. George I c.1714; Studio of Sir Godfrey Kneller
An early English portrait of the first Hanoverian monarch, probably painted in the first month of his arrival in England, September/October 1714. George, as Elector of Hanover, had been a noted military commander, and his depiction as a serious soldier was wholly appropriate.

£760,000 p.a. This was never enough, for in addition to his 'necessary expenses' the King had to bear the costs of the 'civil service' (but not military expenses) out of his revenues. There had been a consistent reduction in the size of the royal household since the reign of Charles I; approximately 500 fewer posts existed by 1714, but nearly 950 officers (with an additional 400 or so servants) made it the largest, most expensive, most extravagant household in Britain. Certain offices, like the Great Wardrobe – by this date primarily responsible for the maintenance and furnishing of palaces and the provision of liveries and clothing payments to various court servants –

were excessively wasteful and laxly managed. The mastership of the Great Wardrobe carried the highest salary at court (£2,000 p.a.), but a high salary did not guarantee high standards of management. The master, throughout George I's reign was the second Duke of Montagu (the Duke of Marlborough's son-in-law), who later in the reign became the first grand master of the revised Order of the Bath, adding yet another untaxing, but financially rewarding sinecure to the network of posts held by the Marlborough family connexions between 1704 and 1749. It is hardly surprising that the Duke of Montagu was able to spend £400 on his clothes for the Prince of Wales's wedding in 1736; his longstanding 'professional' connexion with the courtly offices associated with clothing and chivalry would have required no less.[58]

Under the terms of the Act of Settlement of 1701, no foreigner was permitted to hold public office in England or to take an English title; these measures were intended to prevent an infiltration of Germans in the manner that the Dutch had infiltrated public life under William III. This was no great personal hardship for George I; he disliked the custom whereby relative strangers performed personal tasks on the pretext of maintaining court ceremonial, so he kept key posts vacant before deciding upon suitable appointments. William III's regulations about bedchamber organization and the rituals of dressing and undressing remained in force until the reign of George III, but George I kept to his former habits. His Turkish grooms of the chamber, Mehemet and Mustapha supervised his toilet and dressing arrangements (the formal master of the robes was William Cadogan). Mehemet continued to order and pay for the King's clothing, wigs and accessories, using the same suppliers as his master had used as Elector of Hanover.[59] The King found the privacy and informality which suited him within a group composed of his unofficial family, German courtiers and servants. He left 'the pageantry

and splendour, the badges and trappings of royalty' to his son, the Prince of Wales.[60]

The King's lack of interest in outward show is reflected in official portraiture and sculpture; they provided derivative and uninspired images of kingship, and are an apparent rejection of the powerful visual propaganda produced in other European courts. When Sir Godfrey Kneller died in 1723, the King accepted his Lord Chamberlain's nominee, Charles Jervas, as principal royal painter; no attempt was made to find other, more accomplished artists who might have added glamour or gravitas to the generally pedestrian level of English court portraiture in the first half of the eighteenth century. Signs of interest by the King in his appearance and depiction, or any wish to influence the appearance of others, are non-existent. The creation/re-institution of the Order of the Bath in 1725 owed little to the King's wishes; it was a reflection of Sir Robert Walpole's need to find an extra level of political reward below the Garter, and John Anstis, Garter King of Arms's antiquarian research and enthusiasm for the financial and social rewards bestowed by such an initiative. George I took no part in the selection of colour, style of dress and design of the orders.[61] His personal preference was for a discreet, almost bourgeois appearance, uncluttered by illusory grandeur. The young Horace Walpole was presented to him in 1727, and recalled him as

an elderly man, rather pale, and exactly like his pictures and coins; not tall; of an aspect rather good than august, with a dark tie wig, a plain coat, waistcoat and breeches of snuff-coloured cloth, with stockings of the same colour, and a blue (Garter) ribbon over all.[62]

Initially George I left the ceremonial formalities and winning over of English courtiers to his son and daughter-in-law. Levees, Drawing Rooms and other entertainments were held in the Prince and Princess of Wales's apartments at St James's Palace or at Somerset

House, and occasionally attended by the King. The temperaments and interests of all three were well served by this arrangement, but English courtiers felt that their new King was not fulfilling the social and ceremonial role which provided an important stabilizing influence in court circles. A change occurred in 1717 when, for political and family reasons, the King had to assert his authority and belatedly formulate a court life centred around his activities.[63] He began, in July of that year, to dine in public, hold levees for his gentlemen and to make regular appearances in the drawing room. In addition, there were balls, concerts and card tables. This flurry of activity continued until the autumn of 1720, by which time the political and family disagreements had been resolved. The physical separation of the two royal households – the Wales's were expelled from St James's Palace in December 1717 and settled eventually at Leicester House – required the King to appear, with reasonable regularity, in his Drawing Room on court days for the rest of his reign.[64]

The court perambulated between various palaces, but after the disastrous fire which had destroyed Whitehall Palace in 1698, St James's Palace was never a satisfactory substitute in central London. Daniel Defoe, writing about it in 1727, thought that,

The splendour of the nobility, the wealth, and the greatness of the attendants, and the real grandeur of the whole Royal Family, outdo all the Courts of Europe, and yet this palace comes beneath those of the most petty princes in it.

Despite internal rebuilding to provide a suite of rooms ranging from those open to the public to private apartments, it was not as agreeable in design and location as Kensington Palace or Hampton Court. The months from November to May were spent at St James's; two months at Kensington followed; and then a period usually lasting until late October was spent at Hampton Court or Windsor Castle. Royal birthdays were usually

22 George II 1727; C Jervas
The second Hanoverian king, dressed in coronation robes, enjoyed the public ceremonies, the finery and the etiquette which his father had found so tedious. This style of coronation robe with knee-length surcoat and heavy velvet mantle underwent little change over several centuries. (c.f. Edward VII, fig. 85)

celebrated in London; the King's was in late May, the Prince of Wales's in late October. These dates marked the necessary winter/spring sojourn which any ambitious courtier must be prepared to spend in pursuit of office and favours.[65]

Talent was not an essential qualification for individuals who aspired to office in a royal household or a sinecure in government service. Lady Mary Wortley Montagu thought that, 'a moderate merit, with a large share of impudence is more probable to be advanced, than the greatest qualifications without it.'[66] Family connexions could help, but even when a post was granted, it was but the first of many steps up a long ladder and, in the short term, it added to the individual's expense. The more diverse court life, with a profusion of court entertainments, and birthdays for three senior royals, meant increased expenditure on clothing. Birthday and accession courts traditionally demanded the finest clothes. These were regarded as a compliment to the royal family, a reaffirmation of the wealth and power of the English nobility who attended court, and a support to the London merchants and tradesmen who sold the necessary finery. Theoretically, the highest standards of dress were set by the royal family and their households, as living embodiments of the nation's wealth and grandeur, and as an advertisement for its finest manufactures. The Prince and Princess of Wales happily fulfilled this obligation, as did their courtiers, the latter at considerable expense on limited salaries. In 1715 new clothes for the King's birthday cost a young man in the Prince's household more than £30. In the same year a young law student, Dudley Ryder, went to an ordinary court without incurring any additional expense, 'in best clothes and laced ruffles'. This success emboldened him to 'gate-crash' a court ball by bribing a servant at the door with one shilling.[67] Security was lax, officials and servants were corruptible, and formal invitations were not issued; but no royal servant would have admitted anyone whose appearance and manner might have attracted adverse comment.

The styles of dress worn at court were conspicuous in their use of rich satins and brocades, encrusted, almost three-dimensional embroidery, good lace and fine jewels. Foreigners, such as the Swiss visitor César de Saussure, commented on the great difference between day dress and formal wear. He noticed that

Englishmen are usually very plainly dressed, they scarcely ever wear gold on their clothes; they wear little-coats called 'frocks'... Their cloth and linen are of the best and finest. You will see rich merchants and gentlemen thus dressed, and sometimes even noblemen of high rank, especially in the morning... Englishmen are, however, very lavish in other ways... Peers and others persons of rank are richly dressed when they go to Court, especially on gala days...

De Saussure attended court on several occasions during his visit from 1725 to 1727, but omitted descriptions of his own clothes, merely stating that on the King's birthday, 'everyone (makes) it a rule to appear in new habiliments.'[68] As the century progressed, the basic three-piece suit underwent various changes, eventually becoming a narrow cutaway coat by the 1790s, with a shortened, sleeveless waistcoat and narrower breeches. The simplicity of everyday masculine dress, as described by de Saussure, is more marked when compared with certain styles worn at the King's birthday court in 1722,

most people very fine, but I believe the gentlemen will wear petty-cotes very soon, for many of their coats were like our Mantuas. Ld. Essex had a silver tissue coat, and pink colour lutestring wascote, and several had pink colour and pale blue padesway Coats, which looked prodigiously effeminate.[69]

Gold and silver materials and ornate metal-work embroidery made such clothes very costly, and, being so distinctive, not easily reusable on other gala occasions without considerable alteration and re-trimming. Although styles of dress did not change rapidly in the early years of the century, designs and colours for silks did, making them look old-fashioned very quickly. This knowledge and the protocol of court life is illustrated by the

Duchess of Marlborough's advice to Lady Cowper in 1715, when the latter could not attend the Princess of Wales's birthday Drawing Room for which she had prepared expensive new clothes. She was told to wear them 'on the first day you can easily wait upon the Princess, and shew her how fine you were to have been.' No mention was made of economizing by saving the clothes for a future birthday.[70]

Female court dress was as sumptuous and costly as men's; it demonstrated similar tastes in colour, material and decoration. Lady Sunderland's birthday apparel in 1724 almost matched that worn by men in 1722, 'Her clothes were the finest pale blue and pink, very richly flowered in a running pattern of silver frosted and tissue with a little white, a new Brussels head and Lady Oxford's jewels.' Borrowing jewellery was one acceptable way of economizing. On Queen Caroline's birthday in 1729 Mrs Pendarves went to court with Lady Carteret and her two daughters, 'dressed... in all my best array, borrowed my Lady Sunderland's jewels, and made a tearing show.' Through the good offices of her sponsor, Mrs Pendarves (a noted embroidress) was able to be presented to the Queen, who told her,

> she was obliged to me for my pretty clothes, and admired my Lady Carteret's extremely; she told the Queen that they were my fancy, and that I drew the pattern. Her Majesty said she had heard I could draw very well... she took notice of my jewels. I told her that they were my Lady Sunderland's; 'Oh', says she, 'you were afraid I should think my Lord Selkirk gave them to you, but I believe he only admires, for he will not be so free of his presents.'[71]

This anecdote summarizes some of the reasons why fine clothes were such an integral element of paying one's dues at court. Throughout the centuries the royal eye was quick to spot inappropriate dress but equally willing to admire and voice approval, and to

23. **Caroline of Anspach, consort of George II 1727; C Jervas**
This complementary portrait of George II's Queen, depicts her wearing coronation robes which included the 'stiff-bodied' gown, the fossilized French court fashion which had reached the German Brandenburg court by the 1690s. Caroline was a princess of Brandenburg-Anspach.

show interest in courtiers as individuals. Queen Caroline's witticism about Mrs Pendarves's supposed admirer, Lord Selkirk, was typical of her sharp charm. Possibly the cleverest consort of any English king, she took a lively interest in everything, from the ephemeral pleasures of dress to the mental challenges of philosophy, religion and government. Her court was a place where, 'learned men and divines were intermixed with courtiers and ladies of the household; the conversation turned upon metaphysical subjects, blended with repartees, sallies of mirth, and the tittle-tattle of a drawing room.'[72] The frequency of public Drawing Rooms, and the important birthdays and anniversaries did not invariably provide this congenial mixture of court and salon. In 1728 Mrs Pendarves was dismissive of the court's attractions, at which 'ogling and tweezing, and whispering and glancing... standing and walking and fine airs' were not alleviated by eating, drinking, laughter, dancing or 'smart repartee'. Later that year her description of a Drawing Room recalls Dean Swift's remarks about Queen Anne's Windsor Court, 'I don't believe there were twenty people there besides (the Royal) family'.[73] This was due, in great part, to the lack of formal organization of the public days at court. Numbers were not regulated, no cards were issued; it could be an uncomfortably full or painfully inadequate gathering, or anything between these two extremes.

In addition to the increasing number of diaries, letters and memoirs which described the minutiae of court life and the activities of the royal family in the eighteenth century, there was a marked bias towards satire. In the first three-quarters of the century this mainly took a literary form; later it was matched in ferocity by widely distributed cartoons and caricatures. Typically cruel doggerel characterized the King as 'dapper George' and the Queen, his 'fat spouse'. In fact, this seemingly ill-matched couple were devoted to each other, and had complementary tastes and interests. The King was politically astute, keenly involved in military matters, a patron of the music of Handel, and an enthusiastic participant in masquerades and masked balls which were amongst the most popular forms of entertainments in London from 1715 onwards. The Queen was a patron of the fine and decorative arts, but the portraits of her and the King were usually run-of-the-mill works by artists of the second rank: John Vanderbank, Charles Jervas and Pietro Amigoni. She considered using William Hogarth, despite the fact that one of his satirical engravings deriding masquerades purported to depict George II (when Prince of Wales) disguised as Folly; but a disagreement between the royal architect William Kent and Hogarth ended this potentially imaginative patronage. Hogarth's realistic style of portraiture would probably not have suited the royal couple. When the German miniaturist Frederick Zincke was commissioned to record the royal family the Queen advised him 'to make the king's picture young, not above 25'; in similar vein George II told Zincke that the Queen should look about '28'.[74]

Such vanity was perhaps natural in a couple who had been admired for their youthful good looks when they had arrived in England in 1714. They enjoyed the finery and adulation which accompanied their rank. George II shared with his father a preference for Hanover and a dislike of his eldest son, but was, in all other respects, his opposite. He was interested in appearance, his own and that of others. From him can be traced the almost obsessional Hanoverian interest in uniforms, insignia and the protocol of rank. Assisted by his son the Duke of Cumberland, he introduced uniforms into the British army, specifying in the greatest detail what each regiment might wear, and then had a record of each made by the artist David Morier.[75] He took an equal interest in providing uniform for commissioned naval officers. A delightfully eccentric story about the King's choice of colours was related by the Hon. John Forbes, Admiral of the Fleet, whose opinion was sought by the first Lord of the Admiralty, the Duke of Bedford. The Admiral suggested red and blue or blue and red as 'national colours', only to be told that the decision had already been taken. The King had seen the Duchess of Bedford riding in the park 'in a habit of blue faced with white, the dress took the fancy of His Majesty, who had appointed it for the uniform of the Royal Navy.'[76] What similarity the King perceived between the Duchess and his naval officers is, unfortunately, not recorded anywhere.

The King's dapper appearance is recorded by a number of contemporaries. Mrs Pendarves saw him 'in blue velvet with diamond buttons' at the Queen's birthday ball in 1729. At the wedding of his daughter Princess Anne to the Prince of Orange in 1734 he outshone the bridegroom, 'in a gold stuff which made much more show, with diamond buttons to his coat.'[77] Two years later, at the wedding of his son, the Prince of Wales, he glittered in 'a gold Brocade turn'd up with silk, embroider'd with large Flowers in silver and colours'.[78] The brocaded silk and embroideries of the 1730s and 1740s drew upon botanical sources to create a three-dimensional but naturalistic effect which must, in a crowded court, have dazzled and wearied the eyes. Some 18 months later Queen Caroline died. The King, plunged into misery and purple mourning, could hardly bear to appear in public, leaving a drawing room after a few minutes, early in 1738 'with grief still fixed on his face,' and venting his wrath on those who had the temerity to disregard the rules of mourning – the Duchess of Bridgewater and another lady were turned out of the Chapel Royal for daring to appear in white gloves.[79]

The Queen's interest in personal finery included a shrewd understanding of the expense involved. She often indicated by example and advice the limits within which the cost of clothing for festive occasions should fall, and she tried, whenever possible, to support English manufacturers. She was not extravagant, a sample of her expenses for the quarter years ending 24 June and 29 September 1729 give her personal expenditure as £847 12s and £308 7s 2d, respectively.[80] She might pay 130 guineas for a splendidly embroidered gown, but would reject a sumptuous gold brocade because it was too expensive; she bought the work of Midlands lace-makers, accepted a length of silk from the American colony of Georgia and had it made up to encourage the new industry; she patronized English dressmakers but eagerly examined a fashion doll sent from Paris in order to see what the French princesses were wearing.[81] In 1736, to ensure that the court would be at its most richly elegant for the Prince of Wales's wedding, she 'desired people would not make fine clothes' for her birthday, and was rewarded by the information that 'most of the rich clothes [worn at the wedding] were the Manufacture of England'.[82] For Princess Anne's wedding in 1734 the bridal gown was made from French silk (by an English dressmaker), but the trousseau included English silks, and was available for inspection by the ladies of the court at Hampton Court Palace. This semi-public inspection also took place when Princess Mary was married in 1740.[83]

If accessibility and amiability were two of Queen Caroline's virtues, they were those of a woman who enjoyed the privileges of her rank. As eighteenth-century European courts became more formal and regulated in behaviour and appearance, the ceremonial trappings of royalty became fixed – associated with the continuity of history rather than with the excitement of sudden change. It was, of course, in the interests of the Hanoverian dynasty to emphasize continuity and to revere historical precedents, for, until the early nineteenth century, there was the every-present spectre of the Stuart 'kings across the water'. Male royalties had the traditional appurtenances of rank: political power and influence, membership of select orders of chivalry, and military authority to bolster their position. Female royalties had to create a role for themselves; they were marriageable pawns with an exalted but undemanding place at the apex of the court, and also, should they choose, at the centre of fashionable society.

Court and fashionable society were still inextricably entwined until the death of Queen Caroline; then they began gradually to separate and re-form, running parallel and occasionally criss-crossing, but never again providing one central focus for social aspirations.

It was France, and the French court which provided a model for many European rulers in everything from patronage of the arts to the protocol of court life. The formal etiquette of the French court, which regulated speech, deportment and dress, was copied, in part, by many European courts. It seems probable that the ceremonial dress (worn for coronations, weddings, and possibly on royal birthdays) by the female royalties of the Hanoverian dynasty was based on the French model. This style isolated the fashion of c.1670 (before the looser, less formal mantua became popular) and retained many of its basic features until, in France, the Revolution of 1789 swept away all such anachronisms. It had a boned bodice, fastened at the back, short sleeves and a low, curved decolletage; the chemise sleeves were masked by rows of lace ruffles which usually matched the lace edging around the neckline; the skirt was held back from the petticoat by clasps and had a long train. It was probably this style of ceremonial court dress which Matthew Prior had seen at the Brandenburg court in 1696 and thought so unbecoming. Although materials varied with fashion, and skirts changed their silhouette with the introduction of hoops, many of these elements were found in the English 'stiff-bodied' gown. Mrs Pendarves who saw Queen Caroline and the princesses and peers' daughters who attended her at the coronation in 1727 wearing this style, described it in some detail and considered 'it is a most becoming dress'. She had obviously not seen it before, although she described it again in 1734 when Princess Anne was married. The Princess and her attendants wore stiff-bodied gowns, and Princess Mary's trousseau in 1740 included

'the stiff-bodied gown she is to be married in.'[84] As late as 1777 the *Magazine à la Mode* mentioned Queen Charlotte's dress,

commonly called a Robe de Cour, but more properly the Royal Robe because her Majesty generally appears in this dress. It consists of a close body without pleats or robings ... the stays are cut low before and shaped like a heart.[85]

The majority of women who attended court wore the simpler, more fashionable mantua, its soft, unboned bodice, with pleats or robings as decoration, worn open over a stomacher. When worn at court this style had a train, but not like those worn by the royal family. Surviving examples have short trains or a truncated version, which is folded back, stitched into place and certainly not long enough to be carried by a page – something which César de Saussure had noticed when he saw Queen Caroline's daughters processing to chapel.[86] Sets of lace, caps with the lappets loose or pinned-up, sleeves ruffles, edging round the neckline and a fan, gloves and the best array of jewels that could be mustered, completed the ensemble. It was these elements and the richness of material which separated court dress from fashionable formal dress. Silver and gold thread woven into brocades or complicated embroidery, often using precious metal, gave a solidity of appearance to a style of dress which changed imperceptibly as the century progressed, gradually becoming as fossilized as the stiff-bodied gowns worn by royalty. Certain subtle changes did occur, and those who paid their respects to their monarch once in a very long while and relied on their memories for guidance, attracted gentle mockery. With a change in government in 1742 Horace Walpole noticed, at the King's birthday court,

the numbers of old ladies, who ... have not been dressed these twenty years; out they come in all the accoutrements that were in use in Queen Anne's days ... I met several on the Birthday ... and

24. **Frederick, Prince of Wales c.1732; B Dandridge**

Prince Frederick was disliked by his parents, but inherited their taste for politics, entertainments, formal etiquette and fashionable dress. He was genuinely interested in the arts and patronized a wide range of artists, both English and European, who could depict him sympathetically.

they were dressed in all the colours of the rainbow; they seem to have said to themselves twenty years ago, 'Well, if ever I do go to court again, I will have a pink and silver, or a blue and silver,' and they keep their resolutions.

Walpole took an almost feminine interest in the details of dress. At the previous year's birthday, recently returned from France, he thought himself 'most superb' in a French suit, one of twenty he brought back, but then started to worry in case the opposition newspaper, the *Craftsman* should criticize his extravagant expenditure on foreign finery.[87]

Walpole's letters provide an informed, partisan but witty commentary on the customs and foibles of the fashionable world which clustered around the court of George II, and that of his son, Frederick, Prince of Wales and his wife Princess Augusta. The enmity between father and son was intermittent but deep-seated, much as it had been between George II and his father. Walpole thought the Prince, 'really childish, affectedly a protector of arts and sciences, fond of displaying what he knew... His best quality was generosity; his worst insincerity, and indifference to truth'.[88] The Prince inherited his mother's taste for the visual arts, collected intelligently, and patronized a wide range of artists in pursuit of a suitably regal but relaxed style of depiction for himself and his family. His wife, characterized by Queen Caroline as, 'the best creature in the world, one puts up with her insipidity because of her goodness', developed similar tastes.[89] Initially, however, her youth and inexperience cast her into a subsidiary role to that of her husband. He was something of a social and political gadfly, who had been disappointed in his wish to pursue a military career; this did not stop him demonstrating the Hanoverian taste for uniforms, which found an outlet, albeit a minor one, in devising a style of hunting dress, in the 'national colours' of blue and red. It was worn by him and his close circle, and can be seen in a number of contemporary paintings.

The Prince and Princess flit through the Walpole letters, attending court, being snubbed by the King, ever-present at the 'plays, operas, ridottos and masquerades' which the fashionable world attended in the 1740s. Private balls and masquerades were usually arranged by leading members of the aristocracy, and the presence of royalty was a sign of social approbation. The King had always enjoyed this type of entertainment, and the Prince and Princess appeared to share his enthusiasm for it. One distinction between royalty and other masqueraders seems to have

been that the former did not remove their masks. They were, of course, instantly recognizable, but the conventions of the masquerade allowed a certain amount of *lèse majesté*. In 1742 the Princess of Wales 'vastly bejewelled' chose to attend the Duke of Norfolk's masquerade dressed as one of 'dozens of ugly Queens of Scots'. The jewels, worth £40,000, had been lent to her by a jeweller, Frankz, who would not accept payment for their hire, but on the understanding that she would reveal their source (royalty advertising the wares of exclusive suppliers at minimal or no cost to themselves is not the twentieth-century phenomenon that popular newspapers would like to pretend). Lady Pomfret, disguised as a pilgrim, pertly told the Princess that she thought her 'the Lady of Loreto', a Spanish saint, much bedecked by rich offerings from believers.[90] The Princess's love for jewellery was well-known; at her husband's birthday court in 1739, 'her head and stomacher [were] a rock of diamonds and pearls'.[91] Even the King was not safe from the type of familiarity which was only acceptable at masquerades. In 1749, during the festivities marking the Peace of Aix-la-Chapelle, George II, 'well disguised in an old-fashioned English habit,' was delighted by the success of his disguise when someone asked him 'to hold their cup as they were drinking tea.'[92]

Such transient informality was not captured for posterity to wonder at; there are no pictures of adult members of the royal family in masquerade dress. In fact, of all the portraits of George II the most revealing is the one

25. A Novice of the Order of the Saint Esprit c.1732; after J-M Nattier

This style of dress was copied, in part, by Charles II when he revised the under-dress for the Order of the Garter (c.f. colour plate 1). The flamboyant theatricality which characterized the appearance of French noblemen was not matched by their British counterparts in the eighteenth century when wearing the distinctive full dress of the order of the Garter (c.f. fig. 20).

painted of him without his knowledge, late in his reign. As an old man in his seventies he is still dapper in a befrogged and tasselled coat worn over a heavily fringed waistcoat, wearing, as was his habit, the garter, star and ribbon of the Order of the Garter. The style of dress is a little old-fashioned, but the formality of the attire could hardly have been bettered (excepting portraits in state robes) if he had known that he was being painted. Undoubtedly, his own preference would have been for the portrait of himself in red and gold regimentals – remembered as the last King to lead his troops into battle, at Dettingen in 1743, it is pleasing that he was the first English royal to be depicted in a military uniform of his own devising. His daughter-in-law, the Princess of Wales had every reason to be grateful that she had not been painted in her Mary, Queen of Scots costume, for in 1745 the invasion of 'Bonnie Prince Charlie' took place. The Stuart threat to the House of Hanover was brutally curtailed by the Duke of Cumberland while the English court buzzed with rumours of Stuart sympathisers. After Cumberland's triumph, Horace Walpole was amused to see Lord Rochford at court in November 1746 wearing 'plate buttons for his birthday clothes' patriotically decorated with the Duke of Cumberland's head. Eighteen months later, the Duchess of Queensbury, newly received at court after a 19-year ban, gave a masquerade ball, hoping to attract the King to the event. She seems to have courted a further ban, for her husband was dressed 'in Scotch plaid, which just now is one of the things that is reckoned most offensive...'.[93] The Hanoverian monarchs never ventured into Scotland until 1822, and took an understandably jaundiced view of that part of their kingdom and its odd customs. There was no equivalent to the vice-regal court in Dublin for Scottish society.

The portraiture of female royalties became more varied in the 1730s, but it only served to reinforce the idea of the domestic and/or decorative role of the sitters. A conversation piece, *A Music Party*, by Philippe Mercier, painted in 1733, is of Frederick, Prince of Wales and his three sisters. The Prince is the focal point, playing the cello, and distinguished by his Garter sash despite the informality of pose; his sisters are a discreet chorus, simply dressed, apparently content

26. **A Music Party 1733; P Mercier**

Prince Frederick and his three sisters are, superficially, equals in this informal conversation piece. However, the Prince is the dominant figure, his importance emphasized by his Garter sash and star; his sisters are secondary, dressed discreetly for their role as admiring companions – the fate of every eighteenth century princess who was not heir to a throne.

with their role as accompanists and companions. The Princess of Wales, depicted alone by Charles Philips in 1736, and wearing the 'stiff-bodied' style of dress worn by female royals on formal occasions is, by 1739, accompanied by three small children and three attendants. By the time the Princess was widowed in 1751 (a contributory factor to the Prince's death was, if Walpole can be believed, changing from heavy state robes into 'a light unaired frock and waistcoat'), there was no room in the memorial family group for members of her household.[95] George Knapton painted her holding her youngest child, born after the Prince's death, and surrounded by eight others. The Prince is a ghostly presence, a portrait within a portrait, wearing one of the heavy robes which may, indirectly, have

27. The Wedding of Princess Anne 1733 (O/S); J Rigaud after W Kent

In addition to the usual court ceremonies, the 1730s were marked by two royal weddings. George II and Queen Caroline's daughter married the Prince of Orange early in 1734 in the Chapel Royal, St James's Palace. Extra galleries had to be installed to accommodate the courtiers, dressed in their finest and most fashionable clothes; as etiquette required, the guests had to stand in the presence of royalty.

28. The Royal Family 1733–34; W Hogarth

This preparatory sketch for a royal conversation piece depicting George II, Queen Caroline and their seven children suggests that if Hogarth had not been opposed by William Kent, he would have produced elegant and perceptive portraits of the royal family. Whether his ability to capture their looks and personality would have suited them is less certain; their preference was for uncomplicated flattery.

29. Augusta, Princess of Wales c.1736; C Philips

The second royal wedding of the 1730s was that of Frederick, Prince of Wales to Princess Augusta of Saxe-Gotha. She was painted, possibly just before or just after her marriage, wearing the 'stiff-bodied' court dress worn by royal women. Details, such as the treble rows of frills of her chemise sleeves, were an integral element of this formal, French-inspired style.

caused his death; the Princess is dressed in an informal satin mantua, with the longer sleeve and full cuff which was fashionable in the early 1750s, and a black veil over her hair, but her eldest daughter is wearing a formal stiff-bodied gown and lace ruffles. The portrait is a fascinating summation of the expectations of the young princes and princesses. Below the portrait of the dead Prince is the new, young Prince of Wales and his oldest brother, studying a campaign map; two younger princes play with a model ship; to the right the princesses play with the dogs and strum a musical instrument, and the eldest princess stands by the Princess of Wales's chair, prepared for her role as a marriageable pawn on the chess-board of European royalty.

The Prince of Wales's death resolved the problem of two courts. The new Prince was a minor, and his education, social activities and access to him, were carefully controlled by his mother. In 1754 Walpole wrote wearily to Horace Mann, 'where the monarch is old, the courtiers are seldom young; they sun themselves in a window like flies in autumn, past even buzzing, and to be swept away in the first hurricane of a new reign,' but this did not prevent him garnering gossip about the absurdities of court life and its major protagonists. Standards might seem to have slackened 'at Princess Emily's coming to chapel last Sunday in riding-clothes, with a dog under her arm,' or when 'the noble mob in the Drawing-room clambered upon chairs and tables' to see the lovely Duchess of Hamilton, one of the beautiful Gunning sisters, presented at court, but such behaviour betokened a need for change and excitement in a period of calm. When the King's grandsons began to go into society, to form and express opinions, and flex their political muscles, there were fresh diversions. In 1757 a political caricature depicted the Prince of Wales unfavourably and caused concern; in 1758 Prince Edward entered the navy as a midshipman, the first royal prince to undertake basic

30. **George II c.1737; C Philips**
The interest in dress which earned the King the sobriquet 'dapper' is evident in this portrait. The tan velvet coat with rich gold decoration and matching breeches contrast with a white satin waistcoat, pale, fringed leather gloves and crisp tricorne hat. He always wore his Garter sash, star and garter.

31. **George II, after 1743; S F Ravenet after D Morier**

George II was the last King to lead his troops into battle, at Dettingen in 1743. Both Morier and J Wootton painted him on his charger with battle scenes in the background. He took a particular interest in military and naval matters and spent happy hours devising colours and other details of uniform for his troops to wear.

32. **An Officer of the 4th Troop of Horse; D Morier**

Morier produced a series of paintings for George II and other clients of the new uniforms which were introduced into the British Army. This example provides early evidence of the Hanoverian obsession with uniforms.

naval training, and, in 1760, Walpole agonized, humorously, over whether he should stir himself to be presented to the Prince of Wales.[96]

One of Walpole's supposed reasons for not being able to go to court, was that, 'As I never dress in summer, I had nothing upon earth but a frock, unless I went in black... and pretended that a cousin was dead...'. He had, however, retained his interest in the fashionable foibles of others, telling the Hon Henry Seymour in 1759, 'Remember, everybody that comes from abroad is *censé* to come from France, and whatever they wear at their first reappearance immediately grows the

33. **Augusta, Princess of Wales with Members of her Family and Household 1739; J-B Vanloo**

The Princess and her household are in formal dress; her velvet, stiff-bodied gown, worn over a silver petticoat embroidered in gold, is complemented by an ermine-lined state robe. Mrs Herbert (left) and Lady Archibald Hamilton are dressed in a similar style – brown velvet and silver tissue respectively, suggesting that household officials (not servants) were allowed to wear this royal style. The Princess's Vice-Chamberlain, Sir William Irby, is in a heavily embroidered blue velvet coat and waistcoat of green/blue silk embroidered in silver and colours. Velvet was popular at court during the winter.

fashion.' By the end of the 1750s, the French fashion for blue and silver, so much admired in the 1720s, was again in the ascendancy for court wear. For the King's birthday in 1759 Lady Coventry's clothes were 'blue, with spots of silver, of the size of a shilling, and a silver trimming, and cost my Lord will know what', and the following June, Walpole described the Duke of York, at a ball in honour of the Prince of Wales's birthday, dressed 'in a pale blue watered tabby'.[97] Attention was turning to the new, young generation of royals, and the political and fashionable worlds had high hopes for the changes and rewards that a new reign would ensure.

34. **George II 1750s; G Townshend**
This scribbled caricature has captured George II's indomitable self-regard and dapper appearance which characterized him throughout his long life.

THREE

'A Pageant in another sphere'

Prepare yourself for crowds, multitudes. In this reign all the world lives in one room. The capital is as vulgar as a county town in the season of horse-races.[1]

This was Horace Walpole's warning to his friend George Montagu in February 1761. The excitement, activities and changes which accompanied the early months of a new reign were noted in minute detail by Walpole. The expectations placed upon the new King, George III, combined many elements, but most especially curiosity. He was young, only 22, he had not gone out into society like his brothers and uncles but had only been seen at his mother's side at court functions; his opinions and preferences were hardly known, and he was unmarried. It was a cause for celebration, even if the person who had prompted such an upsurge of festivity was, temperamentally, disinclined to be fêted. With hindsight, it is easy to dismiss this natural euphoria. Popular historians have told us that George III was a political incompetent, the monarch who lost the American colonies – 'Farmer George', a simple-minded man who went mad. It is difficult to imagine him young or as someone who might be interested in personal appearance – his own or that of others; the etiquette of court life or the image of monarchy. To dress historians he is an awkwardly extended overture to the main interest of his long reign – his son, the Prince of Wales, the Prince Regent, the 'First Gentleman of Europe'. This does the King and his consort, Queen Charlotte, an injustice, for

their attitudes changed the direction of English court life, reshaping it in appearance and etiquette in a manner which had a lasting effect.

King George III had one great advantage over both his predecessors: he was the first Hanoverian king to be born, brought up and educated in England. He never visited Hanover, in fact he never once set foot outside of England, but he thought of himself as German, saying in 1786, 'Oh! my heart will never forget that it pulses with German blood.'[2] In other aspects, he was at one with a substantial proportion of his British subjects: cautious, conservative, suspicious of cleverness but interested in new ideas if they indicated improvement rather than radical change. His attitudes mirrored those of many of the less dissolute members of the English aristocracy in the second half of the eighteenth century. He hunted and preferred the country, writing 'I certainly see as little of London as I possibly can'. He also enjoyed family life and saw little reason to worry about his appearance, except on the most formal of occasions.[3] Kingship inevitably presented him with a great deal of formality, and he understood the need to dress

35. George III 1764; A Ramsay
This official portrait of the King in coronation robes is one of a number of copies produced by Ramsay in the 1760s after the success of the initial royal commission. Traditional purple velvet and ermine robes are worn over a fine court suit of gold brocade. Ramsay has invested the King with some of the dignified elegance associated with official portraits of French royalty.

for his role, for, unlike his eldest son, he had a highly developed sense of duty, but little personal vanity.

One of his two unacknowledged sisters-in-law (whose entry into the royal family led to the Royal Marriage Act of 1772), the Duchess of Cumberland, made jokes at his expense, ridiculing amongst other things, 'his ill-made coats, and general antipathy to the fashion'.[4] His approach to fashion may have been that of someone who endured rather than enjoyed its whims, but he was not impervious to change. Portraits of the King throughout his life demonstrate that he was most at ease in the uniforms of his office: coronation robes worn over a rich gold brocade three-piece suit, of coat, waistcoat and breeches, which was the formal court fashion of the middle years of the century; military uniform denoting his role as head of the armed forces, although, like his father before him and his son at a later date, he was never involved in military training or action; and the Windsor uniform, of his own devising, which he wore on every possible occasion, and was undoubtedly his favourite form of dress from the late 1770s onwards. However he was more a follower than a leader of fashion. The richly brocaded pastel silks of the early years of his reign were replaced by darker, more subtle colour combinations and the King kept in step. At the Queen's birthday celebrations in 1788 he 'appeared in the evening in a suit of brown velvet richly embroidered'.[5] By the following decade, Lord Glenbervie was bemoaning the fact that, 'For these last three or four years, if a man has been to Court he cannot go, without some singularity, to dine out or to an assembly without putting on a frock'.[6] The difference between dress worn at court and dress worn privately by fashionable society became distinct as George III and Queen Charlotte tried to maintain a formality of style which they perceived as a mark of respect to the monarchy.

The 'frock' had developed from a style of working class dress worn in the country. It was usually made of cloth, had a turned-down collar, shallow cuffs and was cut away to fit, without bulky padding, over the hips and thighs. There was a general move towards a narrow cut and plainer, more sombre materials and colours in the last 15 years of the eighteenth century. At court functions, younger, fashionable men began to wear plain dark velvets and silks, or dark, striped silks, and the sumptuous embroidery which had been such a feature of men's formal dress earlier in the century was restricted to the cuffs, collar, coat fronts and pockets and was much less flamboyant than previously. A variety of delicately worked floral and pastoral motifs in subtly graduated coloured silks and chenille, with gold and silver spangles or mica glass and fine lace appliqué was used to add definition and sparkle. The comparative sobriety of coat and breeches was offset by a paler silk waistcoat with embroidered fronts and collar. The emphasis in both court wear and less formal dress was towards simplicity of material and decoration which, in turn, promoted the more sophisticated tailoring techniques at which the English were to excel over the next 150 years. Such simplicity was very much in keeping with the King's personal taste and in 1795 he appeared at a reception in 'a prune-coloured coat of broadcloth'.[7] Cloth was a staple English product and as such could be worn by the King without the fear of controversy attached to certain materials.

As in earlier centuries, there were problems in George III's reign about the flood of luxury goods imported from Europe and the east, and the changes in taste and fashion which could adversely affect the livelihood of his subjects. In 1765 he received a deputation of London wig-makers who were concerned about the influx of foreign hair-dressers and the new fashion whereby men wore their own hair rather than wigs.[8] Although as a young man George shaved his head and wore a wig, he seems for a time to have followed the fashion of growing his hair and having it dressed, but in 1773 he reverted to his previous practice. When James Beattie called on the royal 'Peruke-maker', Mr Stewart, to pay a bill, he found the latter 'busied in making wigs for the King, who has lately cut off his hair'. These wigs cost five guineas, and Beattie was obviously impressed by the expense: he paid a relatively modest £1.11.6 for 'a new dress-wig'.[9] Powdered dress wigs continued to be required wear at court long after they ceased to be fashionable, indicating that the deputation of 1765 had had an effect on the styles the King was able to regulate. In 1791 a group of fashionable young men led by Lord Lorne, wore cropped, unpowdered hair and, consequently, were unable to accept invitations to a court ball.[10] It seems probable that they were unwilling to conform by wearing wigs, the most natural solution to such a dilemma. Solecisms in dress and appearance were even less acceptable at court in the 1790s because the new fashions were associated in both the royal and the popular mind with the excesses of the French Revolution, for France retained its role as the arbiter of fashion, despite its bloody social and political upheavals.

Early in his reign the King was made aware of the difficulties which beset the Spitalfields silk industry. English silk weavers were technically as proficient as their French and Italian counterparts, largely owing to the injection of French Huguenot craftsmen into the industry in the years after 1685, but the designs for English silks were rarely as subtle or as sensitive to changes in styles of dress as those of European industries. There were demonstrations by weavers and rioting when the Duke of Bedford managed to engineer the rejection of a bill for raising the import duty on Italian silks in May 1765.[11] In the following year, the pendulum swung in the King's favour; he went to the House of Lords to agree to a bill prohibiting the import of French silks, accompanied by jubilant weavers carrying flags and streamers and playing drums.[12] Royal patronage of the industry, alongside stringent legislation, ensured its survival; Queen Charlotte and her daughters wore silks designed and woven at Spitalfields and by the late 1790s a selection of these, called 'Queen's silk', was being sold exclusively by Harding, Howell and Co. at Schomberg House in Pall Mall.[13] Court etiquette, which required rich silks to be worn at formal occasions long after the fashions for both men and women used plain cloth, light, unpatterned silks, cotton chintzes and gauzy cambrics, played a substantial part in supporting the London-based industry.

Like all members of his family, George III was fascinated by uniforms. The order and precision of military life had been denied him by his grandfather, but he often wore the uniform of the Royal Horse Guards because he approved of its colours, and he spent happy hours memorizing details of military uniforms from illustrations in his collection. This interest took a concrete form when he introduced a new type of official dress, the Windsor uniform. There has been considerable speculation about his choice of colours, 'blue and gold turned up with red', and his reasons for introducing them in the late 1770s. The colours reflected both the hunting livery of blue cloth with red collars and cuffs and gold decoration worn by his father and his friends in the 1730s, and the court uniform worn by his second cousin Frederick the Great. Such uniforms were introduced into a number of European courts in the late eighteenth and early nineteenth centuries and were a natural extension of the developments in military uniform. England was, of course, a maritime as well as a military power and the Windsor uniform might be thought to mirror the blue and scarlet of naval and army uniforms. The new fashion was quickly noticed by the newspaper and journal writers of the time, who, much like their late twentieth-century

Left 36. **Queen Charlotte 1764; A Ramsay**
This companion portrait to the Ramsay of George III depicts the Queen in coronation robes; the dress is similar to that worn by the Princess of Wales in 1739 (c.f. fig. 33). Her jewellery includes the 'stomacher of diamonds, worth threescore thousand pounds' which had impressed Horace Walpole. Such stomachers were usually a row of carefully designed clasps which diminished in size from bust to waist.

37. **Queen Charlotte c.1770; engraving after a portrait by J Zoffany**
The Queen's lack of beauty is hardly noticeable in this depiction in which the highly decorative appearance of her dress, hair-dressing and jewellery is matched by the ornate setting. Although subtly identifiable by the portrait bracelets with the King's miniature, in every other respect she might be mistaken for any fashionably dressed woman of this date.

counterparts, were as, if not more, interested in the clothes worn by royalty, as in their activities.

In August 1779 the *Reading Mercury* reported that:

All the King's suite now wear blue coats with a small red cape and cuff, as does the Queen; the Princess Royal and her attendants (wear) the same coloured riding habit, which is their usual morning dress.

In addition to being apparently bi-sexual in its early phase, the uniform had two classes. At the celebrations for the Prince of Wales's birthday held at Windsor in August 1781, in the morning, at chapel, 'the gentlemen wore the Undress Uniform' but at the ball in the evening, 'The King, the Princes and all those belonging to the King's family, wore the Windsor Full-Dress Uniform.' The distinction was marked by the bands of gold lace applied to the collar, cuffs and fronts of the coat, much in the manner of a military full-dress uniform.[14]

The uniform was regarded as a privilege to wear because it was the personal gift of the King and, therefore, guarded jealously. In 1787 his gentlemen ushers were refused leave to wear it, because 'low personages in the Prince of Wales's family (household) had none', however, 'the Duke of Northumberland had lately applied for it as he hunted with the King, which should be the rule.' Initially the uniform was worn beyond the confines of Windsor. On a visit to Whitbread's Brewery in the City of London in May 1787 the King 'had stick and no sword; common [undress] Windsor uniform.' The Prince of Wales wore it at Wentworth House on a tour of Yorkshire in 1789, and in the same year it was worn by gentlemen invited to Ranelagh by the Spanish ambassador. It was a mark of distinction which conveniently filled the gap for those who, in an age when uniforms added both glamour and gravitas to officers in the armed services, were important government rep-

resentatives with no other entitlement to uniform. When Ninian Home was appointed Governor of Grenada in 1793, he ordered both classes of uniform, but had the foresight to have them made 'of the Thinnest Ladies Cloath'. As a substitute for the formality of traditional court dress it could, on occasion, be almost too simple. Lord Malmesbury was formally presented to the rulers of the Directory in Paris in 1795 and,

was surprised at the politeness and dressed appearance of all about... supposing it would be more suitable to the style of his reception [he] was dressed only in the Windsor Uniform.[15]

It might be 'only... the Windsor Uniform' to Lord Malmesbury, but for the man who had devised it, it was his preferred style of dress in the last 30 years of his active reign. He was painted wearing it by Gainsborough, Edridge and Stroehling – it appears in engravings and cartoons of him on horseback, walking, or in company; and small painted souvenir statuettes were produced of him wearing both undress and full-dress forms. It epitomized his whole approach to dress, which owed little to fashion but a great deal to order, familiarity and comfort. His image is that of a sturdy, straightforward English country gentleman who, by an accident of fate, just happened to be King of Great Britain and Hanover. Sophisticated society did not appeal to him, he was happiest at Kew or Windsor; when he was in London he stayed at the Queen's House (Buckingham Palace); St James's Palace was a place of business but never a home. He was the first English monarch to draw a firm distinction between his domestic life and his public duties and this was symbolized by his use of St James's Palace. He would go there from Kew or the Queen's House and be clothed, according to the traditional etiquette, by the appointed household officer, in court dress for levees. Levees were held on Mondays (while Parliament was in session, but given up entirely after his illness in 1788), Wednesdays and Fridays, and they began at noon and usually lasted for an hour or two, after which the King would conduct business before returning 'home'.[15] He took his court duties seriously, following the traditional practice of receiving any person of rank who wanted an audience with him and celebrating royal birthdays, but apart from visits to the theatre or opera, he did not go out into society.

The King had a high-minded and dutiful attitude towards the role of the monarchy and the royal house and stood alone amongst his uncles, brothers and sons in preferring a quietly domestic private life untouched by the frivolous behaviour of fashionable society. Consequently, the court became a worthy but dull place at which none of the eighteenth century's preferred recreations – drinking and eating to excess, gambling and illicit love affairs – were acceptable. Fashionable society existed as a separate entity from the royal court from the 1760s, although certain royals risked the King's displeasure when they found its attractions irresistible. However, to be presented at court and be eligible to attend levees, Drawing Rooms and so forth, remained an essential passport to social acceptance in England and abroad. Therefore, the etiquette and dress required at court were rituals which could be maintained or altered according to the King's and Queen's perceptions of what was appropriate. These rituals might be archaic or absurd, but to question or contravene them implied denial of access to the court, which few people were prepared to risk.

This innate conservatism meant that the King was opposed to social fluidity, for he upheld the hierarchical nature of society despite the obvious changes it was undergoing. In 1780 he expressed the inherited prejudices of his class (if one accepts the view that he epitomized the apex of the aristocratic oligarchy who ruled Great Britain) by stating,

Lord North cannot seriously think that a private gentleman like Mr Penton is to stand in the way

38. **George, Prince of Wales c.1780; R Cosway**
This miniature of the youthful Prince of Wales is the visual confirmation of the Duchess of Devonshire's description that: 'He is inclined to be too fat and looks too much like a woman in men's cloaths, but the gracefulness of his manner and his height certainly make him a pleasing figure'.

of the eldest son of an earl. Undoubtedly if that idea holds good it is diametrically opposite to what I have known all my life.[16]

The newly successful and enriched members of English society were anathema to him. He made this plain when it was suggested he might sit to avoid the fatigue of walking around the circle of those present at a levee. He said he could not sit, 'for there are so many persons coming to these levees who ought not to come, who ought never to be admitted, the only way I have of not speaking to them is to walk on.'[17] It was well known that if the King did not speak to someone at a levee it showed his greatest displeasure, a useful signal of temporary irritation, or, in this instance, of social unacceptability.

Theoretically, it should have been possible to exclude such persons, for anyone not previously presented to the King was required to have a 'sponsor' when he first appeared at a levee, and to be correctly dressed. There was, however, no prior vetting of those to be presented, and no written formula which dealt with court etiquette. As a result, the impecunious who were acceptable at court solved a variety of financial difficulties by sponsoring others who were not. Lady Bute, the wife of the King's boyhood governor, the Earl of Bute, in 1761 said that attending court was, 'a means of introduction into the world', and James Boswell received similar advice from Lady Northumberland, who told him it was 'a cheap diversion; it costs you nothing, and you see all the best company, and chat away. It is the best coffee-house in town.' She suggested that his friend Lord Eglinton would arrange his presentation.[18]

The 'sponsor' provided the all-important advice about dress, protocol and behaviour, and any rich merchant or nabob could easily be tutored in correct deportment, the management of a sword and the physical attributes of a true gentleman. A hard-up sponsor, a fashionable tailor and a dancing-master were the eighteenth-century equivalent of a crammer on etiquette, although there was no shortage of primers on etiquette for the uninitiated. When James Beattie, Professor of Marischal College, Aberdeen, went to London in 1773 to solicit a pension from the King, his sponsor was the Earl of Dartmouth who referred him to Mr Gray,

who recommended to me a Wigmaker and a Taylor; the former of whom I desired to make me a Bagwig ... and the latter to make me a suit of pale blue clothes in the present court-fashion. Mr Gray lent me buckles, a stock, stockings, and some other little matters for my appearance at the Levee

on Friday; and is also to lend me a sword.

His suit cost six guineas, his wig £1.11s.6d and new shoes 6s 6d, but on the appointed day Lord Dartmouth and he arrived late and the levee had ended; poor Beattie had to wait for nearly two weeks for the next levee as the King was to be out of London. On this occasion he and Lord Dartmouth were early, and the levee went without a hitch; Beattie was presented, kissed his monarch's hand and was delighted by his 'cheerful affability'. It was then decided he should be presented to the Queen, but she did not appear in the drawing-room on the set day, 'on acct. (it is said) of her pregnancy.' A week later, when it was thought the Queen would appear, he made himself ready again. His suit of pale blue clothes were useless 'as the Court is now in mourning', and he had to borrow a 'full-dress suit of Black ... and a black sword'. The Queen did not appear as predicted and Beattie was disappointed once more. In this instance the story ended happily. He was granted a private audience at Kew, had the pleasure of a conversation with both King and Queen and shortly afterwards received his pension. Beattie may have been unfortunate in the experiences or the information of his sponsors, but this is unlikely, and his case shows that it required considerable patience, as well as expense, to be presented at court and to receive the approbation of both King and Queen.[19]

Queen Charlotte's regular appearances at the Drawing Room on Thursdays, and on Sundays after chapel, were disrupted by the successive pregnancies which punctuated her married life until 1783. In that respect, James Beattie's experience must have been shared by many potential presentees in the 1760s and 1770s. The Queen had been an unexpected choice, plucked from the minor German duchy of Mecklenburg-Strelitz when only 17, to marry the greatest Protestant match in Europe. She was young, presumably malleable, spoke poor English and French and was undoubtedly plain. When the marriage was announced in the July of 1761, Horace Walpole considered it 'food for newsmongers' tattle, solicitations, mantua-makers, jewellers, etc. for above two months to come!'[20] The royal wedding was to be followed by the coronation, and London society could discuss nothing but 'robes, ermine, and tissue, jewels and tresses'; even 'Mr Pitt himself would be mobbed if he talked of anything but clothes, and diamonds, and bridesmaids'.[21]

It was a merchant and tradesman's equivalent of heaven. Discovering the Princess's measurements, was just one of the many duties entrusted to David Graeme, the King's envoy who carried the marriage proposal to the court at Mecklenburg.[22] All of her trousseau and coronation garments were made in England, but the strain of the ensuing events, including her mother's death and journey to England accompanied by no German entourage except two *femmes de chambre*, obviously led to a loss of weight. When Walpole saw her at court on the evening of Tuesday 8 September (she had arrived in London only seven hours earlier) she was dressed in white and silver, with:

> an endless mantle of violet-coloured velvet, lined with ermine, and attempted to be fastened on her shoulder by a bunch of large pearls, (which) dragged itself and almost the rest of her clothes halfway down her waist. On her head was a beautiful little tiara of diamonds; a diamond necklace, and a stomacher of diamonds, worth threescore thousand pounds, which she is to wear at the Coronation too.[23]

By the time of the coronation and the subsequent portrait by Ramsay (a pair to that of the King), her clothes had been adjusted satisfactorily and comprised a stiff-bodied gown in velvet and ermine worn open over a richly embroidered and bejewelled petticoat, the double tier of lace sleeves ruffles worn by royal ladies and their attendants, and the 'sumptuous' diamond stomacher which had impressed Walpole.

Initially she appears to have shown some reluctance to conform to the expectations of the English court in regard to appropriate dress for a queen-consort of Great Britain. On her journey to London she was advised by her new English ladies in attendance to curl her toupet. She refused, telling them, 'I think it looks as well as those of the ladies that have been sent for me: if the King would have me wear a periwig, I will; otherwise I shall let myself alone.' In similar vein she was told that the King liked a particular style of dress and responded, 'Let him dress himself; I shall dress as I please.'[25] Gradually, under the guidance of her mother-in-law, the Princess Dowager, and the King's unmarried sister, Princess Augusta, she conformed. Portraits, engravings, cartoons and contemporary descriptions indicate that she followed rather than led fashion, drawing a distinction between formal wear, appropriate for court ceremonies and the styles of dress suitable for informal public appearances and domestic life. According to Walpole, the King gave her many presents of magnificent jewellery, usually of diamonds, and the cartoonists seized on this as a personal obsession, ridiculing her in such prints as *The Queen of Hearts covered in diamonds* of 1786, but descriptions and portraits of her indicate that these were worn only on the most formal occasions. At the drawing-room in honour of the King's birthday in 1792 she wore six large diamonds which *The Lady's Magazine* estimated 'could not be worth less than an hundred thousand pounds'.[26] They can be construed as the symbols of her role, a type of uniform for royal ladies, well understood by foreign rulers. In 1795, the Turkish ambassador drew such a distinction when (on behalf of his master) he gave the King martial gifts – gold pistols, Arab horses and a gold dagger; the Queen received silks and a head-dress of feathers set on a gold band, each feather tip set with diamonds.[27]

Women's dress moved away from the densely patterned brocaded silks of the middle years of the century towards plainer, lighter silks, printed chintzes and, in the 1790s, light cotton cambrics. Many ephemeral styles of female dress were devised, but the two main fashions were the *robe à l'anglaise*–with its closely fitted back and bodice to which the full, often open-fronted, skirt was stitched; and the 'sack' a fashion which appeared at the French court before 1720 and, rather later, was adopted in England. The latter had a loose back panel from shoulders to ankle (or longer, if trained) which was caught into unstitched pleats along the top of the shoulders. Both of these basic styles were subject to variation in the details of construction and decoration, but were usually accompanied by sleeve and neck ruffles, a head-dress of a cap with lappets, gloves and a fan. Throughout the second half of the century there was a diminution in the size of hoop worn beneath the petticoats and underskirts, and a growing sense of relative informality. The subtle distinctions of dress for function and occasion, which by the late nineteenth century meant that a fashionable woman might change five or six times a day, began to evolve in the late eighteenth century. The styles worn at court, however, changed more slowly than other fashions. Queen Charlotte punctiliously observed this distinction, and required those in her household and ladies who attended court to be similarly careful of their appearance. Until the 1790s this was unexceptionable; all European courts were similarly archaically formal in their dress.

The advent of a queen-consort appears to have led, in 1762, to attempts to regularize the style of dress worn by women at the English court. According to Horace Walpole, this was 'to thin the Drawing-rooms', and was to consist of 'stiff-bodied gowns and bare shoulders'.[28] It sounds suspiciously like the style reserved for royal ladies in George II's reign, worn at the Brandenburg court in the 1690s. Order and uniformity in dress suggests a Teutonic thoroughness which may have been reinforced by the arrival of the latest in a line of German consorts. What little evidence can be gleaned from surviving examples of eighteenth-century female court dress do not indicate the 'close body without pleats or robings', which the *Magazine à la Mode* described as a 'Robe de Cour' in 1777. The common features of surviving examples from the period after 1760 are low bodices, a triple row of graduated ruffled cuffs attached to the sleeves, a skirt wide enough to accommodate a hoop 'resembling the shape of a bell and extending its dimensions so large at the bottom', that it could not be successfully drawn on the magazine page, and a train. These trains were usually narrow, truncated tails which were folded back, stitched into place and lacked enough material to trail on the ground. The Queen, princesses and ladies in the royal household had long trains containing two breadths of silk – the Queen's three yards, the others two. At Versailles, trains trailed on the ground as a mark of respect, but in England they were held at the left side of the hoop by means of a button and loop, with the exception of the Queen's.[29] There are no surviving examples of royal court dress of this period and, apart from engravings, few illustrations of what the Queen actually wore at court. Fortunately the one exception is a quite remarkable portrait by Gainsborough, painted in 1781. It is not the *robe de cour*, for it is open at the bodice front, but it has the hoop, flowing train, treble ruffles and would reveal bare shoulders if modesty had not led the Queen to inappropriately tuck a muslin

39. **Queen Charlotte 1781; T Gainsborough**
A rare portrait of late eighteenth-century court dress. The wide hoops, long train, tiered sleeve ruffles and exquisitely over-decorated dress and petticoat are given a romantic delicacy of appearance in Gainsborough's skilful depiction, but were, in reality, heavy, cumbersome and increasingly unfashionable.

fichu around the neck. The dress is an exercise in formal grandeur, taking a fashionable silk gauze dotted with spangles and arranging it over a more substantial silk and contradicting its natural simplicity with ruched robings, scalloped and serpentine tiers of decoration, glittering tassels and large satin bows. Generally speaking, the British, whether royalty or aristocrats had an aversion to being painted in court dress—it did not signify exclusive power and status, as coronation, parliamentary and chivalric robes or military uniform so obviously did. Court dress was just one more type of functional dress, necessary, but

40. George III's Birthday Ball 1782

Royal birthdays continued to provide occasions upon which the richest examples of court dress were worn. The curious mixture of festivity and formality which characterized public royal ceremonial is depicted in this contemporary engraving.

increasingly eccentric. George III was never painted in court dress; for his sittings with Gainsborough he chose the full-dress Windsor uniform which, worn with Garter insignia of ribbon, star and garter, economically summarized his status.

Female court dress, under the observant but ageing eye of Queen Charlotte, varied a little but retained features which eventually made it one of the longest running jokes in Europe. In the 1780s Mrs Lybbe Powys recounted the experience of a friend who had not been to court for many years, 'but luckily on her going to the mantua-maker's she found no alteration in fashions for Court dress for years... Flowers and trimmings, tho' quite out elsewhere...'.[30] Constant reuse of existing court dress was possible for someone like Mrs Papendiek, married to a minor court official, who had various alterations to a dress of puce and white satin, new in 1782, but still

appearing in 1788.[31] It was less possible for a prominent, but spendthrift, member of fashionable society like the Duchess of Devonshire. Writing to her mother in 1780, she regretted not going to the Queen's birthday, having invested in a beautiful 'gown' of 'pale blue, with the drapery etc. of an embroidered gauze in paillons'. By 1795 her circumstances were such that her mother warned her, 'it would be very inconvenient if you was to be in town now as you would hardly avoid the sort of Gala Drawing rooms, which would cost a great deal of money'.[32] Lady Louisa Stuart was of the opinion that, 'Fifteen or sixteen hundred a year, would not do much for two people who must live in London and appear in fine clothes at St James's twice a week', but she was discussing an average couple, not a duchess with an addiction to gambling and an unsympathetic husband, and elsewhere she said, 'A good subject cannot be dressed in these days under one hundred pounds.'[33]

Members of the royal household continued

41. **Thanksgiving Service for George III's Recovery 1789**

Jubilees were unheard of in the eighteenth century; it was usual to celebrate a momentous victory with a church service, but Queen Charlotte advocated a service of thanksgiving at St Paul's Cathedral when the King recovered from his bout of 'insanity' in 1789. The King and princes wore Windsor uniform, the Queen and princesses uniform dresses and 'God Save the King' bandeaux beneath their towering plumes. In this respect, the occasion must have presented a visual coherence akin to that of a military parade.

to receive financial help towards their clothing and, even after the reforms of the Royal Household instituted by Edmund Burke in 1782 – which abolished many sinecures and wasteful elements, including the Great Wardrobe and its highly paid master – the traditional custom of receiving expensive items from the wardrobes of the King and Queen persisted. Such an arrangement was infinitely more beneficial to the servant than the master, a fact which the Queen stressed when writing to Lord Ailesbury, her Treasurer, in 1792 when she was in deficit on her allowance, which also had to cover her daughters' expenses. Given the caveat that the Queen was instinctively a conservative upholder of the traditional forms, it does much to explain

42. The King and Queen at the Royal Academy 1789; engraving by P Martini after P Ramberg

The different approach to fashionable dress by the older and younger generations of the royal family is illustrated in this engraving. The Queen has retained the wider hoop and natural waistline of her youth while the princesses have adopted the higher waist, bustle-pad and pronounced 'pouter-pigeon' fichu of the latest fashions. The King, in conservative long coat and waistcoat is out-shone by the Prince of Wales in narrow cutaway coat and short, straight-edged waistcoat.

the apparent extravagance of all great families on their clothing. She wrote,

> '*The bills I know are high this quarter but etiquette will have it so, for the quantity of lace and linen I am in duty bound to have and the clothes are far more than I want, nay I assure you that I ever wear, and some years ago I meant and wished to have less and change seldomer but was advised against it on account of the noise it would make amongst the Bedchamber women, and if you knew of how little I want of what I must buy you would yourself say that the arrangement made for me was hard.*'[34]

Etiquette ruled the English court like a *deus ex machina*, which even royalty seemed unwilling to challenge, in case the whole fabric of court life collapsed around their ears.

Examples of this can be identified through-

out the reign, but 1786 provides an interesting study across a wide social spectrum. Fanny Burney, the celebrated novelist and also, in earlier and impecunious circumstances, the assistant keeper of the wardrobe (a species of glorified ladies maid) to Queen Charlotte recorded, in July 1786, a typical court day in the life of the Queen and her attendants. The King and Queen were at Kew where 'The Queen dresses her head, (but) put on her Drawing Room apparel at St James's'. The household officials went to St James's 'about an hour before the King and Queen'; on arrival the Queen changed into 'her Court dress', summoned her two attendant eldest daughters, held a private audience and then returned to the private apartments where the bedchamber woman added her ministrations to the Queen's appearance, 'the *etiquette* of Court requiring that one of them should finish her dress.' This was purely ceremonial, 'She only tied on the necklace, and handed the fan and gloves' and carried the Queen's train as far as the ante-room where this duty was transferred to the 'lady of the bedchamber-in-waiting, who then becomes the first train bearer'. While she was at St James's, Fanny Burney could 'never appear, even though I have nothing to do with the Drawing Room, except in a saque; 'tis the *etiquette* of my place.'[35] Belatedly, the sack had become acceptable at the English court, but whether this was a type of 'other ranks' style is difficult to determine. Possibly Fanny Burney's lowly status in the Queen's household might have categorized her dress, or conceivably the distinction between female royalties and all other women was being re-defined. In the same year the actress, Sarah Siddons, was summoned to read to the King and Queen, but, 'could not appear in the presence of the Queen except in a Dress not elsewhere worn called a Sacque or negligée with a hoop, treble ruffles and lappets, in which costume I felt not at all at my ease.'[36] By the late 1780s sacks were distinctly unfashionable, although the Queen

and Princesses wore them as late as 1788 for informal occasions, and hoops were considered an intolerable burden. Jane Austen's sister described a court occasion of c.1786 when she stood 'from two to four (o'clock) in the Drawing Room and of course loaded with a great hoop of no inconsiderable weight.'[37] It was etiquette but it was anachronistic, and the first rule of anachronistic dress, as Charles II demonstrated when revising Garter dress in the 1660s, was to give it historical credence. No-one likes to appear unfashionable but relatively few people, however sophisticated, object to wearing a version of the dress of an admired historical era which pre-dates their individual or collective memories.

This was a truism which Queen Charlotte never understood. Privately she moved with fashion; on formal public occasions she resisted it. Perhaps this reflected the King's wishes. It was he who was angered by Lawrence's portrait of 1790 which depicted her bare-headed; acceptable then and unexceptionable now, but possibly a little too radical for an upholder of the nation's etiquette, and too startling a contrast to Gainsborough's formal portrait of 1781. The portrait was not acquired for the royal collection, but George III was inexperienced when it came to the relationship between patron and artist in the evolution of an agreed visual image of royalty. One of the greatest of late eighteenth-century connoisseurs, Sir William Hamilton, damned him with the faintest praise, regarding him as someone who, 'for want of having formed his taste early and on works of the first class, has never arrived at being sensible of what is properly called the sublime in the arts'.[38] Both he and the Queen (and their children) were painted by nearly every artist of consequence, but the result of this catholicity of taste is an apparently blurred image, veering between the banally domestic and the elegantly formal (and providing the student of dress with a good deal of information about their personal preferences in clothing). Such confusion of

intention is disconcerting but is, essentially, a reflection of the King's lack of understanding of the role of portraiture as a communicator of ideas. He was genuinely disconcerted by the barrage of unflattering cartoons, caricatures and satires which mocked him and his family, but was incapable or unwilling to offer an alternative, coherently structured public image to counter-balance the distortions. He wrote to his son, the Prince of Wales, on his eighteenth birthday,

> *The misfortune is that in other countries national pride makes the inhabitants wish to paint their Prince in the most favourable light, and consequently be silent upon any indiscretion; but here most persons, if not concerned in laying ungrounded blame, are ready to trumpet any speck they can find.*[39]

Such specks could vary in significance, but even in areas where minor modification was wholly within the royal jurisdiction, such as formal royal dress and, flowing from this example, dress for those attending court, there was a conservative inertia which offered considerable scope to caricaturists such as Rowlandson, Gillray and their contemporaries. Men's court dress, for those not entitled to a uniform, retained characteristics of the fashion of the 1770s: powdered wigs, embroidered coats with black silk bags to protect them from the powder, knee breeches, embroidered waistcoats, swords and bicorne hats. This style prevailed, with the minimum of alteration until the second half of the nineteenth century. It was archaic and faintly absurd but women's

43. Queen Charlotte 1789; Sir Thomas Lawrence

The Queen's traditional approach to fashion (c.f. fig. 42) is demonstrated in greater detail in this portrait by the young Lawrence. The taste for lighter, delicate materials and the shift in emphasis to the head and bust are discreetly hinted at rather than accepted wholeheartedly. George III's dislike of this portrait ensured that it was not acquired for the royal collection.

court dress was, increasingly, so ridiculous that male courtiers attracted scant attention. Perhaps Queen Charlotte's desire for certain uniform elements within court dress led to the absurdities of the period c.1794–1820. In 1789, after the King's recovery from his first immobilizing illness, the Queen, Princesses and household ladies wore uniform styles of a 'gown of white tiffany', with a garter blue body; the sleeves were white and ornamented, like the petticoat with three rows of fringe corresponding with that of the bottom of the gown. All the ladies wore bandeaux round the front of their head-dress with the words 'God Save the King'; and on a later occasion they all wore

> *open gowns of purple silk, edged and finished off with gold fringe; (with) petticoats of Indian muslin over which white satin with deep fringe of gold at the bottom (and) white satin bandeaux . . . embroidered in gold letters (with God Save the King).*[40]

At the King's birthday ball, Lady Louisa Stuart's 'uniform' was of white satin, trimmed with blonde lace and bedecked with gold bands and tassels with a crêpe train tied back with gold cord and tassels; the ensemble surmounted by a cap of 'plain crepe with a bandeau of white satin, and 'God Save the King' on it in gold spangles and four very high feathers on the other side.'[41] This quasi-militaristic patriotism did not survive the year; if the King (or Queen) had hoped to introduce a female equivalent of the Windsor uniform for formal occasions, as such careful detailing might suggest, it did not meet with general favour. Only the feathers in head-dresses survived this experiment, keeping pace with fashionable developments. In other respects the style reverted to the traditional hooped and trained formal dress, rich in ornamentation and lavish in its use of materials of 'British manufacture'.

It was the retention of hoops which caused such universal mirth. They would have been

HER ROYAL HIGHNESS THE PRINCESS OF WALES.

44. Caroline, Princess of Wales 1807
This fashion plate of the Princess of Wales in court dress was accompanied by a eulogistic description of her pale lilac dress with its amethyst decoration. The absurdity of this style, with its fashionable high waist but wide eighteenth-century hoops and narrow tail-like train, was admitted by all except Queen Charlotte, who insisted upon hoops for court dress until her death in 1818.

acceptable if the Queen had signalled that female court dress should retain the natural waistline and full skirt of the mantua of the late 1770s, but no such signal was given. As waistlines rose and lines narrowed and became more fluid with the use of soft gauzy materials, the hoop was still required, jutting out awkwardly from just below the bust. It looked absurd, but it used a great deal of material,

for these unfashionably wide skirts were draped and ornamented with every type of expensive trimming; behind, like a tail on a swollen toad, hung a narrow train. If fashionable women had hoped that the Queen would burst out laughing, clap her hands and, in her fractured English, command a change, they were mistaken. One notice, for an evening Drawing Room in April 1805, allowed ladies to wear 'full dress without hoops'. Might reports and illustrations of the formal but fashionable elegance of the ladies at the newly constituted Imperial Court in Paris have influenced this decision? A persuasive advocate may have pointed out that a long, lavishly decorated train, attached at shoulders or waist, could match the absurdly full skirts over hoops in terms of splendour. For whatever reason it was instigated, the result was unsuccessful; the hoop was reinstated and the fashionable magazines continued to illustrate and describe, uncritically, the court dresses which everyone, with the exception of the Queen, found so ridiculous. When Louis Simond visited London in 1810–11, he described the scene as ladies were carried to court in sedan chairs, dressed 'in the fashion of fifty years ago, as more suitable, I suppose, to the age of their majesties' with 'their immense hoops ... folded like wings, pointing forward on each side'.[43] The American envoy, Richard Rush, who attended the Queen's birthday Drawing Room in February 1818, reacted quite differently and his purple prose is an indication of how impressed he was with the spectacle,

Each lady seemed to rise out of a gilded little barricade; or one of silvery texture. This, topped by her plume, and the 'face divine' interposing, gave to the whole an effect so unique, so fraught with feminine grace and grandeur, that it seemed as if a curtain had risen to show a pageant in another sphere.[44]

This theatricality seems at variance with all that is known of Queen Charlotte's charac-

ter and taste. She had a formidable under-standing of all the subtleties of etiquette, but the talents of a pageant-master are more usually ascribed to her eldest and favourite child, the Prince of Wales. In all, 15 children were born to Queen Charlotte and 13 grew to maturity. It was an impossibly large family to direct and control; the sons were educated in England and Germany and, with the exception of the Prince of Wales, given oppor-tunities to pursue careers in the armed forces; the daughters were kept in seclusion under their mother's tutelage and those that married at all were no longer young when they did so. They all appeared, from time to time, at ceremonial occasions and were endlessly painted and caricatured. All of the brothers engaged in those fashionable occupations which George III abhorred: womanizing,

45. **A Drawing Room at St James's Palace c.1805; J Rowlandson**

By the early years of the nineteenth century, court dress for both sexes was a complete luxury – unwearable except on formal court occasions, and an inspiration to caricaturists. Ironically it was the men whose dress retained this fossilized appear-ance. Dark cloth suits with breeches, embroidered waistcoats and silk stockings were still worn in the 1880s.

gambling, drinking and running up debts. The Prince of Wales had an emotional, self-indulgent nature which was tempered by a refinement of taste in artistic matters, but spoilt by personal vanity. The greatest royal connoisseur and patron of the arts since Charles I, he seems, miraculously, to have inherited some of the elusive Stuart charm, but also a fair proportion of their egotism. No eighteenth-century actor could have received so early and thorough an introduction to role-playing and public performance. He was a mere one-week-old when he was created Prince of Wales and shortly after he was on display in his cradle at Drawing Rooms in St James's Palace. Aged two, he was painted with his brother and younger brother by Zoffany, the two Princes respectively masquerading as Telemachus and a Turk; on his fourth birthday, at a fancy dress party, he 'danced a hornpipe in a sailor's dress'. supported by his two younger brothers as harlequin and a 'mademoiselle'.[46] He made regular appearances at Drawing Rooms; on the anniversary of the King's accession in October 1769, aged seven, he and his eldest sister the Princess Royal (aged one) were complimented for their 'graceful deportment and apt performance of the part assigned to them'. The Prince wore scarlet and gold and Garter insignia, his brother Frederick wore blue and gold and Bath insignia and the two youngest Princes were 'elegantly clothed in Roman togas'; the Princess Royal's clothing was, apparently, unremarkable.[47]

Used to adulation and fascinated by all details of dress and appearance (his memory of his god-father and great-uncle, the Duke of Cumberland, who died when he was three, was of an elderly man 'dressed in a snuff-coloured suit of clothes down to his knees'), he was a precociously sophisticated youth and it must have seemed absurdly restrictive when his father wrote to him about his establishment and behaviour when he reached his majority (18 for a prince) in August 1780. Attendance at plays and operas was permitted, so was dancing,

> *but I shall not permit the going to balls or assemblies at private houses . . . . As to masquerades you already know my disapprobation of them in this country, and I cannot by any means agree to any of my children ever going to them.*

There were also instructions about church-going, attendance at Drawing Rooms, riding and general good conduct. It was all too late; the Prince's personal mythology had already passed through its Perdita and Florizel phase, with cartoons exploiting one of his earliest romances with the actress Mary Robinson. The fashionable world offered him an irresistible stage, and dressing-up for domestic masquerades or court rituals had been part of his life as long as he could remember. He liked admiration but he wanted to be involved in everything the world could offer him and plunged with indiscriminating fervour into opposition politics, adopting Charles James Fox's colours of buff and blue, and pursuing all of the interests of fashionable society which his father disliked. He was often drunk, increasingly in debt and unwilling to take advice. As a young man his looks were much admired; he was tall, well proportioned, had an attractive face which lacked the heavy Hanoverian and Brunswick features of his parents, and had thick, glossy chestnut hair. He could have been Prince Charming, concentrating on connoisseurship and collecting, architecture and interior decoration, spreading goodwill and delighting people with his graceful manners, thoughtful conversation and natural elegance. Spasmodically he was exactly that, but it never lasted, and he quickly became the butt of every satirist and caricaturist in London.

In his teens he had recognized in himself 'rather too great a penchant to grow fat' and throughout his life he tried to diet for a brief period, wear corsets and promote styles of dress which disguised his shape rather than resolutely adopt modest habits in eating and

46. The Prince Regent 1819; studio of Sir Thomas Lawrence

The Prince was fascinated by all things military; he frequently wore uniform, and often took active part in its design. He is depicted in field marshal's uniform, his various orders masked by the blue ribbon of the Order of Hanover.

drinking. The Duchess of Devonshire wrote a short character sketch of him in 1782, when he was just 20. All of the personality traits which caused comment later seemed well developed even then: his extravagance, good nature, susceptibility to wine and women, his love of pleasure, his meddling in politics, his loyalty to close companions and his 'ease and grace of... manner'. She described him as,

rather tall ... (with) a figure which tho' striking is not perfect. He is inclined to be too fat and looks too much like a woman in men's cloaths, but the gracefulness of his manner and his height certainly make him a pleasing figure. His face is handsome and he is fond of dress even to a tawdry degree, which, young as he is, will soon wear off. His person, his dress and the admiration he has met, and thinks still more than he meets, from women take up his thoughts chiefly.[49]

In one crucial judgment the Duchess was wrong; the Prince, later King, never grew tired of clothes. He flits relentlessly through the pages of diaries, memoirs, contemporary newspapers and magazines, always exquisitely dressed. For his introduction into the House of Lords in 1783 he wore a black velvet suit embroidered in gold, its pink lining matching the heels of his shoes, his hair dressed in the style he had adopted in 1782, 'flattish at top, frizzed and widish of each side, and three curls at the bottom of this frizzing'.[50] At court he wore the traditional styles with great élan, appearing in a pale ruby coat 'covered with a rich work of white and silver, and beautifully embroidered down the seams with silver... (with a) waistcoat of white and silver' on the Queen's birthday in 1788, and at the King's birthday in 1790 he dazzled in a bottle-green and claret striped silk coat and breeches and silver tissue waistcoat, each item embroidered in silver, spangles and coloured sets with 'Diamond buttons to the coat, waistcoat and breeches'.[51]

Privately, his preference was for the simpler but beautifully tailored cloth coats, tightly-fitting breeches and pristine starched linen, but, like all of his family, he felt happiest in uniform. He wore the Windsor uniform, and the uniform of his regiment, the 10th Light Dragoons, and appeared at court shortly after his marriage in 1795 in full-dress regimentals with the Garter ribbon but 'no diamonds'; on his appointment as Regent he took every possible opportunity to appear in Field-Marshal's dress. His lack of proper military career was a constant irritant, but he expended considerable time and energy on the design or adaptation of uniforms. In October 1811 his daughter Princess Charlotte found him and two of his brothers 'in the *Riding House* looking at and *examining* some soldiers who have got their new dresses'. Again, shortly after her marriage in 1816, she received a visit from him when,

we did not talk on any one disagreable subject or say anything, being fully occupied with discanting and discouraging upon the merits and demerits of such and such a uniform, the cut of such a coat, cape, sleeve, small clothes etc. In short for 2 hours and more I think we had a most learned dissertation upon every regt. under the sun wh. is a great mark of the most perfect good humour.[52]

The Prince could spot any incorrect detail in a uniform, and was always interested in information about foreign uniforms. In pursuit of the excellence of uniformity he issued a decree in 1816, supposedly to support home manufactured textiles, which required,

all his state and household officers to wear costly dresses of home fabrication ... to be made in three classes of uniforms, according to the respective ranks of these officers. The first class consists of suits for the Lord Chamberlain, the Lord Steward, and the Groom of the Stole. The coats are of dark purple, with crimson velvet collars, richly ornamented all over with gold.[53]

It is tempting to speculate about what prompted this move. Possibly the end of the Napoleonic Wars in 1815, which had provided

47. Princess Charlotte of Wales 1816; J Lonsdale

Like her father, the Prince Regent, Princess Charlotte was naturally corpulent, and the few mature portraits depict her in profile, much in the manner of the Regent. Clothes interested her little until she married Prince Leopold of Saxe Coburg Gotha in 1816, and acquired a substantial trousseau.

so many men with elegant military or naval uniforms, led to the feeling that those in royal service must not be left behind. Perhaps it was an attempt to ward off unsuitable applicants for the Windsor uniform; it cannot have been unconnected with the rash of royal and civil uniforms which swept through France, Spain, Italy and many northern European courts in the late eighteenth and early nineteenth century. The Prince Regent's reasons were not known, and at first the uniform was not popular. As late as May 1821, George IV (as he had become on the death of his father in 1820) was irritated by the lack of enthusiasm for his initiative. At Princess de Lieven's he

spotted Mr Planta, principal librarian at the British Museum, in the official style of coat, 'which (the king) had invented a few years ago and which the Ministers generally refused to wear. (The king) went up to him and said he was glad to see him wear it, tho' his principals did not choose to do it.'[54] The obvious answer, which during the lifetime of George III was unacceptable, eventually came to pass. Household officers were given dark blue cloth coats with red cloth collars and cuffs, and government officials had similar coats with black velvet trimmings. As with the Windsor uniform, the coat came in dress and undress versions, expanding to four classes in the 1830s and five in the 1840s.

When he was not devising uniforms, the Prince spent long, happy hours considering his own appearance, and that of those who had to pass before his censorious eye. Linked in popular mythology to George 'Beau' Brummell, briefly the chief dandy of the 1790s and early 1800s, the Prince was as much master as pupil. The Prince was older, started earlier, and lasted longer; the only fashionable area in which he seems to have exercised little influence was that of women's dress. The trousseaux of his wife, Princess Caroline of Brunswick, and his daughter, Princess Charlotte, were left to Queen Charlotte to arrange, possibly erroneously. When his brother, the Duke of York, was to be married in 1793, the Prince was requested to buy diamonds, select a good hairdresser and buy fashionable accessories — shoes, fans, etc. — for his new sister-in-law.[55] Possibly, if his own marriage had been happier, he might have devoted time to developing his wife's tastes in line with his own.

It was, sadly, a disastrous mismatch; the Princess (first cousin to the Prince of Wales) was strong willed, excessively familiar, gauche and graceless. Her lack of personal fastidiousness was such that the English envoy Lord Malmesbury had to prompt her to wash more often and change her linen regularly. In

England matters did not improve; she was brash, 'utterly destitute of all female delicacy', and apparently uninterested or incapable of dressing properly or behaving well.[56] During the short-lived marriage (the Prince and Princess separated after little more than a year) there were those, like the Prince's friend the Duchess of Devonshire, who were prepared to be charmed by the new Princess of Wales and to blame the Prince for the disunity between them. At a private presentation at Carlton House in late February 1796 the Duchess and her sister met the Princess, whose manner,

was affectionate and coaxing almost . . . She enquir'd after you (the duchess's mother) and

48. Princess Charlotte of Wales 1817; G Dawe
The Princess is dressed in a blue silk sarafan trimmed with gold braid. The sarafan was the traditional dress of Russian women. This portrait is a compliment to Czar Alexander I, under whom her husband had served, but whom her father disliked. On her left breast is the star of the Order of St Catherine of Russia. This dress, without its lace sleeves and modesty-piece, is in the Museum of London.

admir'd our dresses very much, and appear'd, I find, at the Queen's house in one like them last Saturday . . .[57]

The Duchess was noted for her innovative elegance so the Princess had chosen exactly the right subject upon which to compliment her. Despite the separation, the Princess appeared at court functions (which the Prince usually avoided) and her style of dress was publicly admired in newspapers and magazines. Privately she was thought to dress, 'very ill, shewing too much of her naked person'. Eventually she retired abroad, shocking English visitors and officials by her improprieties and absurd or immodest dress. She returned to England and was tried before the House of Lords for misconduct – a fat, raddled woman with a black wig and a ferocious expression; she was refused entry to her husband's coronation in 1821 and died the same year. She was a constant embarrassment to the Prince, but he had married her only to settle his debts, and was quite unprepared to charm and guide her. She was wickedly indiscreet about his short-comings, on one occasion exclaiming that she should have been the man and he 'the woman to wear the petticoats . . . He understands how a shoe should be made or a coat cut . . . and would make an excellent tailor, or shoemaker or hairdresser but nothing else.'[58]

There was enough truth in this remark to wound. If the Prince had followed his usual habits during their short time together, he would have occupied himself for hours on end with his suppliers, ordering clothes, jewellery, cosmetics and so forth, leaving the Princess to amuse herself as best she could. When he was low-spirited, for instance after the death of Fox in 1806, he lost all interest in his usual pleasures – eating little and ordering practically nothing – but when he was high-spirited and emotional he was extraordinarily generous, loading mistresses and friends with presents ranging from expensive jewellery to a carefully chosen card-case. His debts always included large sums owed to tailors; in the early 1790s various tailors–Joseph Weston of Old Bond Street, Schweitzer & Davidson of Cork Street, Louis Bazalgette and Winter & Co.–had unpaid bills amounting to over £30,000. He bought everything in quantity: dozens or scores of everything from pairs of gloves to waistcoats and pantaloons. Furs, masquerade costumes, swords, sticks, uniforms; presents of lace or shawls for his sisters and female friends, and cosmetics, scent, wigs, false whiskers and jewellery for himself. A large fortune was expended upon maintaining his position as the best-dressed prince in Europe. Inevitably, because his weight fluctuated so much, his clothes were in constant need of replacement; it would not have occurred to him to have garments altered–fine tailoring depended upon cut and fit, and he was a walking advertisement of what could be achieved by careful corseting and exquisitely cut garments. When the Princess of Wales saw him for the first time, she said, with characteristic lack of tact, 'I think he's very fat and he's nothing like as handsome as his portrait.' The Prince may not have liked his wife, but he was fond of children, and they of him; they accepted that he was fat but liked his 'wonderful dignity and charm of manner', as the young Princess Victoria expressed it later in her life. The Hon. George Keppel remembered, as did the Princess, the wig he wore, but also that:

> *His clothes fitted him like a glove; his coat was single-breasted and buttoned up to the chin... Round his throat was a huge white neck-cloth of many folds out of which his chin seemed to be always struggling to emerge.*[59]

It was the combination of obeseness and dandification which fascinated the cartoonists, and they found him irresistible subject matter: 'A voluptuary under the horrors of digestion', 'The Prince of Whales'; they were indefatigable in their pursuit of his foibles. The Prince tried to suppress them or to buy off the perpetrators but to little purpose. Princess Charlotte, whose relationship with her father was not easy, wrote in January 1812, 'The print shops are full of *scurrilous caricatures* and infamous things relative to the Prince's conduct in different branches'; in the same letter she had, however, noted that 'No family (the Royal family) was ever composed of *such odd people*, I believe, as they all *draw different* ways, and there *have happened* such extraordinary things, that in any other family, either public or private, are never herd of before'. In the previous autumn, at the request of the Prince, his daughter had begun sitting to George Sanders for a portrait; her vanity was patently no match for her father's, for she wrote, 'I have left dress and everything to him (Sanders)'.[60] When the Prince was painted, as a young man, as Regent and as King, it is quite plain that he chose exactly the style of dress and type of portraiture which might develop a refined visual record of royalty in its public and private capacity. He also made particular use of Lawrence to present a coherent record for posterity of his appearance and manner, although there are attractive contributions to his visual iconography from Gainsborough, Stubbs, Beechey, Hoppner and Wilkie. He was fortunate in reaching his maturity during the golden age of English portrait painting, but there is no indication that the artist rather than he dictated his stance or style of dress. He is usually in profile or three-quarter face, which made him appear less fat; the fashionable high-necked collars and cravats which he did so much to popularize act as the equivalent of corsets for his jowls, and his ample proportions are disguised by corsetry, excellent tailoring and the artistic use of elongation. As an antidote to cruel cartoons it was obviously an ineffective tool, but as an example of enlightened patronage in pursuit of historically credible propaganda it stands alongside Van Dyck's vision of Charles I.

One of the ironies of the Prince's life was that although he liked and was liked by children, his relationship with his only child, Princess Charlotte, was strained and distant. Her upbringing and education was supervised by the Prince and his mother, Queen Charlotte. There were occasional, awkward meetings with her mother, Princess Caroline, but much of her time was spent closeted at Warwick House (close to Carlton House) under the watchful eye of her governess and small household, or at Windsor where her grandmother and spinster aunts led a sheltered and humdrum existence. Perhaps she reminded the Prince too much of her mother; she was certainly outspoken, high-spirited and hoydenish. Czar Alexander I's sister, the Grand Duchess of Oldenburg, thought her, 'rather like a young rascal, dressed as a girl'.[61] She was also bright, intelligent and interested in politics and current affairs, but apparently without personal vanity. She admired contemporary heroes as disparate as Lord Byron and the Duke of Wellington, applauding the latter's modesty in always wearing a plain coat rather than flashy regimentals.

Her letters reveal relatively little interest in fashion; she is gracious in her thanks for presents such as a gown or hat; like her father she felt the cold and expressed the need for a warm pelisse; and on one occasion in September 1814 while at Weymouth, forgot her responsibilities in a high-spirited note about 'a smuggler... who sells the most delightful French silks at 5 shillings a yard. I am going to be after him.' The most detailed information in her letters was about jewellery, that essential 'prop' for all female royalties. She received occasional presents of it from her father and grandmother and was equally generous with gifts to her friends at the time of her proposed marriage to the Prince of Orange in 1814, incurring considerable debts. By the time of her engagement to Prince Leopold of Saxe Coburg Gotha in 1816 she appears to have changed her opinion about the necessity for rich jewellery. The trousseau, supervised by Queen Charlotte was decided and being prepared by March 1816 and a 'fine diamond necklace' was on order (for £3000). To go with this were a diamond belt and two 'head ornaments', two strings of pearls for bracelets which 'with what I have in jewels, will do very well, as I would rather less money were spent on them, and more upon plate, furniture and such like things'.[62]

The Princess's future husband was penniless; as a younger, albeit talented son of a minor German principality, he had made a great match. He was not much liked at court— the Regent nicknamed him 'le Marquis peu à peu'— and he had the innate caution of someone who was not prepared to let himself or his great prize be ridiculed and derided like his father-in-law. The Princess wrote, 'he has a great horror of debt and I have had a good lecture upon economy and extravagance already.' He was also 'particularly observant about my dress' and while she and the Regent discussed diamonds and jewellery to the value of £15,000 ('I don't wear earings and bracelets are not seen'), Prince Leopold 'wishes to give me something but does not know what'.[63] Their brief marriage–the Princess died 18 months later shortly after giving birth to a still-born son–was happy. 'Le Marquis' kept the Princess's allowance of £50,000 a year, their residence, Claremont, arranged the marriage of his widowed sister to the Duke of Kent (the brother of George IV) and was well ensconced as favourite uncle to the heiress-presumptive to the throne, Princess Victoria, before returning to Europe in 1831 as King Leopold I of the Belgians.

As a 'peu à peu' career, it was quite remarkable. However, it is almost certainly owing to his careful habits that the small group of garments worn by Princess Charlotte were cherished rather than dispersed, as was the usual royal custom. A childhood dress, a court dress (presumably altered for it lacks the width to accommodate hoops), her glistening silver tissue and lace wedding dress and train and the blue satin Russian-style dress in which she was painted by George Dawe in 1817, provide the first substantial group of English royal clothing to survive. The Princess was 21 when she died, but both the clothes and the surviving portraits and engravings indicate a buxom woman of above average height who, had she lived, might quickly have become fat and ungainly. The most intriguing garment is the Russian-style sarafan—a type of formal peasant dress. The fashion for military, foreign and revivalist styles in women's dress was a feature of the teens and twenties of the nineteenth century. The Czar and his sister, the Grand Duchess of Oldenburg, had visited England in 1814 but he and the Regent had not liked each other; the Russian style affected by Princess Charlotte, glamorized in satin and gold braid and worn with exquisite Brussels lace sleeves, suggests a compliment to an ally (with whose forces Prince Leopold had served) and a snub to her father. A gesture almost worthy of her mother, although infinitely more elegant.

There was, however, no-one more dedicated, more knowledgeable and more eclectic in his tastes than the Prince Regent when it came to devising and wearing traditional or quasi-historical forms of dress. Performances theatrical and military fascinated him, as did court ceremonial and etiquette. His whole life had been dedicated to the idea of visual excellence and spectacle, and when he became king he was offered an irresistible opportunity: a coronation. The influences upon his choice of dress for himself and all the leading 'players' for coronation day in July 1821 rather foxed contemporaries: those who had seen the designs had expected the spectacle 'to convulse the whole of Westminster Abbey with laughter'. They imagined the King would be overinfluenced by Walter Scott novels or an illdigested diet of Tudor fripperies; it was all thought absurdly theatrical – until the actual day. The King had spent considerable time

49. Queen Caroline c.1820; Sir George Hayter
This study of Caroline of Brunswick, estranged wife of George IV, is related to Hayter's painting of the Queen's trial for adultery in the House of Lords. Fat, ageing, over-flowing her fashionable dress, the black-wigged Queen had the sympathy of many who regretted her behaviour but felt that she had been badly treated by her husband.

studying the details of James II's coronation. He had an unexpected interest in the Stuarts – rendered wholly acceptable by the death of the last of the legitimate line descended from James II in 1817 when the Cardinal of York had died, leaving him a fine sapphire from the Stuart royal jewels. The garter underdress, introduced by Charles II, provided one source of inspiration; another was the French King Henry IV, 'whom I admire almost to the point of extravagance'; a third was the coronation dress and uniforms worn in 1805 when Napoleon became Emperor of the French.[64] This last provided an occasion of quite unparalleled splendour, with every style

of dress and uniform carefully designed to create a dramatic and rich brilliance of colour and texture. Napoleon had consciously created a new style of coronation because he wanted no comparison with the ceremonial ritual and dress of the Bourbon Kings of France. George IV could have followed his father's example, permitting peers, ministers and household officers to wear their traditional coronation robes over court dress or, had he wished, their various uniforms: military, naval and household. It would have been customary but immemorable, and having waited so long to become king (he was 59 when he was crowned), George IV determined upon a pageant which would be unforgettable.

There were no rehearsals, such an idea for great state occasions developed later in the nineteenth century; it was only in the theatre where, after coronations had taken place, re-enactments were staged for the delectation of the paying public, that there could be any certainty of a smooth progression of events. Although the peers and privy councillors felt absurd in their fancy dress and the King worried about his wife gate-crashing his great

50. George IV in Coronation Robes 1821; E Scriven after Stephanoff

As an example of ceremonial theatre, George IV's coronation equalled that of the Emperor Napoleon I in 1805. All of the clothes were a quasi-historical amalgam of Bourbon French robes (see fig. 17) and Tudor styles. The pages – in white satin with gold decoration – wore one style of the costumes required for all participants, although colours and details varied according to rank.

by Bourbon kings), they do not seem to belong to a fat man. Vanity had caused him to be corseted more violently than usually; he is said to have sweated through handkerchief after handkerchief, and, when looking close to collapse, been revived with *sal volatile*. This 'gorgeous bird of the east' or 'more like an Elephant than a man' – depending upon the spectator – had a popular triumph.[65] Engravings of individuals and scenes, lavishly illustrated books and portraits recorded the participants and events. Many families retained their unique garments (could they possibly have thought this would become the form for English coronations?), and it is possible to reconstruct a representative group of participants. There is a coherence and colour balance when these garments are brought together which is an impressive testament to the King's strong visual sense.

He undertook other successful enterprises, including a visit to Ireland in 1821, a tour through France and Belgium to Hanover in the same year and, in August 1822, a visit to Scotland. He prepared himself for the last visit by re-stocking his wardrobe, tactfully acquiring a variety of Scottish items (including royal plaid in satin, velvet and cashmere) from a London supplier, George Hunter, who had a business in Edinburgh. His appearance as a Scotsman, however, was not entirely convincing, although he liked its novelty well enough to be painted in kilt, plaid and bonnet by Wilkie.[66] As on this occasion, the King had a propensity, when not appearing royally dignified, to seem like an actor in a part which

day, the series of ceremonies, the procession from Westminster Hall to the Abbey, the coronation ceremony and the banquet afterwards impressed most of the spectators. Wearing a tight-laced cloth of silver doublet and trunk-hose worn with a crimson velvet surcoat and parliamentary robe (later substituted for a purple coronation robe), and exhorting his pages (all peers' sons) to 'Hold it [the train] wider' as he processed, the King entered the abbey. The garments survive today, and although immensely heavy (the robes were made in the French fashion worn

51. John Thorp, Lord Mayor of London 1820–21

Thorp is depicted wearing the formal robe and chain of his office which was, traditionally, and still is, worn over court dress. Such suits – the breeches and coat of velvet or fine cloth, with embroidered decoration on coat and pale waistcoat – changed little until the 1880s, but were worn less as more and more men became entitled to civil uniform.

he wanted but was incapable of playing well. In December 1826 Prince Pückler-Muskau attended the state opening of Parliament, at which the King only was in full dress 'truly covered from top to toe with the ancient kingly decorations'. The occasion struck Prince Pückler-Muskau as tragi-comic,

to see how the most powerful monarch of the earth was obliged to present himself, as chief actor in a pantomime, before an audience whom he deems so infinitely beneath him. In fact, the whole pageant, including the King's costume, reminded me strikingly of one of those historical plays which are here got up so well . . .[67]

The foreign prince also had his reservations about levees and Drawing Rooms, those ceremonial aspects of kingship at which the Hanoverian royals met their courtiers formally. George IV as Prince of Wales, Regent and King was not known for his punctuality; in February 1790 James Hare wrote letters to the Duchess of Devonshire criticizing the Prince for keeping courtiers waiting, drawing unfavourable comparisons between him and George III.[68] He would, however, have considered himself a rigorous upholder of correct dress and etiquette, if not manners.

While he was Regent, George maintained the styles of dress which had been acceptable to his parents. In the *London Gazette* in 1812 a levee notice stated that, 'The same regulations of dress will be strictly observed as at His Majesty's Levées', and in the same year Robert Chester, assistant master of ceremonies, advised Count de Lieven that 'powder tho' optional was generally worn at Court'.[69] Powdered wigs, ceremonial swords, flat bicorne hats and dark suits of cloth or silk, embroidered lightly, often matching the embroidery on the paler silk waistcoats worn beneath, silk stockings and light pumps were the 'uniform' for courtiers without an accepted martial or household uniform. Pückler-Muskau wrote in March 1827 that,

almost everbody is admitted to these levées if they can but appear in the prescribed dress, there cannot be better sport for the lover of caricatures. The unaccustomed dress, and no less unwonted splendour of royalty, raise the national awkwardness and embarrassment to their highest pitch.[70]

There were caricatures, but there had also

been attempts to tighten up regulations concerning those permitted to attend. Although more than a thousand 'gentlemen' often attended, only a proportion – comprising ministers, generals, and diplomats – were allowed a brief private audience. The general assembly then passed the King, taking several hours and congesting the public rooms at St James's Palace in the process. Formal cards were instituted in 1825, submitted in advance to the Lord Chamberlain's Office with the names of the person to be presented and their sponsor. Despite this method of weeding out the ineligible, later sets of regulations suggest that illegible handwriting and brazen cheek were not unheard of methods of gaining access. The problem, of course, was the emergence of industrialists, manufacturers and entrepreneurs–the 'nouveau riche' who wanted the social cachet of being presented at court. Finding a sponsor, learning the etiquette and buying or hiring the appropriate clothes were easily within their grasp, but the traditional nature of English court life placed them below the salt – they made their money rather than inherited and spent it. That rules were flexible for friends of royalty infuriated those who were not. Gradually, a system emerged whereby the sons of these wealthy businessmen, if educated at the right schools, recruited to a fashionable regiment or living on a private income, might be presented at court. Their social acceptability, however, depended on their not being associated with their fathers' businesses. It was a typically English compromise, hypocritical but apparently more democratic than those stuffy European courts where even a gentleman had to prove his ancestry had been impeccable for several generations.

By the 1820s the most obvious feature of men's court dress was its increasingly old-fashioned, late eighteenth-century appearance. If this was intended to deter fashionable social aspirants from attending court, it applied to men only, for women's court dress was allowed to mirror current fashions. In

52. Female Court Dress 1821
After George IV had permitted the abandonment of hoops under court dresses in 1820, such dresses were similar in all respects to fashionable evening wear, with the addition of a light silk train, fine jewellery and a plumed head-dress.

1820 George IV's first Drawing Room announcement included the rubric, 'His Majesty is graciously pleased to dispense with Ladies wearing Hoops.'[71] Queen Charlotte had been dead for two years, and there was no acknowledged consort to arbitrate in such matters. Was the King influenced by his sisters, his sisters-in-law or his female friends? Or did he simply not like hooped skirts?

The new order was no less formal than the previous, but it was more elegant. Fashionable high-waisted dresses were lavishly decorated on the bodice, sleeves and hem, often with costly gold or silver embroidery; there were lace or tulle over-dresses softening plain, coloured silks and proper trains attached at the back of the waist. Accessories of long gloves, fans, jewellery, lappets and towering feather plumes – four, five or six, like the most exquisite performing horses – were instituted. Prince Pückler-Muskau commented:

> *A drawing-room and a presentation at Court here are as ludicrous as the levée of a Bürgermeister of the ancient Free Imperial cities of our fatherland; and all the pride and pomp of aristocracy disappears in the childish 'embarras' of these 'ladies', loaded – not adorned – with diamonds and fine clothes.*

The King, however, liked the female decoration but not always the ladies; as a result he instituted regulations about presentation cards and prior application for women as well as men.[72]

It was the most memorable occasion for someone newly married and wholly acceptable, like Mary Lucy. In her memoirs, the details of her presentation at court in May 1824 are more extensive than those of her marriage five months earlier. She was presented by Lady Warwick, who had the entrée, and wore a dress of,

> *white tulle covered with small silver stars, and round the skirt flowers worked in shades of lilac, the underneath petticoat was of white satin, and the train too of the richest white satin trimmed with a broad blond lace and edged with a thick silver cord. On my head a plume of ostrich feathers, blond lappets and diamonds. On my neck the large ruby (in form of a heart) with diamond centre, and my splendid diamond earrings worn for the first time.*

The King kissed her cheek (as was customary) asked her name and gave 'a most gracious smile' and she was set for celebration, a week of 'fearful . . . dissipation: four balls, concerts, the play, dinners and parties every night.' Before she returned to Warwickshire, having spent her first 'season' in London, she had acquired an attractive souvenir from her cook's aunt who was housekeeper to the King, 'thirty of the finest Holland damask table-cloths very little the worse for wear . . . we readily gave the £50, there never was such a bargain!'[73] All the royal table linen was a housekeeper's perquisite and could obviously be re-sold advantageously.

George IV's personal debts far out-stripped the sums that could be made by his servants' judicious use of their customary perquisites, and he died penniless. His brother the Duke of Clarence, (who became William IV in 1830), when inspecting some of the late King's treasures, said forthrightly, 'Damned expensive taste.' Prince Pückler-Muskau dismissed George IV as innately frivolous, writing,

> *It sounds ludicrous to say, (but yet it is true) that the present King . . . is a very fashionable man; that his father was not in the least degree so, and that none of his brothers have any pretension to fashion; – which unquestionably is highly to their honour: for no man who has any personal claims to distinction, would be frivolous long enough to have either the power or the will to maintain himself in that category.*[74]

It was easy to be disparaging and it is easy to forget that George IV's delight in visual excellence, in both its subjective and objective forms, enhanced many elements in national life which are taken for granted today. Amongst these, he may be especially remembered for developing pageantry and ceremonial, state buildings, Buckingham Palace and Windsor Castle most notably; and fine public and private art collections, such as the National Gallery and the Royal Collection. A minor but happy contribution was his

53. George IV 1822; W Finden (1829) after Sir Thomas Lawrence

This informal portrait of the King is indicative of his care to retain his position as 'a very fashionable man'. His expensive, exquisitely cut coats and breeches were a testimony to English tailoring, but his interest in fashion, connoisseurship and delight in spectacular ceremonial was generally ridiculed.

promotion of English tailoring and all the associated activities connected with men's dress. His clothes and personal effects (with the exception of certain souvenirs and perquisites) were auctioned over three days in December 1830 and ran to 438 lots. The range of items is revealing in its diversity: 'whips and sticks; wearing apparel; black and white silk dress stockings; dress coats, military jackets, Windsor uniforms; beautiful plumes of ostrich and other feathers, and miscellanies, expensive military and other dresses, etc.' State items worn at his coronation and at the opening of parliament, the exclusive Windsor uniform in dress and undress versions, and military uniforms of Hussar regiments were not thought worthy of preservation by his family, and were mixed up with his personal property. The latter included, 'A complete Highland Dress, formed of Scotch plaid, and lined with green silk', matching jacket and trousers and, 'A Scotch cap of velvet, with a beautiful plume of black feathers'; masquerade costumes, brown and blue cloth coats, pantaloons, and monogrammed items including stockings, cambric handkerchiefs and five Irish shirts were also included. The most pitiable item is the 'pair of invalid's crutches with velvet cushions', a testament to his last pain-racked years. If Mrs Lucy had thought £50 a bargain for 30 royal tablecloths, surely the King's clothes were almost given away: 50s for the undress Windsor uniform coats dating from the King's years as Regent; for a rose-coloured satin robe with a Garter star worn at the coronation £7.5s; £6. 6s for a silver-laced Hussar jacket; 50s for six white waistcoats.[75]

As one of the brothers without 'any pretension to fashion', William IV exorcized his late brother's ghost as thoroughly as he knew how: economizing in every way, from sacking French cooks to dressing unexceptionably. He had undergone a naval rather than a military training as a prince but, like all his family, he was interested in uniform and rigorously

54. George IV 1830; Sir David Wilkie

For his visit to Scotland in 1822 the King acquired Royal Stewart tartans in satin, velvet and cashmere, but his appearance and pose conjure up the 'chief actor in a pantomime'. He took a life-long pleasure in 'fancy-dress', as his masquerade costumes and, most obviously, his coronation robes testify. This set of clothing – 'A complete Highland Dress, formed of Scotch plaid, and lined with green silk' with 'A Scotch cap of velvet, with a pleasure plume of black feathers' – was auctioned in December 1830.

formal about ceremonial etiquette. He was a hearty, moderately intelligent man with a large family of illegitimate children – the Fitzclarences, to whom he was devoted – and a modest, understanding, much younger wife, Queen Adelaide (who was a princess of Saxe-Meiningen). He intended that the royal court should be active, not a reclusive enclave for a few favourites as it had become in George IV's last years. The Hon. Emily Eden considered that, 'the Court is going to swallow up all other Society' because 'all the great people who intrigued for court places', expecting effortless sinecures, were kept hard at work from early in the morning until late at night arranging 'reviews, breakfasts, great dinners and parties all following each other'.[76] Prince Pückler-Muskau was of the opinion that by reading 'the best of the recent English novels', it was possible, 'to abstract from them a tolerably just idea of English fashionable society.' He added various caveats which indicate that the novels did not capture completely the combination of 'vice and boorish rudeness' which he had observed in English society.[77] Perhaps he did not read widely enough, for nineteenth-century novels are replete with every type of venality, poor behaviour, arrivisme and snobbery. The containment of social revolution within a rigid class structure is one of the most interesting aspects of English life in the nineteenth century. It was a structure which should be surmounted by an active royal family but,

> the prolonged deficiency of a Court has naturally suspended the influence of royal supremacy over the private circles of the nobility; . . . A few years will now suffice to show in what degree the supremacy of a resident Court may avail to alter the existing order of things.[78]

Neither William nor his Queen were leaders of fashion; they wished to see a revival of the formal etiquette and central role of a royal court, but they understood the need for a judicious modernization of the old forms. The

55. **George IV and the Duke of York c.1827; Crowhurst of Brighton**
The 'grand old Duke of York' of the popular rhyme was the King's favourite brother. Both he (left) and the King were excessively fat in old age. Unflattering depictions turned the king into a virtual recluse in his last years. It is worth comparing this with the Lawrence (no. 53); the coat is similar, but artistic licence and painful reality are all too evident.

King was most often to be seen in a plain green cloth coat and beaver hat (when not in uniform) and had even to be warned by Lord Hertford that his 'dress might be taken exception to' when he appeared so dressed in St James's Street two or three days after his brother died.[79] Image did not interest him, and there are caricatures but few formal depictions of him or Queen Adelaide. She was a plain but good-natured woman who supported British manufactures assiduously, requesting that they be worn at the coronation

Published by Fisher, Son & C? Caxton London May 16. 18...

in September 1830 and the Drawing Room which followed it. Princess Victoria, the young heiress-presumptive, followed her aunt's example, appearing at a Drawing Room in 1831 wearing a dress 'made of materials entirely manufactured in England.'[80] French fashions dictated women's dress and were illustrated in the women's magazines, appearing in increasing numbers after 1815. Such fashions were made up in Spitalfields and Macclesfield silks, English cloth and printed cottons, and fine Lancashire lawns; and were worn with shawls woven in England (using eastern styles of decoration) and hand-made or machine-woven laces. Queen Adelaide appears to have had a particular liking for lace, both English and continental; the fuller styles of the 1830s with their wide over-sleeves, gauzy collars, shawls and extravagant head-dresses were attractively (and expensively) formal when lace was used.

Women's court fashions could be illustrated without fear of ridicule alongside full-dress for evening wear, the only perceptible difference between the two being the long, handsomely decorated train and the exuberant group of feathers and lappets which were worn on the head for court-wear. The feathers and lappets were becoming an unfashionable anachronism and were challenged by enough women to merit censure. In May 1834 the London Gazette carried the notice:

56. The Royal Dukes 1827; C S Taylor

A visual summary of some of the many styles of dress, ceremonial and civilian, to which male royalties could aspire. The Duke of Cumberland (later King of Hanover) and Duke of York wear military uniform; the Duke of Clarence (later William IV) is in parliamentary robes over naval uniform; the eccentric Duke of Sussex has adopted Highland dress; and the Duke of Cambridge wears a discreetly fashionable cloth coat. However, unlike George IV, none of these was celebrated for their interest in fashion.

Some ladies have appeared at Her Majesty's Drawing Rooms in hats and feathers and turbans, and such head-dresses being contrary to Court Etiquette, notice is hereby given that all ladies . . . must appear in feathers and lappets, in conformity with the established order.[81]

There were similar difficulties throughout the 1830s about the wearing of breeches or pantaloons by men who attended court. Men's clothes became business-like foils to women's dress as the nineteenth century progressed and were 'distinguished only for exquisite neatness and delicacy of texture'.[82] Etiquette books warned would-be gentlemen that it was 'bad taste to dress in the extreme of fashion'.[83] However, as pantaloons, those slim-fitting precursors to trousers, replaced breeches for general wear, there was a move to have them accepted at court.

Distinctions were made about appropriate dress for the all-male levees and the drawing rooms and state balls at which the Queen and other ladies were present. Thomas Creevey, appointed treasurer of the Ordnance in 1831, was urged to go to court by his patron, Lord Grey. He balked at the cost, but was assured that £120 was for the grandest (most embroidered) versions and he could get away with expending £40. He was presented to the King, 'in Blue pantaloons, an immense broad gold lace stripe down the sides, and BOOTS'; for the Queen he wore, 'white demididdles (breeches), white silk stockings, shoes and gilt buckles, and a hat with feathers all round the edges', lent to him for the occasion.[84] Perhaps Creevey had hoped that pantaloons – so convenient for levees, their natural elasticity of cut allowing the necessary obeisance of kneeling upon the right knee, kissing the King's hand, rising, bowing and retiring, to be executed elegantly – would be permitted wear at drawing rooms, thus saving him extra expenditure. They were, but not for the likes of him.

All men entitled to wear a full-dress uniform

57. **'What's in the wind now?'** 1831; **'HB'**

This sketch, one of a series on political subjects, depicts William IV and Lord Melbourne. Unlike his brother, the last Hanoverian King was not a fashionable man, preferring plain cloth coats and pantaloons leavened by uniform when protocol required it. Melbourne is dressed in an early version of plain cloth court dress – a wig-bag at the coat nape, a bicorne hat and sword were required accessories but purely ornamental.

which included pantaloons (in essence, every uniform except the Windsor uniform by the mid-1830s) were permitted to wear 'uniform pantaloons and boots agreeably to regulation' at levees, Drawing Rooms and state balls. Those who wore the Royal Household uniform, civil uniform or court dress 'must appear in shoes with buckles and breeches with knee buckles.'[85] As practically everyone was eligible for some type of uniform by this date – the lowliest government official, deputy lieutenants of counties, officers in every branch of the services from yeomanry to navy and all Royal Household appointments – the effect must have been to drive anyone in cloth court suits with embroidered waistcoats to a state of anxious rage in case they be thought ungentlemanly social climbers.

1. *Left:* <u>CHARLES II</u> c.1682/3; E HAWKER

Painted at much the same time as new works on St George's Hall, Windsor Castle were completed, the King is depicted in Garter robes, his favourite form of ceremonial dress. He wore this quasi-historical style with an élan worthy of his half-French blood and his cousin Louis XIV.

2. *Right:* <u>GEORGE III</u> c.1780–85

This naive portrait of George III in court dress has captured the King's forthright traditional qualities. The style of his court suits changed little until the early 1790s; he continued to wear the decorated silk materials of his youth with powdered wigs and the distinctive Garter ribbon.

3. *Left:* <u>GEORGE, PRINCE OF WALES 1795; R. DIGHTON</u>

Issued in the year of his marriage to Princess Caroline of Brunswick, this idealized aquatint may be one of the depictions which caused the Princess to say, 'I think he's very fat and he's nothing like as handsome as his portrait'. All of the elements of the plainer style of the court dress of the 1790s are carefully recorded.

4. *Right:* <u>GEORGE III 1810; R. DIGHTON</u>

This good-natured caricature was issued to celebrate the King's golden jubilee. From the time of its introduction in the late 1770s, the King wore the Windsor uniform on every possible occasion, and in the public mind it was inseparable from his public appearances. This is the full-dress version decorated with gold lace.

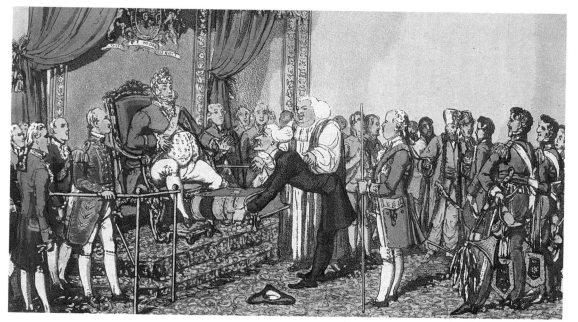

5. *Above:* <u>DOCTOR SYNTAX PRESENTED AT COURT 1820</u>

This well observed humorous illustration of a court presentation – in this instance a levee – captures all of the key elements. Household officials, courtiers, army officers, foreign visitors and clerics provided a colourful pageant in the centre of which the King 'held court'. By this date George IV was accustomed to such unflattering cartoons of himself, although he never liked them.

6. *Left:* <u>QUEEN ADELAIDE 1830</u>

Fashion plates occasionally included idealized images of royalty. In this instance, the Queen-Consort of William IV jostles for attention with the French ballerina Marie Taglioni, Italian regional dress and the latest hairstyles. The Queen was an enthusiastic patron of Spitalfields silks, which were particularly suited to formal styles such as this.

7. *Above:* THE ROYAL FAMILY AT THE GREAT EXHIBITION 1851; C. WELLS

The curious mixture of formality and informality at public events visited by royalty is apparent in this conversation piece. The formal evening dress of the Queen and Prince is at variance with the smart day clothes of those around them; their two eldest children are similarly formal, although not yet in their teens.

8. *Left:* QUEEN ELIZABETH II 1986; M. LEONARD

This portrait celebrated the Queen's 60th birthday; it was based wholly on photographs, not sketches. Photography – still or moving – is the best known medium for recording royalty in this century. The Queen's sumptuous brocade sofa, the bright-eyed corgi and the Queen's dress harmonize and convey a reassuringly crisp but untheatrical idea of modern monarchy.

FOUR

'Full-dressed confusion'

Writing to her recently married daughter, the Princess Royal in 1858, Queen Victoria, stated, irritably, 'I am not a dwarf'.[1] She was responding to the criticisms of her daughter's diminutive stature which were being voiced at the Prussian court in Berlin, knowing that the Princess was taller than her. It had been an obsession of the Queen's early years when her uncle, King Leopold of the Belgians, had written coaxing her to grow taller; in late 1835 she had written to tell him that as a result of a recent illness, 'I am grown... a little taller and Dr Clark says I shall grow quite tall after this. I should be glad if it were the case, if it was only to please you, dear uncle.'[2] She never grew above a height of approximately 4 feet 10 inches, and with her Hanoverian relish for the delights of food and drink she had a constant battle to maintain a neat, well proportioned figure. After the death of her husband the Prince Consort in 1861, she gradually allowed her body to assume that astonishing rotundity which was such a gift to late nineteenth-century cartoonists.

It is one of the more endearing qualities of the Hanoverians that however much they tried to strengthen the line of succession with tall, handsome partners for their princes and princesses, the throne was invariably occupied, from Victoria's reign onwards, by a small monarch dwarfed by a tall or statuesque consort. Queen Victoria's father was tall and portly, her mother short, pretty and plump; the genetic mix gave her the least appealing combination – short stature, a Hanoverian head and face, and a propensity to corpulence.

With such physical disadvantages it is hardly surprising that the Queen, until widowhood solved the problem for her, struggled with the almost insuperable difficulty of dressing stylishly.

Almost every last detail of the Queen's long life and reign has been analysed and published, and there has been discussion of her clothing in a variety of biographies, memoirs, diaries and articles. It would be inappropriate to pre-empt the work which is presently being undertaken on the large, surviving collection of her clothing at the Museum of London. It is possible, however, to consider the image of royalty that she wished to foster; to consider her attitude towards appearance – her own and that of those who surrounded her; and to examine contemporary opinions of her style, or the lack of it. During the course of her reign there were three developments which are particularly pertinent for the dress historian. All three were visual developments: the advent of photography as a medium for recording people and events, the triumph of English men's tailoring throughout Europe, and the rise to undisputed superiority of the French couturier.

Photography was a process which fascinated both Queen Victoria and the Prince-Consort; he was first photographed in 1842, and thereafter it became a favourite royal method for recording both formal and informal occasions. As an irresistibly cheap record of anything that did not move, its popularity was assured throughout society, and for the

first time there were a great many accurate depictions of female court dress. This may not be unconnected with the desire to have a momento of the expensive, Paris-inspired dresses which were worn to court functions. Men's court dress, which had retained its anachronistic links with the eighteenth century, inspired few of its wearers to acquire a record of themselves when they had the option of discreetly elegant everyday clothes. Even exquisite tailoring and French chic could be rendered absurd in the photographic studio, for unlike portrait painters, photographers found it less easy, at first, to flatter their sitters. Both Queen Victoria and the Prince Consort suffered this ignominy, and their photographic images are rarely a convincing advertisement for fine English tailoring or the art of the French dressmaker (or the English dressmaker's version of the current French styles).

One of the truisms of nineteenth-century appearance is that a distinct visual and functional division developed in regard to the clothing worn by men and women. The superb tailoring in sombre-coloured cloth for men's coats and trousers became increasingly popular and, gradually, the colourful or contrasting elements in the male wardrobes – pantaloons, waistcoats, gloves – were eliminated or relegated to purely domestic, informal items such as dressing gowns and smoking jackets. The message was a simple one: serious men of business – politicians, public officials, industrialists – had to work in grimy and polluted towns where dark suits were both functional and a reflection of the sober nature of their public duties. Exuberance was con-

58. The Presentation c.1838; H Robinson after A E Chalon

An idealized impression of the young Queen Victoria, which suggested that she was tall, slim and conventionally pretty. It supports Alfred Chalon's assertion to the Queen when questioned about the effect of photography on the livelihood of painters, 'Ah, non, Madame, the *photographie* can't *flattère*'.

fined to gilded uniforms, and even country clothes were made of discreet, camouflage-coloured cloth. In contrast, women's dress, from the mid–1820s onwards, became noticeably more restrictive, with a battery of styles and structures which enhanced areas of the anatomy – arms, shoulders, bust, hips – but always to the disadvantage of the wearer. Corsets, crinolines, bustles and extravagantly full, or uncomfortably tight bodices and skirts, lavishly decorated with frills, ruffles, braid and lace, turned women into little other than exquisite ornaments for their menfolk. These developments made no concession to the fact that there was a female ruler of England; the Queen firmly believed in the superiority of men, and had no sympathy for movements concerned with extending the franchise to women, or dress reform. Indeed, like many of her contemporaries, she dressed to please the man in her life. Once she had found her ideal partner in Prince Albert of Saxe Coburg Gotha, who was, fortunately, not only one of the most handsome European princes of the time, but also intelligent, well-educated and extremely industrious, she relied upon his advice in everything, rarely making any decision of consequence, including the selection of her clothing, without consulting him.[3]

As a young princess she took great interest in the dress of women whom she thought might provide appropriate mentors. She particularly admired the French chic of her aunt-by-marriage, Queen Louise of the Belgians, who was only seven years older than her, and 'a very elegant little figure'. After their first meeting in 1835, when Queen Louise, responding to the Princess's admiration, had given her small presents of clothing and advised her upon her hairstyle, there was a stream of gifts from the Queen to the Princess. The dresses and bonnets came from Paris and were the work of Mlle Palmyre, the leading dressmaker of the day. This natural kindness appears to have been prompted by King Leopold who, instrumental in grooming his nephew Prince Albert to be Victoria's consort, was equally anxious that his niece should be an elegant rather than a dowdy ornament to the English throne (it was, of course, a role he had fulfilled for Princess Charlotte 20 years earlier). The dresses were in the soft shades and materials which flattered the young Princess – grey satin broché, plain and patterned pink silk, and pale blue flowered silk. The fashions of the late 1830s were particularly suitable for a diminutive princess; the close-fitting bodice, natural waistline and moderately full skirt gave a well-balanced silhouette which suited most women. It was an agreeably ingenue style for an 18-year-old queen; the Prussian

59. Queen Victoria 1840; F A Heath after E Corbould

The Queen's lack of inches and tendency to plumpness meant that she looked her best in simple, well-tailored clothes. The severe lines of a riding habit and the additional height of a top hat gave her a favourable distinction.

envoy thought her, 'beautifully, tastefully and becomingly dressed' when he saw her in the procession for the state opening of Parliament in July 1837.[4]

The novelty of being young, admired and powerful after a repressed and secluded youth found expression in energetic pursuits: riding and dancing, alongside the necessary duties of her new role, in which her mentor was Lord Melbourne, the Prime Minister. He advised her about everything – affairs of state, court etiquette, and dress. When she was worried about where to place her Garter order, he referred her to the Duke of Norfolk, who showed her a portrait of Queen Anne wearing the garter. Lord Melbourne was at her side when she rode, wearing a chic black velvet riding habit; when she reviewed her troops, dressed in a female adaptation of the Windsor uniform; at her coronation, when she wore the specially designed robes of gold tissue, woven with the emblems of England, Scotland and Ireland; and at the state opening of Parliament, when she complained of the tremendous weight of the crimson velvet and ermine robes.

As the novelty of the new reign began to wear off for both Queen and country, the court was criticized for being too foreign (that is, German), and the Queen for patronizing French materials and French fashions. The Queen began to put on weight and became bored with the duties of her new life. Melbourne chivvied her, suggesting that English dressmakers were not comparable to French, but that she should watch her diet, be careful about her dress, and be prepared to conduct the required levees and Drawing Rooms, for, 'A queen's life is very laborious; it's a life of moments, hardly any leisure'. As a mentor, Lord Melbourne was not ideal; he did nothing to develop an unpartisan political attitude in his protegée, or to introduce her to the many social and economic problems that afflicted the vast majority of her subjects. He was, however, relatively successful in persuading her of the need to take her ceremonial role more seriously. In July 1838 Prince Albert wrote to his tutor that what he had heard of his cousin was not much to his taste, for she 'delights in court ceremonies, etiquette and trivial formalities.'[5]

The Prince assumed the role of mentor to the young Queen when they married in February 1840. He had many excellent qualities–he was genuinely fond of the queen and he lent her invaluable support in the business of government – but he was never popular in England. The latent xenophobia re-emerged, and memories of King Leopold's long and expensive sojourn in England after Princess Charlotte's death, made penniless German princes, especially Coburgs, unwelcome. In his heart the Prince believed that he would never 'cease to be a true German, a true Coburg and Gotha man', and unfortunately for him there was no sympathetic reception committee, of the type that greeted female German royal consorts, equipped with a wardrobe of 'British manufacture', which could turn him into an unexceptionable English gentleman. The Queen found his foreign good looks, tall, slim physique, and style of dress fascinating. She accorded him the honour of wearing the Windsor uniform during his visit in October 1839, but when he attended a military review with her, he wore his green Coburg uniform with 'tight cazimere pantaloons [nothing under them] and high boots'. A variation of these boots, made of red leather and designed for the Coburg hunt, were worn with an open-necked shirt and soft cravat when the Prince hunted in England (recorded in a Landseer group, *Windsor Castle in Modern Times*, in which the tightly-fitting pantaloons indicate that drawers were omitted for this activity as well), but such outré fashions were regarded as the equivalent of operatic stage costume by most Englishmen.

When wearing British military uniforms, court dress, the Windsor uniform or even the kilt (which the royal family wore in Scotland),

the Prince always seemed rather exotically foreign. In 1843 a fashion plate of the Queen, the Prince and the Duchess of Kent illustrated this un-English, dandified appearance, which is reminiscent of Count d'Orsay or the young Disraeli, rather than a discreetly tailored member of the English aristocracy. As Baron Stockmar, adviser to the Queen and Prince Albert, wrote in 1854, the Prince

did not dress quite in the orthodox English fashion . . . did not sit on horseback in the orthodox English way . . . did not shake hands in the true orthodox English manner . . . all this, even by those who were in closer contact . . . who knew and esteemed him, could not easily get over. One heard them say: 'He is an excellent, clever, able fellow, but look at the cut of his coat, or the way he shakes hands'.[6]

It was as insuperable a problem for the Prince as the Queen's short, plump stature was for her. Neither of them had a suitable English example upon which to base their idea of how a Queen regnant and her consort should dress. Queen Adelaide had been a consort, and much older, and there had been no male consort since Prince George of Denmark (Queen Anne's husband) had died in 1708. So the Prince, unadvised or unadvisable, retained his un-English manners and style of dress, and met with the whole-hearted approval of his wife. In 1862, recalling their life together, the Queen wrote a careful reminiscence of every detail of her late husband's daily habits. She described his hunting clothes: green cloth coat, light breeches and high black boots; his shooting jacket (he shot three or four times a week); and his short coat of black or 'Balmoral mixture', worn with 'checked or other trousers'. She described his trousers as having straps under the foot (which went out of fashion in the 1850s), which 'made him look so nice and gentlemanlike', and he 'always wore the blue ribbon of the garter under his waistcoat which looked so nice'. He also wore uniforms, both English and German, although he had never undergone any military training, but the cult of uniforms in the nineteenth century was a feature of all European courts, although less pronounced in England than elsewhere. In fact, the Germanic obsession with uniforms was not at all to the taste of the English. In Berlin in 1858, Sir James Clark was depressed by the sight of 'the perpetual uniform... none of the Royal family, or princely class, ever appear out of

60. **Windsor Castle in Modern Times 1840–45; after Sir Edwin Landseer**

The relatively uncluttered fashions of the early 1840s suited Queen Victoria. Prince Albert's hunting clothes – red leather Coburg boots, skin-tight pantaloons, open-necked shirt and loose cravat – were ridiculed by English gentlemen who thought he looked like an Italian tenor.

the stiff military dress, the whole country seems occupied in playing at soldiers.'[7] The Queen, unlike her subjects, liked uniforms. As a young girl she had written in her diary, 'Count Zichy is very good-looking in uniform, but not in plain clothes. Count Waldstein looks remarkably well in his pretty Hungarian uniform.'[8] It was a sign of the Hanoverian pleasure in the glitter and colour of uniforms; a style of dress which added spurious glamour to all but the most nondescript of men.

Uniforms for female royalty were a rather different matter; Queen Victoria experimented with various possibilities before finding a solution for her descendants to follow. As a young woman she wore a version of the Windsor uniform for reviewing her troops, but by 1856 she was recorded on horseback

at an Aldershot review in a scarlet and gold military-style tunic, navy riding skirt and small felt hat with plumes.[9] The neat, severe lines of riding dress had always flattered her, and it was a stroke of genius, which her ancestors would have applauded, when she identified so elegantly with her troops. Designs for more imposing Germanic uniforms with metallic head-dresses were prepared, but her taste did not run to such overtly masculine formulas. Generally, she did not expend a great deal of thought on her clothing and its consequent effect on her public image. In 1842 she told King Leopold, 'I ... hate being troubled about dress', although she had a life-long admiration for the beauty and fashion sense of others.[10] At first she had been content to be guided by her aunt, Queen Louise, but then the Prince took over this role, so that the French chic of the Queen of the Belgians was overlaid by the German sentimentality of Prince Albert's taste. She bought and wore

61. **The Ambassador's Reception 1844; H Melville**

One of a series of engravings depicting formal occasions and events held at Buckingham Palace and St James's Palace. Foreign ambassadors and envoys await the arrival of the royal party. The importance of uniform as a mark of office was well-established by this date.

both French and English fashions and, from time to time, as on the visit to Ireland in 1848, paid a graceful compliment to national interests by wearing a dress of green Irish poplin at a levee and a pink poplin ornamented with gold shamrocks for a Drawing Room.[11] It was consistent with the wearing of tartan satin or cloth, woven in the Balmoral and Victoria checks that she and the Prince designed for their holidays in Scotland, but it was also an erratic sensibility, for, like many women who are not beautiful, do not have fashionable physiques, and have not had a thorough grounding in the art of dressing well, the Queen got her image wrong more often than she got it right.

The two most beautiful and fashionable royal ladies in Europe in the period after 1850 were the Empress Elizabeth of Austria and the Empress Eugenie of France. Both devoted considerable time and energy to the business of looking exquisite, something for which Queen Victoria had neither the time nor the inclination. She met the Empress Eugenie twice in 1855; the Emperor and Empress

visited England in April, and the Queen and Prince Albert visited France in August. She was entranced by the Empress's beauty, particularly her limpid kohl-ringed eyes, and by her elegant clothes, about which she wrote in favourable detail in her journal. Others did not share her enthusiasm; Lord Cowley considered Eugenie, 'very handsome, very coquette', and Florence Nightingale dismissed her as 'the Empress who was born to be a dressmaker.'[12] This did not deter Queen Victoria; she and the Empress became life-long friends, but the Queen always had a taste for the raffish and exotic. Once she had met the Empress, the Queen became concerned about her clothes for the state visit to France, understandably so. She had always had a propensity for draping herself in shawls, wearing over-decorated dresses cluttered with lace, ribbons, bows and flounces, and under the prince's guidance (sometimes to his designs, and certainly to his taste) she had taken to swathing her dresses in huge floral trimmings – convolvulus, geraniums, grasses – sometimes real, sometimes artificial or embroidered. The wider sleeves and tiered skirts of the 1850s, often decorated with additional ribbons and ruffles, were not flattering to tiny women. Fashion decreed horizontal emphasis, which can rarely, except with great discretion, be worn as successfully by small women as fashions which rely upon vertical lines for their impact. Entering Paris, swamped by a massive white silk bonnet trimmed with streamers and maribou feathers, weighted

62. Queen Victoria in Fancy Dress 1845
The mid-nineteenth century interpretation of eighteenth-century dress is far from accurate, but the overall effect was admired. Even when not in fancy dress, the Queen, influenced by Prince Albert, liked the fussiness of tiered skirts, flounces of lace and ribbons and a good display of jewellery. This style of evening dress, the decorated Christmas tree look, has enjoyed successive waves of popularity amongst female royalty.

down by a green mantle over a flounced white dress, and carrying a green parasol and large silk reticule embroidered with a gold poodle – a handmade gift from her daughters – the Queen amazed and amused the sophisticated Parisians.[13]

Her formal evening wear was often as unflattering as her day clothes. In 1847 Mary Lucy was invited to 'the ball of the Season' at the Duchess of Sutherland's house. The Queen arrived with the royal party shortly after 10 o'clock, and Mrs Lucy took the opportunity to observe her. She thought the Queen:

dances beautifully and is very graceful, though short and a bad figure. Her dress was white tarlatan embroidered in colours round double skirts, with a wreath of flowers mixed with many diamonds on her head, and in her hand she carried a bouquet nearly as large as herself.

In contrast, the Duchess 'looked an empress in a dress of white silk and fine lace trim'd with bunches of stephanotis and a profusion of diamonds on her head'.[14] As well as being an acknowledged beauty and stylish dresser, the Duchess was Mistress of the Robes and a long-standing friend of the Queen's, but ironically the Queen never chose to consult her about her costume. By the 1850s, Victoria's evening dresses were even more decorated, with swags and flounces of lace, ribbon and flowers cascading over her short body, and slashed, diagonally, by her blue Garter ribbon. In addition to diamonds in her hair, she also wore a range of pearl and gemstone jewellery – tiaras, pendant ear-rings, necklaces, brooches and rings on nearly every finger. The overall effect was akin to one of the highly decorated Christmas trees which were introduced into royal festivities by the Coburgs. Later in her reign, one of her favourite prime ministers, Disraeli, referred to her as the Faery, a flattering allusion to the great Queen Elizabeth, Spenser's 'Faery Queen', but Disraeli's sense of humour may well have been tickled

by the diminutive figure bedecked with jet, pearl and diamond jewellery in a theatrical, stage-fairy manner.

The Queen's collection of jewellery was sparse at her accession but magnificent by the end of her life, although many of the pieces, like her bouquets, were inappropriately large for such a small woman. The most suitable pieces were the delicate creations designed and commissioned by Prince Albert; jewellery design was more his métier than dress design.[15] With this collection of jewellery at her disposal, and the softly feminine clothes of the 1850s as a foil, quite by chance, or so it seems, Queen Victoria evolved a type of formal uniform for royal ladies which amalgamated all of the rarest and most costly elements at hand – low-necked, wide-skirted dresses of French silks and lace; exuberant embroidery in silks and metal threads; hot-house flowers; and quantities of precious gems set into every type of jewelled accessory. It combined fashionable elements with a revivalist pastiche of late eighteenth-century court dress, and it both dazzled and astounded observers.

Interest in historical dress was a nineteenth-century enthusiasm, and there was considerable antiquarian research, pioneered by J R Planché. His work found its earliest expression on the stage, in Charles Kemble's productions of Shakespeare's plays in the 1820s, but it also influenced painters and provided a type of historical verisimilitude for guests invited to fancy dress balls. Such balls became fashionable once more in the 1830s, and the royal couple, with their interest in painting, history and the theatre, and their pleasure in dancing, gave three such balls in 1842, 1845 and 1851. The first was combined with a half-hearted attempt to assist the declining Spitalfields silk industry by requesting that guests wore costumes made from British materials.[16]

Such balls, temporarily, allowed the Queen to assume the role of the minor partner: Queen Philippa to the Prince's Edward III in 1842; an eighteenth-century court lady in 1845; and a lady of the court to the Prince's Louis XIV in 1851. In reality, the Prince was forever destined to be the junior partner, and was considerably less fortunate than his uncle King Leopold, with an allowance of £30,000 per year rather than £50,000; additionally, he was not created Prince Consort until 1857, although increasingly conscientious in his work to reform the royal household, advise

63. **Prince Albert in Fancy Dress 1845**

The Prince's unwillingness to shave his side-whiskers and moustache, combined with the remarkable shortness of his breeches are delightful anachronisms. It is all too easy to see why British contemporaries found his brand of good looks so unacceptably foreign.

the government of the day, chair various advisory committees, accompany the Queen on tours at home and abroad, and catalogue and enhance the royal collections. His interest in the arts was genuine and informed, and under his guidance a number of important acquisitions was made for the royal collection and for the nation. He and the Queen patronized contemporary artists, both English and German, commissioning many works, particularly of royal subjects, depicting individuals, groups and particular occasions. Their fancy dress costumes were captured for posterity, as were many other formal and informal moments in their lives; a large proportion of these are of unsurpassed banality in terms of content and execution. Portraits of the Queen and the Prince minimize her small stature; she stands while he is seated, enhancing her regal grandeur, or she is in the foreground with him in shadowy attendance. Albert is frequently in uniform, while Victoria is more variously dressed, in day clothes, evening gowns or court dress with jewellery, feathers and train. Portraits by Winterhalter (who glamorized the French Imperial court) manage to give the Queen a girlish beauty and gravitas, despite the fussiness of her dress; the Prince always contrived to look melancholically impressive. Photographs reveal how tall he was in comparison with the Queen, but many of these were not for circulation. They were private family 'snaps', although they do not instantly conjure up 'our *happy domestic* home – which gives such a good example' that Queen Victoria felt was the key to her public popularity.[17]

High moral tone at court, and comfortable domesticity in private, were the essence of the Queen and the Prince's attitude towards their role. The distinction between public life and private life was drawn more firmly than in previous reigns. With the Prince's support and encouragement, the Queen was prepared to travel more widely at home and abroad than any English monarch had done since the middle ages, but she valued the privacy that could be found at Windsor, Osborne and Balmoral. She and the Prince did not lead society; certain sections of society came to them, by invitation, but their example was not much admired or copied by the English aristocracy, to whom agreeable entertainment did not, generally, revolve around family life. It was a bourgeois concept, and by the time Walter Bagehot's *The English Constitution* was published in 1867, it was thought that:

> *A family on the throne is an interesting idea . . . It brings down the pride of sovereignty to the level of petty life . . . a royal family sweetens politics by the seasonal addition of nice and pretty events.*

His analysis, within an historical framework, led him to the view that (fashionable) society did not need one leader; it was aristocratic rather than monarchical, partly through historical circumstances and partly through its inherent nature. It had become an 'upper ten thousand' in which 'Great ladies give the tone to it with little reference to the particular Court world'. He accepted that levees and Drawing Rooms continued as 'Formal ceremonies of presentation and attendance,' but felt that:

> *they no longer make a part of social enjoyment; they are a sort of ritual in which nowadays almost every decent person can if he likes take part. Even Court balls where pleasure is at least supposed to be possible, are lost in a London July.*[18]

The only observation that Bagehot failed to make was that presentation at court was an essential qualification for acceptance into fashionable society, and that many 'decent person(s)' continued to be ineligible for this social accolade.

The subtle nuances of acceptability at court are charted in the etiquette books which had become such an essential prop to those newly-risen in the world. Early in the century they were anonymous, but later they were often the acknowledged works of impoverished 'ladies'

and 'gentlemen' whose bitter resentment of the changing face of fashionable society is all too evident in their texts. To the late twentieth-century mind the distinctions which were made seem petty-minded and incomprehensible, and a gradual blurring of social categories owed much to the Queen who detested 'snobs'. Initially, however, she made no changes to the rules of presentation observed by William IV and Queen Adelaide. Finding a respectable sponsor, notifying the Lord Chamberlain's Office of the intention to attend a levee or Drawing Room, purchasing or borrowing the appropriate traditional styles of dress and learning the correct movements and forms of obeisance were becoming sanctified rituals, as were the actual occasions which continued, less frequently, to be held at St James's Palace. A set of engravings produced in the mid-1840s illustrates the state rooms and some of the presentations to the Queen at levees, Drawing Rooms, diplomatic receptions and so forth. They look elegantly arranged, rather sparsely attended functions at which everyone, as in the theatre, was well rehearsed. In reality, they were often uncomfortably hot, full, unpleasant gatherings at which a reserved sovereign, surrounded by members of her family and household, would tolerate rather than enjoy the parade of dutiful, expensively dressed subjects.

Presentation at court was an accepted signal that a young man or young woman had become an adult and was ready to take his or her place in society. Girls aged 17 or 18 left the school-room, acquired a wardrobe of new clothes and were presented at a Drawing Room, usually by their mother or a female relation (who had been presented themselves – it was, supposedly, an inviolable caste), then they were able to accept invitations to dinner parties, balls, country house weekends, closely chaperoned, at which they were assessed by potential husbands. On marriage they were presented again, by a female member of their husband's family and, no longer single, could

64. The Dancing Lesson c.1856

There were many popular prints of the royal family in the 1840s and 1850s which emphasized 'our *happy domestic* home – which gives such a good example'. They presented an idyllic view of a perennially youthful queen and prince, with pretty, well-behaved children. In fact the Queen and Prince aged rather quickly in the 1850s, and their enlarging brood of children provoked cartoons questioning whether the state could afford to support so many young royals.

themselves make presentations. An interesting feature of the Victorian period was the number of young women who were presented for the first time after their marriage, often wearing a modified version of their wedding dress. Many of these young women would have been ineligible for presentation before marriage, for the 'wives and daughters of general practitioners... solicitors... merchants... men in business (excepting bankers) are not entitled to presentation'.[19] It was the ambition of the wives of such professional and businessmen to see their daughters marry into the 'aristocratic professions' of the clergy, military and naval officers, physicians and barristers, or even into the country gentry or the nobility. A daughter's beauty was of less interest than her potential dowry and her father's wealth, and many mutually satisfactory bargains were struck. Divorcees were totally excluded until late in the reign, although one or two slipped through the net. Young men usually went to their first levee somewhat later, after university, or as they began to make their way in a smart regiment, or in public service. Americans, both men and women could be presented by the American minister and his wife, and, as they were less stuffy than their European counterparts, the background of presentees was less closely scrutinized.

In May 1842 the English actress Fanny Kemble and her husband, the southern American slave-owner Pierce Butler, were presented at court. This was partly prompted by the Queen's 'curiosity', but assisted by the Butlers' friendship with the American minister Edward Everett, for neither of them would have been eligible in normal circumstances. Fanny Kemble's memories of the event are refreshingly free of the usual sentimentality. She was nervous and felt awkward, but managed the necessary obeisance without actually seeing the Queen, 'I kissed a soft white hand which I believe was hers; I saw a pair of very handsome legs in very fine silk stockings which I am convinced were not hers, but am inclined

to attribute to Prince Albert', and left with no more memorable an impression than 'of a crowded room of full-dressed confusion.' The whole episode had also been costly, for she had already spent her annual dress allowance before the summons to court. She hired her diamond necklace and matching ear-rings, and wore the latter, with theatrical flair, in her hair, stitched to a scarlet velvet bandeau and matching bows. Her dress of 'white satin and point lace, trimmed with white Roman pearls' resulted in a bill of £97 from her dressmaker Mme Dévy, and prompted the comment, 'If I could earn £200 now I should be glad.'[20] The crowds and confusion noticed by Fanny Kemble become more marked as the reign wore on. In 1848, 'The Queen was for once a little tired with the great heat, and 284 Presentations, the average number being 110'.[21] Two years later, Mary Lucy took her daughter Carry to court for the first time. It was the last Drawing Room of the season, but when the Lucys reached the first room,

the crowd and crush of ladies fat and lean was so great that it was simply impossible to make one's way through the door. I did all I could to protect poor Carry, but was almost squeezed to death myself, and when at last we did get into the large room or gallery next to the throne room, Carry fainted away.

By the time she had revived the Queen had left, and the spectre of Carry not being invited to the royal ball on 9 July lay heavy on Mrs Lucy; invitations to royal balls, banquets, concerts and receptions were dependent upon potential recipients having been presented. Fortunately, the circumstances were relayed to the Queen via the Lord Chamberlain, and her majesty was graciously pleased to consider Carry 'as having been presented.'[22]

In the 1850s *Punch* magazine made much capital out of the impossibly large numbers of people who attended Drawing Rooms. They ran before-and-after cartoons, tongue-in-cheek notices and editorial comment. In June

1855 there was a short, illustrated article 'The Crush Rooms at St James's', which suggested that Drawing Rooms should be moved to 'the more spacious apartments of Buckingham Palace'.[23] This suggestion was not acted upon until the late 1860s, and it was not until 1873 that the Lord Chamberlain's Office started to count everyone present, not just the presentees. By the following year even the 'spacious apartments' were not large enough; on 5 May 1874 1269 people attended a drawing room, and the clerk noted, 'This was the D. Room which was so overcrowded and about which there was so much comment in the newspapers'.[24] Unfortunately, comment did not

65. Queen Victoria Presenting Medals to the Guards 1856; W Bunney after Sir John Gilbert

The great disparity in height between the Queen and the Prince-Consort is evident in this group study, as is the latter's increasingly middle-aged appearance. The various events of the royal couple's life were minutely recorded in paintings and subsequently made available through engravings and lithographs.

lead to action and, by the end of the century, there were sometimes as many as 3000 people present at some Drawing Rooms. Such confusion and inaction is typical of a good deal of the unrehearsed pageantry of the nineteenth century. It had a recklessly amateur quality which was an obvious inheritance from the time when posts in the royal household were viewed as sinecures rather than serious posts which presented opportunities to implement necessary changes.

The clothes which were worn were as magnificently impractical as the arrangements for the events. In 1838 *The Ladies Cabinet* predicted, with remarkable foresight, the re-introduction of hoops into fashionable dress, but opined that, 'it is expected to be first introduced at her Majesty's drawing-rooms'.[25] In fact, the hooped petticoat or crinoline did not reappear until the late 1850s, but from the late 1830s onwards skirts continued to enlarge. This increased circumference, married to a wide train, meant that one woman probably needed the amount of space at St James's Palace which had been comfortably

66. **The Prince Consort in Highland Dress**
c.1855–60; J A Vinter after K Macleay

Queen Victoria and the Prince spent many holidays at Balmoral Castle; they designed Balmoral and Victoria tartans to supplement Royal Stewart for both wear and soft furnishings. Although, as a child, George III had worn tartan, it did not become an essential element in royal wardrobes until Victoria's reign.

occupied by two or three in the 1820s. Such fashions were sanctified by royal decree, for the Queen requested, in the 1840s, that all women appearing at Drawing Rooms should wear clothes of British manufacture. This decree was, apparently, in abeyance by the late 1850s; an etiquette book of 1859 says nothing of nationally produced goods, but mentions a dress of 'some plain, but costly silk'; a petticoat of 'rich Brussels lace, or of Honiton lace, or tulle'; and a train of 'moiré or glacé silk'. The train was becoming a vast almost three-dimensional confection, 'about seven yards in length (from the waist) and wide in proportion', trimmed with festoons of lace and bunches of flowers.[26] All of these items could have been made of Spitalfields or Macclesfields silks, but many were not, and there was no attempt to check their British (or other) manufacture.

Contemporary magazines and illustrated newspapers often recorded, in considerable detail, exactly what was worn by the royal family and other distinguished ladies of the court. This was thought vulgar by European courts, who frowned upon such information being circulated, but it seems to have fulfilled two purposes: first, it was the British elements which were specifically identified, for instance, 'The petticoat was of white moiré antique with deep flowers of *Honiton* lace, trimmed to correspond with the train'; and secondly, it gave up-to-date information of the style of dress and accessories which were worn – a verbal appendix to the unauthorized etiquette books.[27]

Men's levee dress and the dress worn at court functions when women were present was dominated by uniform, including the fifth class of civil uniform devised by Prince Albert in the mid-late 1840s when he was reforming the royal household. The hapless few who had no claim to any uniform had to wear a cloth or velvet court suit in subdued tones of mulberry, claret, dark blue or bottle green (or black if they were barristers) with the cutaway coat and breeches of the early years of the century, complete with black silk bag at the nape of the coat collar to protect it from non-existent powder, flower embroidered waistcoat, sleeve ruffles, silk stockings, sword and bicorne hat. It was as absurd as the mandatory hoop had been for women in the early years of the century, and sober-minded Englishmen must have felt pangs of envy at the sight of American diplomats and visitors who were allowed to wear plain black evening dress. Many men hired or borrowed their clothes, as anyone not entitled to the many varieties of uniform was unlikely to be expected to make regular appearances at court. Prince Albert presided at most levees from 1843 onwards, at the Queen's express wish, but made no attempt to vary the form of dress required.

It is very noticeable, when studying photographs of Queen Victoria and Prince Albert, how, in the late 1850s, they became prematurely middle-aged. The Prince, in particular, appeared stooped and care-worn, and the Queen's incipient matronliness became more pronounced. Portraits still flattered both of them, and the many engravings taken from these perpetuated the illusion of comparative youth. Although their youngest child, Princess Beatrice, was only a year old when their eldest, the Princess Royal, married Prince Frederick William of Prussia in 1858, the focus of attention, in their minds and those of the public began to shift to the younger generation of royals. All nine children lived to adulthood, and the popular, sentimental prints of the growing family (and the witty cartoons of the apparently limitless brood) were gradually replaced by closer private and public scrutiny of the individual princes and princesses. In portraits and photographs they were depicted wearing everything from miniature kilts and sailor suits, both of which set juvenile fashions, to fancy dress for private theatricals. Privately, they were inculcated with the need to take care of their clothes, which were usually plain

BEFORE PAYING HER RESPECTS AT ST. JAMES'S.   AFTER PAYING HER RESPECTS AT ST. JAMES'S.

and fairly serviceable garments, some of which may have been 'run up' on the sewing-machine that was installed in the nurseries in the late 1840s.[28]

Both parents were anxious that their children should not emulate the example of George III's family–the sons running wild in society and the daughters kept in virginal seclusion; the spectre of the Queen's 'wicked uncles' haunted the royal couple despite their own unexceptionable domestic harmony. This fear gripped both of them to the extent that they did not deal intelligently with the two eldest children, the Princess Royal and the Prince of Wales. The former was a precociously bright young woman, the favourite of her father, but married off too early, just two months after her 17th birthday. Dressed in white silk moiré, swathed in Honiton lace and floral trimmings, her ample court train carried by a row of maids of honour, the tiny Princess married her tall, uniformed Prussian prince.

67. Court Dress: Before and After, 1855

The crush and confusion of overcrowded Drawing Rooms at St James's Palace attracted both serious and satirical attention. Increased numbers and the amount of space required by court dresses meant that the experience was more an endurance test than an agreeable social occasion.

Like all of the momentous events of Queen Victoria's life – marriages, christenings, important anniversaries – this ceremony was recorded on canvas. The occasion is crowded with women in court dress, the men in uniform (military and royal household), even the Queen's sons have been accorded a sort of uniform, Scottish dress with smart black velvet jackets. After a brief honeymoon at Windsor, the young couple returned to London for a court at which they received the felicitations of fashionable society – the Princess dressed once more in white moiré, ruched with white satin and decorated with Honiton lace, white

68. **Queen Victoria Presenting a Bible c.1861; T Jones Barker**

The Queen was fascinated by the exotic and took an active interest in the far-flung territories over which Great Britain was establishing influence during her long reign. She is depicted in formal court dress, her small stature swamped by the decorative fuss of feathers, flowers and flounces.

roses and jasmine.[29] Three days later she left for Berlin, while her parents pondered the problem of what to do with the Prince of Wales.

Whereas the Queen and her husband had positively relished the preparations surrounding the Princess Royal's entry into society and her subsequent wedding – the Prince had designed the dress for her first formal party, and the Queen's journal was full of details about 'Vicky's' clothes and trousseau – they were far less understanding about their eldest son's interest in dress. It was almost as if they had read the etiquette books which opined that women must, necessarily, be fascinated by dress and appearance, but that this was a failing when demonstrated by men. The example of George IV was often cited, but without admiration, for he was 'a king and a beau, and in debt to his tailor'.[30] The Queen thought the Prince of Wales was a caricature of herself, in both the physical and temperamental sense, and her and her husband's lack of faith in their son did little to encourage him to apply himself to serious study. The manner in which he was given written instructions by his father, and his own wishes about his future ignored or over-ridden, are similar to the lack of understanding shown to the Prince of Wales by George III in the late 1770s. Prince Albert expected his son to behave impeccably, and to improve his mind through programmes of literary and artistic appreciation; there were to be no opportunities for gossip, cards, billiards or practical jokes. The young Prince might enter the army, but not to learn the profession; he was to spend a short time at Oxford University but was on no account to mix with other students. The Prince's gentlemen were also given instructions on 'The qualities which distinguish a gentleman in society', which owed not a little to the fashionable etiquette books which laid emphasis upon discretion, good manners and a well-rounded education.[31] It is hardly surprising that, feeling incapable of becoming a paragon, the Prince of Wales found solace in dress, practical jokes and the exercise of his princely social charm. By the time he visited his sister in Berlin in November 1858, his father was fore-warning the Princess Royal that: 'Unfortunately, he takes no interest in anything but clothes, and again clothes. Even when out shooting, he is more occupied with the cut of his trousers than with the game.' The visit was a success, and the Prince returned full of news about his social engagements, the Prussian uniform that he had been given, and with a short, centre-parted German hairstyle.[32]

His interest in his appearance ran alongside his mother's criticisms of his poor looks, his knock knees, his dullness, and his attempts to improve himself are an understandable reaction. Sadly, he had no friends outside his family circle with whom he could easily discuss his problems. His charming manners, a characteristic of the last Prince of Wales, George IV, were combined with a social isolation which prompted Prince Metternich to write, 'Le jeune prince plaisait à tout le monde mais avait l'air embarrassé et très triste.'[33] It was lucky for the Prince that, being in every particular the opposite of his father,

the developing clash of interests and ideas was ended with the Prince Consort's premature death in December 1861.

There was profound sympathy for the Queen, and even those members of society who had never liked the Prince Consort speculated about her ability to cope without his constant guidance and support. All court functions were cancelled in 1862; at the beginning of the season a notice issued by the Lord Chamberlain's Office stated that 'The Queen will this year hold no levees or Drawing Rooms.' Certificates of presentation were issued to applicants who were travelling abroad and wished to attend foreign courts. The widow was, however, still Queen of Great Britain, and the social element of her role might seem ritualistic, but it was important. Queen Anne had been devoted to her consort, but after his death she had continued to perform all of her public duties. Queen Victoria viewed matters differently; she had a large family who could fulfil the social obligations of the monarch while she lived reclusively, retaining her grasp on affairs of state but eschewing all forms of wider social intercourse. It is hardly unexpected that the young woman who had told Lord Melbourne that she was bored with dressing suitably, the happily married matron who wrote to her uncle that she disliked being troubled about clothes, should discover that the undemanding simplicity of a widow's black dresses and caps suited her admirably; it was one thing less to worry about as she grappled with the work of government and the affairs of her large family. The lack of a focus for national pageantry, and the depressing example that the Queen's sombre appearance created caused hostile comment in the newspapers, which felt that such seclusion and mourning were having an adverse effect on dressmaking and allied trades. The Queen and court were closeted at Osborne for Princess Alice's wedding in July 1862, and Princess Alice described the event as being 'more like a funeral' when she wrote to the Princess Royal; the Queen also viewed the wedding of the Prince of Wales from the box-like privacy of the Royal Closet in the Chapel at St George at Windsor, wearing, 'for the first time since December '61, the ribbon, star and badge of the Order of the Garter, the latter being one my beloved had worn...', and thinking herself very brave.[34]

She was outraged, therefore, when early in 1864 it was rumoured in the newspapers that she would come out of mourning and resume all of her former social duties. In a personal letter to *The Times* she stated firmly,

This idea cannot be too explicitly contradicted... The Queen heartily appreciates the desire of her subjects to see her, and whatever she can do to gratify them... she will do... But there are other and higher duties than those of mere representation which are now thrown upon the Queen, alone and unassisted....[35]

She was alone and unassisted because, like her Hanoverian forebears, she would not share the affairs of state with the heir to the throne, virtually condemning him to a life of social irresponsibility which the Prince-Consort had tried to prevent. For 40 years she presided over the government business of the monarchy, dressed in her mourning black. She eventually abandoned the heavy black crape of first mourning for lighter silks and plain black cloth (except for those occasions when other family deaths requires swathes of crape), sometimes leavened with the addition of lace, jet decoration, silver and gold, miniver or ermine. It was a comfortable uniform, and the tragic widow eventually became a national symbol for the values of historical continuity, and even the caricatures and cartoons were more often affectionate than not.

Released from the vagaries of fashion, she generally wore:

black silk, with very full skirts, the bodice buttoned down the front, and a square décolletage which was filled in with a dainty chemisette of white lisse (similar to tulle). The sleeves were rather wide, reaching to just below the elbow, and to them were attached full sleeves of white lisse –

69. Queen Victoria, mid-1860s; D J Pound
Photography became popular with the royal family from the early 1840s onwards. Many photographs were engraved and reproduced in magazines and books, allowing many more people to become familiar with the unidealized appearance of royalty. Queen Victoria in widow's weeds symbolized the British monarchy at home and abroad for nearly 40 years.

rather like those of a bishop–fastened at the wrist with a small button and loop.

With this simple style were worn flat, black satin pumps with crossed ribbons (like ballet shoes) over black silk stockings with white soles, and a white widow's cap with long streamers.[36] An anonymous publication, *The Private Life of the Queen*, which appeared in 1897, and was promptly banned, suggested that, 'About her own clothes the Queen never showed any particular taste, and nowadays she only fancies the plainest of gowns and mantles', and goes on to illuminate a habit which quickly became established within the senior echelons of the royal family once the old system of perquisites had ended. The Queen's 'wardrobe woman' was able 'almost without exception' to produce,

the gown, bonnet or mantle (worn) on any particular occasion. The Queen's collection of clothes would form the most accurate and interesting commentary on the modes of the past sixty years. Her Majesty also keeps with great care and pride a large number of articles worn by the late Prince Consort and by her mother the Duchess of Kent'[37]

It seems feasible to assume that the Queen's hoarding instinct, for she kept every sort of memento and commissioned souvenirs of every type, may not have been unconnected with the idea of a permanent memorial of her reign. Her last public act, in 1899, was to lay the foundation stone of the Victoria & Albert Museum and, in 1898, the State Apartments in Kensington Palace (in part occupied by her as a child) were opened to the public. Either location could have provided a suitable setting for a royal museum, and the latter did, to a limited extent, fulfill this function when inhabited by the London Museum, which enjoyed the enthusiastic patronage of Queen Mary. However, the purges of Edward VII, and the changed attitudes of later royals to whom 'the monarchy is not a museum piece'

have vitiated this possibility, and the collections which illustrate the public and private life of British royalty over four centuries are irretrievably scattered and will, presumably, remain so, unless powerful and informed patrons agree that this is an appropriate subject to analyse and display coherently.

The Queen's decision to wear mourning garments for the rest of her life did not dull her interest in, and strong views about, the clothing worn by others. She disliked extravagance and slavish subservience to the latest fashions, and she developed an innate conservatism which conveniently disregarded her own youthful experiments and pleasure in new styles. The ladies in her household were obliged, permanently, to wear mourning, initially black, then in its more moderate colourways, shades of grey and lilac and some white, but there was always the possibility of being plunged into black if a foreign royal or relative of the royal family died. The first third of the Queen's reign was colourful and festive, marked by royal christenings, balls, concerts, and state visits which encouraged vivacity in clothing; the last two-thirds contained as many funerals as weddings and christenings. Even weddings did not guarantee a relief from mourning attire or colours. In 1879 when the Duchess of Teck (the Queen's cousin) wrote to Lady Elizabeth Biddulph, asking if the latter would attend her at the wedding of the Queen's son, the Duke of Connaught, she said, 'You can wear violet, lilac, or grey, or white, I believe, if more agreeable to you'.[38] Such restrictions, in a period which saw a plethora of new colours made possible by the invention of chemical dyes, provided an almost water-colour effect of subtly selected tones. Fortunately for the women in fashionable society, they did not have to take their lead from a mournful, middle-aged recluse, but could look to the beautiful young Princess of Wales, Alexandra of Denmark for their inspiration. The Princess had won the Queen's goodwill when they met

70. Princess Alexandra of Denmark 1862
Queen Victoria was entranced by the beauty and
modest demeanour of Princess Alexandra. The
simplicity of the young Princess's clothes was a
reflection of the relative poverty of the Danish royal
family, not of the Princess's personal preferences.

in Brussels in 1862; her beauty and tact were
enhanced by her suitably mournful appearance in:

> *a black dress, nothing in her hair, and curls on
> either side, which hung over her shoulders, her
> hair turned back off her beautiful forehead. Her
> whole appearance was one of the greatest charm,
> combined with simplicity and perfect dignity.*[39]

Bagehot may have been correct in believing
that society did not require the monarch to
influence and orchestrate its activities, but a
royal family wholly isolated from society,
except on rare public occasions, is unlikely to
be viewed as other than a tiresome and
expensive anachronism. Such criticisms were

voiced in the 1870s; it was thought that the
Queen was not fulfilling her duties correctly,
and hoarding her annual civil list allowance.
On the other hand, the Prince of Wales
was almost too enthusiastic a member of
fashionable society, involved in public
scandals associated with divorces and gambling. The Princess of Wales, however, was
both a favourite of society and of the population at large. She had two inestimable

advantages, apart from her sweet temper: she was a great beauty and she had impeccable dress sense. Fashions that looked awkward or absurd on others suited her, and the camera loved her. She is one of the earliest examples of a public figure who understood the power of photography to create or enhance a public image. There are traditional, formal portraits of her, some of which are charming, but they do not capture the range of her beauty and

71. **Arrival of Princess Alexandra at Gravesend 1863; H O'Neil**

'Alexandramania' swept the nation when the Princess arrived (on her second visit) to prepare for her wedding. Even on a festive occasion such as this, discretion required her to wear the colours of half-mourning – purples and mauves – in deference to Queen Victoria's wishes.

stylishness; photography did, and in her case is the most potent record of her individuality. It is regrettable that she never sat to John Singer Sargent, arguably the last great portrait painter in the grand manner, but portraiture and the British royal family after 1861 was generally bland and uninspired. Photography had become the most inventive medium for capturing the royal image, and in the Princess of Wales it found its first genuine star.

A eulogistic biography, written in 1902 shortly after the Princess had become Queen, stated: 'Rarely, if ever, has it been the good fortune of a nation to have the greatest queen in history followed by the most popular and beloved queen consort.' This hyperbole is interesting because it begins to demonstrate that bias towards women and the monarchy which is such a feature of that institution over the last 150 years. There is an identifiable shift in emphasis away from the grey, sombre-suited male royalties, who might easily have been politicians for all the interest they generated, towards the softer 'sweetness of character and ... womanly compassion for the poor and suffering' to be found in female royals. This movement was assisted by the considerable public propaganda – in women's magazines, newspapers, officially authorized photographs and plethora of line drawings which drew attention to the 'good works' and attractive appearance of royal women. A matriarchal society in which the bourgeois values of a

72. **The Prince and Princess of Wales and Prince Albert Victor 1864**

This official study of the Prince and Princess and their first child is dominated not by the Princess's beauty and growing reputation for elegance, but by her husband's very fashionable appearance. Lounge suits for men were a new development, and the Prince was demonstrating a life-long fascination with clothing, which had been frowned upon by the Prince-Consort, but flourished after his death.

sound, happy home life (of the type pioneered by Queen Victoria and the Prince Consort) was allied to the idea of kindly but glamorous regality, which took charitable work and formal court ritual in its stride. This image began to permeate English life at much the same time as the movement for women's suffrage gathered momentum, and has had an equally long-lasting effect on national life. The irony was that the Prince and Princess of Wales were not interested in social issues and a changing role for royalty, for they were both innately frivolous young people, concerned with their appearance and the excitements of fashionable society. Their tastes were in accord, and from the earliest days of their marriage their London residence, Marlborough House, and their country home at Sandringham, provided the setting for entertainments which brought them into closer proximity with fashionable society than any royals since the hey-day of the Prince Regent.

The Princess had been brought up at the relatively spartan and impoverished Danish court, where she had received an inadequate education. She was a decorative and charming lightweight who never developed any intellectual interests, and like many beautiful women she was self-centred and capable of steely determination. Such determination was a prerequisite for anyone who cared enough about her outward appearance to look exquisite through the changing fashions from 1863, when she arrived in England, up to the time of her death in 1925. Like the Empress Elizabeth of Austria, who met her in 1868 and thought that the two of them were the only royal ladies in Europe who knew how to dress well, she was slim, dark and graceful. It was not, however, Queen Victoria's intention that her future daughter-in-law should compete with glamorous foreign royals, or become enamoured of finery in the same manner as the Prince. Advice on the Princess's trousseau was forthright, 'three or four trains and *grandes toilettes* will, the Queen thinks, be sufficient.'[41]

73. The Opening of the Royal Infirmary, Bishop's Waltham 1865; 'F.W.'

Public or semi-public royal occasions, laying foundation stones, opening buildings etc., increased in frequency in the late nineteenth century, and younger members of the royal family were introduced to the public in this manner. Queen Victoria insisted upon simplicity in dress for her children and Princesses Helena (*left*) and Louise are clothed in identical sturdy tan cloth dresses and jackets rather like the uniforms worn in orphanages.

74. The Prince of Wales 1868

The tradition of wearing tartan at Balmoral continued after the death of the Prince Consort, and the Prince of Wales who was fastidious and fashionable, saw no absurdity in a Germanic royal family pretending to be native Scots.

During her pre-marriage visit to England in 1862 the young Princess consulted her friend and cousin Princess Mary Adelaide of Cambridge (later Duchess of Teck) about suitable clothes. The more important items, including her wedding dress, were made in London using British materials, but her lingerie was prepared and exhibited at the establishment of the Danish milliner, Mr Levysohn.

She arrived in England dressed in mauve Irish poplin and purple velvet, in mourning for the Prince Consort she had never met, and was married in a dress of silver moiré festooned with Honiton lace woven in a design of roses, shamrocks and thistles, which Lady Geraldine Somerset thought 'très bon gout, light, young and royal.'[42] It was, in fact, one of those over-decorated extravaganzas which the Prince Consort had favoured, and very similar to the dress worn by the Princess Royal in 1858. The Princess must have longed to wear the chic wedding dress of Brussels lace which had been King Leopold's present, but which was thought unpatriotic. She may have found an opportunity to wear this dress 10 days later at a reception at St James's Palace, when Lady Waterford admired 'her coronet of diamonds and a very long-trained gown of cloth of silver trimmed with lace, pearl and diamond bracelet and stomacher'; another source described the same dress as 'a petticoat of white and silver moiré, covered with a dress of Brussels lace.'[43] In contrast with this grandeur, the simplicity of her day clothes and easy, unaffected grace were observed a few days later when she visited the zoological gardens; she wore grey moiré with violet velvet trimmings, a white bonnet and a fine shawl – the last was probably a wedding present, for it was usual for brides to be given cashmere shawls. She was described as:

> quite as tall as the Prince of Wales, and in a very long dress and a high bonnet looks more important than he does, and is so elegant that she need not fear the competition of the other beauties, the Empress of France and the Empress of Austria.[44]

75. **The Princess of Wales c.1873**
The Princess was photographed throughout her long life, and always appeared poised and elegant. Her dress sense was impeccable, and styles she adopted quickly became popular. This light-hearted, quasi-naval fashion was one of many that was associated with her.

It was a competition which Queen Victoria would not have wanted the Princess to enter; but she, understandably, was enjoying the freedom and adulation of her new life. Wearing 'a pale blue dress (with) a blue bonnet trimmed with white... all smiles and graciousness to everyone', she enchanted the people of Sandringham; and two thousand people and over 500 presentations marked her first Drawing Room in May 1863 at which she wore white silk and Honiton lace.[45] By 1865, her enjoyment of fine clothes and a tendency to over-spend were accomplished facts. One of her dressmakers, Mrs James of Hanover Square (who had made her English wedding dress),

> *was the type of milliner, so bland, so persuasive... she would run you up such a bill that would make you cry out, as the Princess of Wales is reported to have done when she saw her first milliner's bill. 'Oh, Heaven forgive me for such extravagance!'*[46]

There was no public outcry, no overt criticism; the English dressmakers and textile manufacturers were delighted to have such an elegant advertisement for their wares, and fashionable women were pleased that there was a member of the royal family who shared their tastes. None of Queen Victoria's daughters, of whom a number remained in England after mar-

76. **Court Dress c.1876–78; C Silatte**

The seasonal Drawing Rooms or courts provided considerable business for court dressmakers. This drawing is one of a small group showing the ingenuity of decorative effect which could link dress and train – the latter became increasingly substantial towards the end of the century.

riage, attracted the same degree of attention and admiration as the Princess of Wales. Amongst the royal family, only Princess Mary Adelaide of Cambridge shared the Princess's relish for clothes and shopping, and she, in the words of Mrs James, the dressmaker, 'is such a darling, only she is too large.' The latter was an understatement; the Queen and her relatives were both amazed and pleased when, at the age of 33, she was finally married to the Prince (later Duke) of Teck. The Princess of Wales wore Cambridge blue to the wedding, a typically elegant compliment, as when she wore Irish lace and green poplin on a visit to Ireland in 1868.[47]

In 1868/9 the Princess paid two visits to Paris – at the beginning and end of a six month tour of the Near-East with the Prince. She found it delightful 'and went about all day long and to a great many shops, which was most amusing', using the first visit to plan a major shopping excursion on her return at the end of the tour. Queen Victoria cautioned her son and daughter-in-law, 'not to vie in dear Alix's dressing with the fine London Ladies, but rather to be *as different as possible by great simplicity*, which is more elegant'.[48] It did not occur to the Queen that her daughter-in-law was the very finest of London ladies, and one of the most innately elegant women that she would ever know. Change, variety and experimentation upset the Queen as much as they interested the princess; in 1874 Queen Victoria took exception to the characteristic hair-style which the Princess helped to make popular, describing it as 'too high and pointed and close at the sides for her small head. The present fashion with a frizzle and fringe in front is *frightful*.'[49] The Princess took little notice, moving effortlessly from the full crinolines of the 1860s into the bustles of the 1870s, and, flattered by the great couturier Charles Frederick Worth naming his princess line for her, paid her first visit to his salon in 1878. These narrower styles of the late 1870s and 1880s suited her slim, well-proportioned

77. Queen Victoria and Princess Beatrice 1882

Although she never abandoned the mourning black of her widowhood, the Queen wore lace and jet decoration on her simple black silk dresses, and a delightful ruched tulle white cap. The fashionable line of Princess Beatrice's dress indicates the vagaries of changing style which the Queen was happy to ignore.

figure, but long before this her innovatory approach to fashion had inspired a number of successful novelties. She introduced, or made popular, high collars and deep chokers (to disguise a small scar on her neck), jaunty navy and white suits, and a witty habit of dressing in identical clothes to her sister 'Minny', Empress of Russia, whenever they could be together.

Her beauty did not fade, on her 25th wedding anniversary her ten bridesmaids thought, 'We all looked old ladies, but the

Princess as fresh and young as she did on her wedding day.' Photographs of her with her three daughters suggest that she might be an older sister, certainly not a mother. None of them inherited her stunning looks or her fashion sense. In 1889 her daughter Princess Louise married the Earl of Fife; patriotically 'The trousseau was ordered with due reference to the promotion of home industries which has always distinguished [the Princess of Wales], and orders for lace and lingerie were given to charitable institutions.'[50] In reality, the Princess was far less of an ally and promoter of home industries than the Duchess of Teck; she used both French and English dressmakers and suppliers – Mrs James of Hanover Square, then Madame Elise of Regent Street, with Redfern for tailored clothes; and Worth, Doucet and Fromont in Paris. Her constant travels in Europe made it relatively easy to patronize foreign dressmakers; she was, by temperament a cosmopolitan woman to whom this would not have seemed unpatriotic. As she grew older her tastes changed, the brighter colours she had once favoured, especially shades of blue, were abandoned after the Duke of Clarence's death in 1892. She adopted discreet, subtle semi-permanent mourning, wearing 'a pale grey dress and many diamonds' to her daughter Princess Maud's wedding in 1896, and lilac for the diamond jubilee procession the following year.[51]

By the time she became Queen in 1901 she had devised a personal style which was summarized by an early biographer:

Tall and graceful, and invariably dressed in what appears just the right thing for the occasion, devoid of all exaggerations of style, (she) has that easy and reposeful demeanour which perfect dressing gives. Every detail of her costume seems to have been made for her and her alone. She has an artistic sense of the fitness of things ... (but) has so far conformed to modern fashion as to abandon her old favourite, the close-fitting princess-shaped bonnet, for a small toque ... she has adhered to the curled toupée ever since she first adopted it twenty or more years ago. High collars and ruffles at the throat are greatly liked ... of late years she has preferred silver grey and pale shades of heliotrope. She is extremely particular about the fit of her bodices and jackets, and never wears a material which has a tendency to crease; for this reason she likes tailor-made costumes in cloth or tweed, and prefers a velvet gown to a silk'.[52]

The flattering hyperbole does not disguise a rigorous approach and care for detail which only a very rich, determined and essentially vain woman would have contrived. It was a style of dressing which relied upon an expensive amalgam of the best of English and French dressmaking, ornamented in the evening and on formal occasions by a magnificent collection of jewellery. She had a sure sense of the style which would be enhanced by a rich display of pearls and gemstones on the head, neck and arms; the Christmas-tree effect, pioneered by Queen Victoria, was simplified and given grandeur by the Princess, and copied throughout fashionable society. Alongside her, the Prince of Wales, his girth increasing with the passage of years, as his mother's had done, also retained his youthful enthusiasm for clothes. Although he lacked the height and physique to be the perfect model for the art of English tailoring, he was always keen to try new styles. From 1859, when as a student he had worn his first bowler hat, he was seen in every type of new clothing for men: the softer 'lounge suit' of the 1860s; the new black evening coat and trousers; tweedy Norfolk jackets and knicker-bockers for country sports; trousers with creases; and

78. The Prince and Princess of Wales 1882
By the 1880s the Prince and Princess were well-established as the leaders of fashionable English society, and their innate stylishness excited admiration at home and abroad. The Prince's beard and portliness gave him a distinguished appearance that he had lacked as a young man.

Homburg hats. He was married wearing Garter robes over military uniform and, until the end of his life, was happily addicted to every uniform available to him. He was rigorous in applying his extensive knowledge of correct uniform and insignia, chiding those who had the temerity to appear before him with the minutest detail incorrect. He was not handsome but after he had grown a beard and moustache in the 1860s, masking his receding chin and adding balance to a face dominated by a prominent nose, he acquired an air of distinction which won praise throughout Europe.

Society, which Queen Victoria and the Prince Consort had viewed with great suspicion, took the Prince and Princess of Wales to its unreliable heart. This was not approved of by the Queen, or by old-fashioned observers like Lady Geraldine Somerset who thought the couple 'too little royal.'[53] They were not stuffy, but neither were they undignified; no-one forgot who they were, but merely rejoiced in their youth, gaiety and stylishness. The Queen blamed 'society' for leading the Prince and Princess astray; she wrote to the editor of *The Times* in 1870, asking that he 'frequently *write* articles pointing out the *immense* danger and evil of the wretched frivolity and the levity of the views and lives of the Higher Classes.'[54] The freer, more relaxed attitudes of younger people also infuriated her; in a letter

79. The Duke and Duchess of Teck with Indian Soldiers 1883; S P Hall

The portly, extrovert Duchess of Teck was a popular member of the royal family. She undertook many public and charitable engagements and did not let her size deter her from wearing fashionable styles of dress. Her conscientious and informed approach to her public duties influenced her only daughter, Princess May, later Queen Mary.

to the Princess Royal she criticized the type of behaviour which was not unknown to the Princess of Wales,

one of the new fashions of our very elegant society is to go in perfectly light-coloured dresses – quite tight – without a particle of shawl or Scarf (as I was always accustomed to wear & to see others wear) – & to dance within a fortnight of the confinement even valsing at 7 months!!!! Where is delicacy of feeling going to![55]

Queen Victoria's dislike of pregnancy and child-birth was so ingrained that anything to do with it invariably brought her out in a rash of exclamation marks; when younger women challenged the idea that it was an illness which should be disguised she saw this as symptomatic of declining standards in manners and dress, rather than as a healthy acceptance of a natural occurrence.

Her bourgeois, insular view of changing social mores was not shared by the Wales's, but neither should she have worried that they would be less respected for encouraging new attitudes. The Prince and Princess went into society, but were never wholly identified with it. The increased opportunites for fast and comfortable travel meant that European royalties could constantly visit and be with each other, and in each other's company they could be relaxed and at ease in a way which was less possible in the houses of the hybrid mixture of old nobility and newly wealthy businessmen who vied to entertain them, but who the royals never considered as other than a wholly separate species outside their exclusive caste.

In February 1863 the Prince of Wales began to assume certain of the ceremonial functions of the monarchy, holding the first levees since the death of the Prince Consort in 1861. He decided to abandon the old procedure whereby the presentee knelt and kissed the royal hand, substituting the more democratic handshake. This proved as time-consuming as the previous method – about 2000 people with 1010 presentations marked his first levee –

80. **The Prince of Wales 1883**
Uniforms became increasingly elaborate in the nineteenth century, and princes often wore the uniforms of foreign powers when visiting their countries. The Prince of Wales is dressed in a German uniform and looks convincingly Hanoverian.

and a new formula of bowing and then retiring was adopted. Supported by his brothers and, later, by his sons, he was gracious and dutiful, but change of any significant variety was slow to arrive. The old restrictions concerning eligibility for court presentation were guarded jealously, although the Queen by knighting or ennobling various artists, musicians, actors and industrialists, confused the issue over who was or was not an acceptable member of society.

During court ceremonials the old guard still glittered in the embroidered and gilded grandeur of their uniforms, outshining anyone condemned to regulation court dress. The curious cloth suits and pale, embroidered waistcoats were replaced by discreeter black

velvet court suits in the 1870s, but looked no
less like fancy dress. Whatever their style of
dress, the discomfort engendered by too many
aspiring courtiers packed into too small a
space, affected men as much as women,
although the former were spared the burden
of bulky dresses and heavy trains. Trains were,
in fact, an increasingly inappropriate and
cumbersome type of garb for ceremonies
which took place in the early afternoon.
Drawing rooms were resumed at the same
time as levees, with the Queen's daughters
and the Princess of Wales deputizing for her.
This arrangement continued until the end of
the 1867 season, but in 1866 and 1867 the
Queen held 'Courts' at Buckingham Palace
for limited numbers – 250 in the first year
and 260 in the second. The Queen, having
overcome her nerves at re-establishing this
very slender link with fashionable society,
held traditional Drawing Rooms from 1868
onwards but only at Buckingham Palace. The
usual regulations about eligibility, appropriate dress and time of day were unaltered, and
the Queen was usually present for only the
first hour before being replaced by her
daughter-in-law or daughters.

   The accolade of presentation at court lost
none of its appeal, and if Queen Victoria had
hoped that her five-year absence would render
such ceremonies less pertinent, she was mistaken. Numbers of aspirants for presentation
continued to increase; it had been calculated
that by the end of the century the number of
families actively involved in the pursuits of
fashionable society and the events of the

81. The Royal Family 1887; L Tuxen

This picture commemorated the family reunion
which marked Queen Victoria's golden jubilee.
The Queen referred to her extended (and extensive) family as 'the royal mob'. The men in their
uniforms, the women in luxuriant dinner dresses,
the little boys in kilts or sailor suits, and the little
girls in fluffily pretty party dresses, personify the
apparently indestructibility of royalty as the apex
of European society.

82. The Duke of York c.1892–95

The second son of the Prince and Princess of Wales, Prince George, became heir presumptive on the death of his brother in 1892. He was a straightforward, conventional young man, with none of his father's taste for stylish or innovative clothes. He had, however, inherited his mother's slim physique and something of her symmetry of features.

London 'season' was approximately 4000.[56] Such families could provide a stream of sons and daughters who wished to be presented, but the 4000 was only a small proportion of the 30,000 families who were listed in the Court Guide in 1900. Such listings were often speculative, an insurance for a future in which the daughter of a wealthy businessman might make the happy transition into the top 4000. This possibility began to be endangered by the influx of statuesque American heiresses, with their wardrobes of expensive Worth dresses and apparently limitless resources – a species immortalized by Charles Dana Gibson, whose sister-in-law became Lady Astor. The changes in society deplored by Queen Victoria in the early 1870s were an established fact by the 1890s, despite the conservative attitudes enshrined in the flow of etiquette books which continued to appear. The continued popularity of this type of book was unaffected by the fact that their authors often ridiculed or despised the major section of their readership. Lady Violet Greville epitomized this type of author, complaining in 1892 that:

> Thirty years ago none thought of going to Court unless they were great personages for whom it was a duty.... (Now) rich merchants; people in business; country squires; American cousins; people of no estimation except in their own; people who are never under any possible circumstances likely to be invited to State balls or parties – all of these crowd and press and gather together... The father attends his levee, the mother and girls the Drawing-Room, notwithstanding the expense of the dresses, at which, however, they would think it an act of treason to grumble.[57]

Dresses for a first London season were very important for young girls who were competing for attention with the handsome, confident and statuesque beauties who ruled fashionable society in the last quarter of the century. Few debutantes were as assured or contrary as the young Margot Tennant (later Asquith), whose wardrobe for her first season came from Worth, and included only two pale ingenue styles – one of which she wore to her presentation. Worth was the de luxe end of a scale which, at an English court dressmaker, could start as low as £20 for 'a girl's white presentation frock', or might easily run up to £300 if a proud Mama wanted complicated lace and embroidery on the dress. Court dressmaker was a general term applied to fashionable London dressmakers; it meant that they were *au fait* with the regulations governing court dress, and could provide three-dimensional representations of the styles described in the etiquette books. Debutantes and brides usually wore white (the latter economizing by having their wedding dress re-modelled), older women could wear any colour they wished, but black was taboo unless as a sign of family or court mourning. The dress had to have a low-cut bodice with short sleeves, and a skirt trimmed with lace or tulle, decorated with embroidery, flowers or pearls. Two or three feathers were pinned to the back of the head with lappets or a veil suspended from them. Long white gloves covered the arms (suede was prohibited by the Queen in the early 1880s, although her grand-daughter Princess Marie Louise had to be reprimanded for wearing them at court in Berlin in the

1890s), a bouquet or fan was carried, but the *tour de force* was the train. Not less than 'three and a half yards long ... cut round or square, fastened from one shoulder (or both), or put on at the waist,' it was 'made of a more costly and handsome material than the other part of the dress; velvet or satin is chosen, and it is trimmed with lace, and feathers or flowers...'[58]

Many of the most impressive court trains which survive in museum collections date from the period c.1890–1910, and the combination of their size, three-dimensional decoration and rich materials provides stunning

83. A Drawing Room at Buckingham Palace 1896; S Begg

The Princess of Wales frequently deputized or assisted Queen Victoria at drawing-rooms. The royal ladies wear mourning for the Queen's son-in-law, Prince Henry of Battenburg. Something of the glamour and glitter of these occasions is conveyed by the uniforms, dresses and jewellery shown here.

examples of exquisite but totally useless dress-making, for few wearers had the wit of the woman mentioned in the *Illustrated London News* in 1902, who had her crimson velvet, gold embroidered train 'made into a cover for her grand piano afterwards'. During the 1870s and 1880s the train was often designed as an integral feature of the dress, but when trains were separate, the English tended to prefer them fastened at the waist or diagonally from shoulder to waist. When, in 1863, Princess Alice wore a 'violet velvet train from the shoulders, trimmed with . . . miniver' this style reflected the more Germanic tradition, although it was also worn in this manner at the Imperial court in Paris.[59]

Presentation at court was often a more memorable occasion for many young women than their wedding. This explains, in part, the survival of the specific elements of court dress as features in twentieth-century wedding dresses. Royal brides and their guests invariably wore court trains; the exception to this rule came later in Queen Victoria's reign when her daughter Princess Beatrice married her Battenberg prince at Whippingham Church on the Isle of Wight, and guests wore formal day dresses. Generally, however, royal ladies were upholders of the established forms, recognizing that any deviation from the etiquette of correct dress would be a signal to society to follow their lead. Dressing correctly was a complicated affair in the late nineteenth-century because there was an ever-growing range of women's clothing – informal tea gowns, day dresses, tailored suits, sports clothes (for tennis and croquet or, more daringly, for cycling), dinner dresses, ball gowns, and court dress. The work involved in producing fashionable clothes that changed every season meant that there could be considerable profits for fashionable dressmakers, and for the new department stores (the latter aimed mainly at the middle classes), and poor pay and appalling conditions of work for many seamstresses. It should also have provided a

great boost to native textile industries, an area in which royal patronage might usefully play an important part.

Such patronage could easily have been co-ordinated by the Princess of Wales, a natural role for the most elegant and admired female member of the royal family; instead it was her cousin, the Duchess of Teck who espoused the cause, through personal example – she always insisted upon English silks, Irish poplins, and Scottish tweeds, and by direct action. She was a prime mover behind the formation of The Silk Association of Great Britain and Ireland writing letters, sitting on committees, urging her wide circle of friends and connexions to support this area of British industry, paying factory visits, organizing exhibitions, praising when it was deserved and criticizing if she felt that British manufacturers were showing less originality than their European competitors. Her efforts attracted considerable praise from within the industry, who thought,

> *It was chiefly owing to the exhibitions at St James's Square and Stafford House, and the patriotic action of the Duchess of Teck in ordering the material for her daughter's bridal and trousseau dresses from British looms, that the public were induced to encourage home production.*[60]

This was just one of many charitable causes and active patronages that the Duchess developed; she provided a new pattern for royal involvement and encouragement in matters of a non-political nature which had a lasting influence on her daughter Princess May, who became Queen Mary in 1910.

If Queen Victoria and Queen Alexandra

84. The Princess of Wales 1897
Amongst the many festivities which took place in diamond jubilee year was the Devonshire House ball. All London society ordered extravagant and luxurious disguises. The Princess's usual style of evening dress was modified to include a type of early seventeenth-century sleeve decoration and standing collar, and is a foil for her remarkable collection of jewellery.

demonstrated wholly different images of queenship – in appearance, style and interests, Queen Mary was closer in temperament and attitude to the former. The frivolity and fashionable pursuits of her mother-in-law (she married the Duke of York, the only surviving son of the Prince and Princess of Wales, in 1893) were not to the liking of the thoughtful, intelligent Princess May of Teck. Her large, vibrant, active mother and moody, artistic father were 'poor relations', forced to live abroad in the early 1880s in order to retrench; they returned to London for their only daughter's confirmation in 1885 and subsequent debut in 1886. Princess May was tall, statuesque, handsome; contemporaries considered her graceful but 'never thought of her as pretty. She did her hair wrong, too high and tight at the sides'. Her own opinion was, 'I am too much like Queen Charlotte ever to be good-looking'. The camera did not love her and it was thought, 'She ought never to be photographed, as [photographs] do not do her justice' – living confirmation of the artist Alfred Chalon's supposed reply to Queen Victoria when she asked if photography might ruin his profession, 'Ah, non, Madame, the *photographie* can't *flattère*'.[61]

As a young princess, just launched into society, Princess May had two major disadvantages: her parents' relative poverty, and the fact that she was Her Serene Highness rather than Her Royal Highness. The first disadvantage meant that her clothes did not come from Worth or Doucet or from a fashionable London dressmaker, but from a peripatetic French dressmaker, Madame Mangas, who did not charge inflated sums for her designs. Even so, the Princess's uncle, the Duke of Cambridge, grumbled at what he thought of as absurdly high dress bills. He was prepared to give her £40 for three dresses, but not for one ball-gown which was the agreed price.[62] Being Her *Serene* Highness meant that although in England she could be positioned with the royal family at courts and

other formal occasions, in Germany and at other status-conscious European courts, she would be relegated to the category of minor royalties. The combination of these two elements made the likelihood of a 'great match' improbable. Consequently, it was a great shock to foreign courts when Queen Victoria sanctioned her engagement to the Duke of Clarence in 1891. He was the eldest son of the Prince and Princess of Wales; a weak, hapless youth, whom, it was thought, would benefit from Princess May's sense and intelligence. The match was popular in England, for the Tecks were much-liked and, at her most xenophobic, the Queen agreed, 'I must say I think it is far preferable than ein kleines deutsches Prinzesschen, with no knowledge of anything beyond small German courts.'[63]

This attitude was not a new one for the Queen; she had agreed to her daughter Princess Louise marrying a commoner, the Marquis of Lorne, in 1871, and had given her blessing to the Wales's eldest daughter, another Louise, marrying the Earl of Fife in 1889. Princess May was, however, singular in various ways, she was the only princess in English history to have had two fiancés, two wedding dresses and two trousseaux, for the unfortunate Duke of Clarence died in January 1892. Eighteen months later the Princess married his brother, and the patronage of British materials and dressmakers for the bride's second trousseau was recorded in great detail in *The Lady's Pictorial*. The Grand Duchess of Mecklenburg-Strelitz, the Princess's aunt, gave £1000 and some expensive black lace towards the trousseau, which was crammed with patriotic silks, poplins and tweeds. *The Lady's Pictorial* was not unduly impressed; its writers thought that the Princess 'cannot be called a dressy woman and has no extravagant taste in dress, preferring always to look neat, lady-like and elegant, to keeping in the forefront of fashion.' Married in a dress of Spitalfields silk, and leaving for her honeymoon dressed in creamy Irish poplin, the new

Duchess of York was an impeccable advertisement for English products. Then, almost immediately plunged into black mourning for a Teck aunt, she was delighted to be summoned to Osborne to be fêted by Queen Victoria. Her pleasure in her new wardrobe was expressed in letters to her mother; she described which clothes she wore on particular occasions, and how she was able to complement them with items from the splendid collection of jewellery which had been given to her as wedding presents.[64]

She settled quietly into her new life, making the ritual visits to Balmoral and Osborne (she and the Duke had homes in St James's Palace and on the Sandringham estate), appearing at court, taking her part in the royal round of banquets, receptions and balls. She was not, however, comfortable in the world of fashionable society, and it, in turn, did not feel comfortable with her, finding little in common with her serious, thoughtful dignity. Sir Frederick Ponsonby, who spent three evenings in her company in September 1894, thought her 'pretty and what you would call voluptuous, but decidedly dull'.[65] It is a curious description, but it certainly fits some of the photographs of her taken at this time. Hers was the type of statuesque good looks admired in the 1890s and early 1900s, but there was an aloof, controlled quality to it, almost as if it embarrassed her. It seems probable that she had already decided that she wanted to develop a different image for royalty than that associated with the Princess of Wales – a return to the quiet, self-contained dignity of Queen Victoria. Even in costume for the Devonshire House Ball in 1897, one of the greatest of all nineteenth-century fancy dress balls, she appeared strained and awkward, while her mother-in-law and all the fashionable society beauties suggested by their poses and expressions that this type of event was the most delightful fun, an expensively ephemeral game of charades. To the young Duchess, being royal was much more than a pleasurable game, it was a great privilege and duty, a commitment to life-long standards which owed nothing to fashionable society and its fads. She had not yet found a personal style with which she might adorn rather than detract from her rank, or been given the opportunity to mould the image of royalty as she thought appropriate.

85. Edward VII, Queen Alexandra and Members of the Royal Household, 1902

The first British coronation at which the participants were photographed. The King and Queen were leaving Buckingham Palace; Edward VII is reminiscent in stature and dress of Henry VIII in late portraits, but Queen Alexandra is exquisitely fashionable.

FIVE

'Daylight upon magic'

The death of a monarch is an arbitrary point at which to divide a study of dress and manners, but the death of Queen Victoria in 1901, so conveniently close to the beginning of a new century, seemed to contemporaries to signal the dawn of a new age. Society, manners and dress had changed with increasing rapidity since 1837; houses were more comfortable, foreign travel was relatively easy, the motor car and aeroplane were in their infancy, and telephones and telegraphy made intercontinental communication fast and efficient. A reign of 64 years had seen more sophisticated innovations than had occurred in the two previous centuries. In November of 1896 the Queen had seen her first 'animated pictures' and thought their production 'a very wonderful process, representing people, their movements and actions as if they were alive.'[1] By 1900 photography was a well-established medium through which royalty was made familiar to its subjects, and 'animated pictures' and, at a later date, radio and television, were to focus attention on those aspects of royalty with which few were familiar – their voices, actions and personalities. Such inventions had the potential to revolutionize the image of the royal family and their immediate circle, making them accessible to millions rather than hundreds of people at home and abroad. Social and technical revolutions are often more insidious than political ones because they are less easy to identify as revolutionary in intention until radical change has permeated an institution so thoroughly that it cannot be stopped.

In earlier centuries, English monarchs had gradually distanced themselves from their courtiers and subjects, devising arrangements whereby their private and public lives were separable. Regulations about behaviour and dress sanctified the special nature of this relationship, and the commissioning and circulating of official images provided a confirmation of the grandeur of royal life. This edifice had begun to break down in the late nineteenth century; cartoons, satires, scurrilous or unflattering diaries and memoirs, comment in newspapers and journals, and the absorption of some royals into the very heart of fashionable society were letting in the 'daylight upon magic'–the very danger that Walter Bagehot had warned against in the late 1860s. His view had been that, 'Above all things our royalty is to be revered, and if you begin to poke about it you cannot reverence it.'[2] The poking about had started before 1900 and gathered momentum, halted occasionally by happy accidents of individual endeavour, but no serious strategy was developed by twentieth-century royalty and their courtiers to safeguard the institution of monarchy and preserve its magic.

Although Edward VII had waited a little longer, was slightly older and ruled for a year less than George IV, the comparisons between them are worthy of brief consideration. Like his great-uncle, Edward VII was a stickler for correct etiquette and ceremonial forms; he was equally fascinated by dress, and to a slightly lesser extent by uniforms. He was not, however, a connoisseur, but more fortunate in being on good terms with all of his numerous relations in England and Europe. Unlike George IV, he had no thought of retiring into semi-seclusion, and he positively relished the opportunities presented to him for innovation and change. The old order was swept rapidly away and, in its place, a fashionable, light-hearted sociable style of monarchy emerged. It had been so long since a new monarch had acceded to the throne that no-one knew what to do. The journals and letters of that consummate courtier and public servant, Lord Esher, record the uncertainties that prevailed as Queen Victoria laying dying at Osborne. Esher went to Windsor Castle on the 21 January 1901 and noted, 'To-day all has been confusion. Precedents date back sixty years!', and the following day he added, after his return to London, 'The ignorance of historical precedent in men whose business it is to know is wonderful.' Gradually a sort of order began to emerge, in which Esher, to his obvious delight, played a major role as a species of Grand Vizier, sorting out royal papers, answering queries from the King, assisting with the organization of the coronation, acting as an intermediary between the King and politicians and multifarious other tasks.[3] At much the same time, the Duchess of York was writing to the Grand Duchess of Mecklenburg-Strelitz, asking for information about the coronation and etiquette of William IV's reign; the Grand Duchess was the only surviving British princess who could remember the court of a king and a queen-consort. It soon became apparent, however, that the new King and his consort would arrange all such matters to suit themselves.

Once he had accepted the post of Deputy-Governor of Windsor Castle, a post which, as the King informed him personally, qualified for a uniform of 'Blue and scarlet, a tunic and a hat with a straight plume, with a sash round the waist', Lord Esher was able to observe closely the style and manner of his royal master, who, he thought, looked, 'wonderfully like Henry VIII, only better tempered'. Clothes played a significant part in this new life, and were regulated according to the place and occasion. From the day of the accession council, when all present wore their uniforms (royal household, civil and military), there was a rigid formula which suggested uniformity of appearance, if not actual uniform. Significance was attached to all manner of seemingly trivial changes, for instance the fact that the King wore his kilt during the daytime at Balmoral, as well as in the evening, a garment which when he saw it in October 1904, Lord Esher thought, 'not very well cut. The stuff is too light and thin and does not hang well.'

The kilt, and the tartans designed by Queen Victoria and Prince Albert, were becoming a 'Balmoral uniform' worn as regularly in Scotland as the Windsor uniform at Windsor Castle. The latter was still impressive and popular; it was worn at a ball held at the Castle in June 1903 and Lord Esher thought it to 'look so well, and add to the decoration very materially.' Knee breeches were still worn with the uniform, and were required wear for anyone attending a gala function at which royalty were to be present. The King, of course, had clothes for every eventuality – naval uniform when he was setting out to join the royal yacht, *Victoria and Albert*; once on board his courtiers would wear:

> blue serge and dine in a queer sort of smoking-jacket with brass buttons. Rather smart – E.R. and a crown on them. The King wears his navy mess kit – which oddly enough does not sit ill upon him.

Informally, the King wore yachting clothes and a jaunty white cap; his extensive wardrobe contained every type of uniform, formal and informal day clothes, and a range of sporting and country garments.[4] When he travelled abroad, as he did nearly every year, to France or a German spa, he was accompanied by trunks containing more than 40 suits and no fewer than 20 pairs of shoes.[5] He grew increasingly rotund; briefly, after his appendicitis operation in 1902 he was on a strict diet and lost two stones in weight and eight inches from around his waist, but whatever his size he rarely looked other than impeccably dressed. Photographs of him leaving Buckingham Palace for his coronation, wearing state robes, suggest a rather friendly, velvet-and ermine-covered bear, and his Masonic regalia invites mirth, but these were forms of dress over which he had little influence. On other occasions, in clothes of his choice he appeared as a short, portly man whose stylishness enhanced rather than detracted from his natural dignity.

He expected and received respect, and he surprised many with his ability when he became king. Those who had dismissed him as an easily bored, pleasure-seeking leader of fashionable society, and an internationally recognized advertisement for the excellence of English tailoring, were both startled and impressed by his metamorphosis into a states-man. The Marquis de Soveral once told him, 'Vous êtes un grand diplomate, un homme d'état remarquable', and this opinion was not just restricted to friendly foreign envoys and obsequious courtiers. This greatness was, as so often in the royal family, not unmixed with an interest in more mundane matters, including an informed and meticulous eye for the niceties of dress. Princess Victoria, the King's daughter, might merely fix her disapproving eye on a pair of brown boots worn in her presence; the King would have commented, however, as he did, regularly, when he saw uniforms, insignia and orders incorrectly arranged and worn.[6] He was even-handed in his criticism; on one occasion he told Queen Alexandra that she must change her Garter star from the left of her bodice to the right. She assured him that it was only worn in that manner in order not to interfere with the arrangement of her jewellery, but he insisted upon change, and she obeyed him.[7]

He was less successful with her Garter ribbon, which she wore from right to left or vice versa, as the dress she chose seemed to dictate. From the beginning of the reign, when she took exception to the correct usage of queen-consort, preferring the more majestic queen, and later when she wrote to Sir Arthur Ellis about her coronation dress, 'I know better than all the milliners, and antiquaries. I shall wear exactly what I like, and so shall all my ladies – Basta!', she followed her own innate sense of correctness in regard to dress and ceremonial. The Grand Duchess of Mecklenburg-Strelitz's memories of the etiquette associated with Queen Adelaide were graciously ignored, as the Queen fretted over the height of her foot-stool for the state opening of Parliament; decided upon the appropriate four duchesses to attend her at the coronation, 'tall and well-matched'; and ignored the King's wish that she should watch but not be part of the birthday parade: 'after the King had started, she drove out of the Palace, and followed – and went round in the procession!'[8] She had an almost theatrical flair for knowing what was expected of her, and a delightfully idiosyncratic disregard for the humbug of precedent. Her increasing deafness, an inherited problem, made it possible for her to appear to misunderstand instructions, or simply not hear them.

It is often the case that as one sense diminishes it is compensated for by the increasing acuteness of another. In Queen Alexandra's instance, an already highly developed sense of visual symmetry (in terms of her appearance only, since the knick-knackery of her homes was comfortable rather than elegant) she became imbued with a strongly pictorial quality. She became the story-book queen, perpetually graceful and elegant, apparently ageless and capable of the most imperial grandeur on formal occasions. Even wearing 'a most extraordinary hat, like a squashed mushroom', she looked, 'perfectly regal as usual', and unlike the King who disliked

public demonstrations of excitement, she enjoyed the approbation of an audience, whose 'vast astonishment (at) her youthful appearance' was so gratifying.[9] She looked her most magnificent in the evening, shimmering in silk or satin, and ablaze with all of the jewellery she had acquired when Queen Victoria died, in addition to her own, not inconsiderable collection.

Her coronation as queen-consort afforded her an opportunity to play a central role in a ceremony of the greatest significance, and her idiosyncratic approach to this occasion was worthy of George IV. Newspapers and books of the time implied that she wanted to patronize British manufacturers, and Warners of Braintree did receive various orders for cloth of gold, cloth of silver and purple velvet.[10] In fact the velvet for her train was supplied by Marshall & Snelgrove, and had been woven by an elderly Huguenot; it was in a shade of purple not traditional for consorts, but which pleased her, and the embroidery (executed by the Ladies Work Society) incorporated royal emblems reserved for the monarch, alongside the decorative roses, shamrocks and thistles. The dress was of gold tissue overlaid by net embroidered with gold and silver floral motifs and gold spangles, and was woven in India under the supervision of the Vice-Reine, Lady Curzon. This glittering imperial fabric was made up in Paris by a firm called Thorin-Blossier into a fashionable fitted bodice, with low decolletage and pointed waistline, and a gored skirt – lovely but unexceptionable wear for a Drawing Room.[11] There are features, however, which indicate other influences –

86. Queen Alexandra 1902

The Queen's coronation dress of gold tissue, overlaid by net embroidered with spangles and floral motifs was made in Paris using Indian fabrics. Her purple velvet train was wholly British in manufacture and execution, but the overall effect was similar to her fancy dress for the Devonshire House ball in 1897 (c.f. fig. 84).

the wired, standing collar is reminiscent of the fancy dress worn by Alexandra to the Devonshire House Ball in 1897 when she impersonated the sixteenth-century Marguerite of Valois; and the hanging sleeves of net and simulated open-fronted appearance of the skirt, achieved by pendant chains and matched bow and drop brooches, bear some resemblance to the style of Russian court dress worn by her sister Minny, the Dowager Empress. It is a cosmopolitan *jeu d'esprit* typical of Queen Alexandra, and everyone present in Westminster Abbey on 9 August 1902 was dazzled by the slender, radiant and remarkably youthful Queen 'ablaze with light' who processed down the aisle.

The Queen had the uncanny ability to inspire admiration rather than envy in women as well as men. Margot Asquith who stayed at Windsor Castle with her husband, the Prime Minister, in 1908, thought, 'She looked divine. She wore a raven's wing dress contrasting with the beautiful blue of the garter and her little head was a blaze of diamonds'. The Queen was 64 but continued to look exquisite until her husband's death in 1910 changed her, suddenly, into a fragile old woman. Margot Asquith had her own, idiosyncratic and expensive dress sense; she continued to buy many of her clothes from Worth, and was able, on a visit to Windsor, early in 1910, to wear one of her loveliest Worth dresses, of silver tissue with a blue sash, to the investiture of the King of Portugal with the Order of the Garter.[12] Queen Alexandra shared Mrs Asquith's interest in the chic Parisian couturiers; on a state visit to France with the King in 1907, after an 18-year absence from the French capital,

She walked about the Rue de la Paix with Lady Gosford, and delighted in all the shops. She thought everything very cheap, and bought up half the town. At the 'receptions' she was at her very best ... The Parisians had never seen anything like her. Of course the Faubourg St Germain was

*in ecstasies and mocked poor Mme Fallières,
dressed in plum-coloured velvet, who trotted and
waddled alternately behind her.*[13]

The Queen's high standard of elegance and well-known extravagance was imitated by many women in fashionable society. Lady Curzon, the American Vice-Reine of India was a celebrated customer of Worth, and wore a dazzling dress with embroidery simulating peacock feathers at the Delhi Durbar in 1903, but vice-regality was considered the equivalent of licensed extravagance. Lady Cynthia Asquith, a visitor to the vice-regal court in Dublin in August 1915 and January 1916, was much impressed by the jewels and 'fabulous' wardrobe of 'Queen' Alice–as she called the Vice-Reine, Lady Wimborne. She recounted a story of Lady Wimborne's outrage when someone estimated that the Vice-Reine's annual expenditure on dress was *only* £10,000.[14]

In 1901 Lady Agnew, writing in *The Cornhill Magazine*, believed that 'an ordinary well-favoured couple' with a house in the country and a 'medium-sized mansion' in London might live on £10,000 a year. They could entertain and be entertained, give their children a good education and participate in the season. The 'cream' of the season was considered to be the 'courts, levées, state dinners and balls, Royal garden parties', but in addition there were dances, balls, banquets, dinners, the opera and theatre, concerts, exhibitions, fashionable sporting events, and innumerable charitable committees and functions. The expense of this social round could be compounded by anyone who aspired to entertain royalty. Daisy, Countess of Warwick considered that:

The extravagance involved in country house entertaining was so considerable that some of Royalty's friends... had to economize for a whole year, or alternatively, get into debt, that they might entertain Royalty for one weekend.

Perceptive social commentators understood how devisive this spend-thrift grandeur was in a country where poverty was widespread and social conditions for the majority had worsened since the 1890s. C.F.G. Masterman wrote:

At the one end of the scale the lives of a large proportion of the rich are far from satisfactory. Separated from many of the realities of life, they are unable to find natural ways of expending their money, and, in consequence, are driven to indulge in sumptuous living or in vulgar display.[15]

The majority of fashionable society, living in clean, well-appointed London mansions and on carefully tended country estates, surrounded by rosy-cheeked, well-fed servants, would have disputed Masterman's opinion. They would have believed, quite sincerely, that their way of life provided, directly or indirectly, employment for thousands of people–servants, tradesmen, manufacturing businesses. The comfort and glamour of their lives would have been interpreted as the finest possible advertisement for English prosperity, not as an ostrich-like perpetuation of a privileged and exclusive caste system; the irony was that most people still believed in the inviolability of the social structure, and wondered at, rather than envied the pageantry and display of fashionable Edwardian society.

Dress was one of the most obvious ways in which this hierarchical superiority continued to be demonstrated. Fine tailoring and complicated dressmaking were not bought cheaply; the number of changes of clothing and variety of necessary garments were less subject

87. Lord and Lady Carrington 1902

Lord Carrington wore full-dress first class civil uniform beneath his coronation robes; his wife is dressed in the fossilized eighteenth-century style of female coronation robe which Norman Hartnell replaced with an inappropriate velvet 'dressing-gown' in 1953. The page was more than a charming accessory; he carried the train of Lady Carrington.

to the whims of fashion for men, but it was expensive, and it required a very thorough knowledge of what was 'gentlemanly'. Men's dress continued to reflect the mid- to late nineteenth-century development of the three-piece suit into various formal and informal permutations. Colours, with the exception of country tweeds and light summer suits of the informal variety, were uniformly sombre. It was women's dress that changed rapidly, evolving from the tightly-fitted princess-line of the 1880s, with its large, shelf-like bustle, into a fuller, more balanced line in the 1890s. Tightly-fitted bodices with wide sleeves and gored skirts were worn into the early 1900s, but over a new, S-shaped corset, which gave a characteristic undulating silhouette.

Woollen suits and dresses of simple cut vied with softly-draped silk dresses overlaid with tulle or chiffon, in the soft pastel shades made popular by Queen Alexandra in the late 1890s. It was a mature, sophisticated style, often complemented with a wide-brimmed hat, and a carefully chosen bag, parasol and gloves. Between 1908 and 1910 there was an apparently sudden and dramatic change in style; the waistline began to rise, skirts narrowed and lost their trains (for day wear), and a tunic-length jacket or over-dress emphasized the new, vertical line, which was softened by fluid materials and topped by hats which grew ever larger and were smothered in flowers, feathers and veiling. The changes in dress which took place between 1911 and the early 1930s contrived to flatter slim, moderately tall, younger women, and the era of the statuesque, mature beauty ended before the onset of the First World War. Older women had to fend for themselves as best they could in this period, which favoured young women, and many of them continued to favour a slightly shorter, pared down version of the princess-line, tunic and overdress of c.1908; this style, surmounted, from about 1914 onwards with a distinctive toque hat, was the preferred dress of both Queen Alexandra, and her much younger daughter-in-law, Queen Mary.

The change of direction in women's fashions coincided with the death of Edward VII. Fashionable society was once more without royal leadership, for neither the new King or his consort were comfortable in the circles in which Edward VII and Queen Alexandra had moved so effortlessly. The reintroduction of a Victoria & Albert style of monarchy, with the emphasis on domestic harmony and high moral tone, did not mean the abandonment of all the innovations in style from the previous reign. There was, for instance, no return to the outmoded afternoon Drawing Rooms. In 1901 Lord Esher had been asked for his views on the arrangement of Drawing Rooms and levees; it had already been rumoured that the former were to be abolished and replaced by, 'five enormous evening parties instead – to which people will be invited.' He was perturbed by this idea, for those whom royalty would wish to invite were unlikely to be the people who expected to attend in the natural course of events. It may well have been the King's intention to invite, from amongst his wide and varied acquaintance, exactly those 'Actors one never met socially, nor people in trade and business' that hide-bound courtiers considered were not members of society because society consisted solely of 'those who were eligible for presentation at Court.' The leviathan of in-built privilege and prejudice defeated any thought of flexibility; Lord Esher supported the notion of invitations as a way of strengthening the status quo, and

revising a system full of abuses; notably the receiving of payments for presentation at Court, and the irresponsible introduction for political or social reasons to the Sovereign of persons who should not be admissible.

The old restrictions were retained, but one of Lord Esher's suggestions, within a range encompassing everything from the *mise-en-scène* (Esher was an enthusiastic theatre-goer)

to the style of obeisance, was implemented. His suggestion was that the Queen might

modify the form of 'low-necked dress' worn hitherto – and allow women to wear sleeves – at any rate to the elbow. The décolletage hitherto in vogue being one of the most trying and unbecoming costumes ever invented for women.

'High court dress' for the elderly and infirm was sanctioned in 1903, with elbow-length sleeves and a modest neck-line. Esher's other suggestion regarding dress – that the train should be 'a regular official garment of some selected material ... not ... of "chiffon" which looks like an elongated housemaid's duster – was ignored.[16] Court dressmakers continued to dress their clients in every type of material for dress and train, just as long as the garments conformed to the relatively loose specification included in the latest edition of Dress and Insignia Worn at Court.

88. **Court Dresses and Trains 1903; E Vincent**
This illustration from The Lady's Pictorial indicates why such garments were preferable for evening courts rather than afternoon Drawing Rooms. The influence of Queen Alexandra's wired coronation collar can be seen in the high, semi-collar-like sleeves. By this date, trains were massive three-dimensional confections.

This remarkable publication, which first appeared as a pamphlet in the 1880s and grew into a major work by the time the last edition appeared in 1937, concentrated principally on men's dress, with never more than two pages devoted to women. The complexity of the uniforms; dress and undress, levee and Drawing Room, northern and tropical, the wearing of orders and medals, and the variations in velvet court dress ensured this publication substantial sales. Levees were more functional occasions than the new evening courts; at the latter, after the presentations had been made, a light, buffet supper was served. Men could not attend a court unless they had been presented at a levee, but their eligibility was scrutinized closely, and many requests were routed through senior officials in the armed forces or public service rather than the Lord Chamberlain's office. Despite the formal setting, in St James's Palace, they were routine affairs, but they maintained the useful fiction, described so fulsomely when the Duke of York held his first levee in March 1894:

89. George V and Edward, Prince of Wales, 1910

The new king and heir to the throne, dressed respectively as Admiral of the Fleet and midshipman in the funeral procession of Edward VII. The British royal house's fascination with naval rather than military service began with George V who had entered Dartmouth Naval College in the late 1870s.

it was remarked that HRH possessed the quality which distinguishes the whole of his family, of recognition of anyone with whom he has ever come into contact.[17]

Edward Marsh, a junior colonial official, who attended a levee in 1902 would not have agreed; he thought it, 'a most wearisome performance', which took over an hour to accomplish as '1500 of the educated classes,' moved through, 'successive pens... just in time to make one's bow to the red, bored, stolid sovereign.'[18]

Such *lèse majesté* amongst younger members of society was widespread in the era after 1901. The King and Queen were not young, neither were their circle of courtiers and friends, but the relaxation in social attitudes which they represented had a liberating effect on young men and women. This found expression in more youthful fashions, entertainments and artistic innovations; new ideas generally met with acclaim rather than criticism. It was thought witty to poke fun at or be unimpressed by royalty. Lady Diana Manners (later Cooper) was presented at court just before the First World War, and had been reared on her mother's admiration for Queen Alexandra's great beauty; Lady Diana saw 'an old woman with red hair and terrible teeth, because no-one bothered about teeth in those days.'[19] Approximately ten years later, Cecil Beaton saw Queen Alexandra at Sandringham flower show, 'still beautiful, thinner and haggard' with her face 'painted scarlets and whites and black and magenta'.[20] Beaton thought the Edwardian age glamorous, and was dazzled by royalty, but to young women of the era both Queen Alexandra and Queen Mary seemed relics of a past age, fossilized in both manners and dress. Lady Cynthia Asquith, a fashionable beauty, but without the means to dress lavishly, expended time and energy on keeping in the forefront of fashion – buying at sales, accepting clothes from richer friends, and having gar-

ments re-modelled. In May 1915 she went to
her tailor and 'told him he must do something
to my white coat and skirt to make me look
less like Queen Mary.' In the previous month
she had noted that, 'clothes have undergone
enormous changes since the war and have
become practically early Victorian with real
full skirts. I thought war would produce
reactions to womanliness.'[21] The war produced many changes in women's clothes,
but in fashionable circles the most noticeable
difference were the acceptance of the fuller,
shorter skirts, hair cut in a waved bob à la
Irene Castle, and strong, rich colours, which
gave vibrance to gatherings where soldiers
now dressed in functional khaki.

Amongst the younger female members
of the royal family, there was no natural
leader of fashionable society; instead there
were various fashionable young aristocrats
and some stylish young actresses, like Zena
Dare and Gladys Cooper who were admired
and emulated. Princess Mary, the only
daughter of George V and Queen Mary
dressed in a simple, unostentacious manner,
and was overshadowed by her mother. The
Queen, like Queen Victoria, found clothes
troublesome; in Paris in May 1908 she avoided
the couturiers and concentrated on sightsee-
ing. When she wrote to her aunt, the Grand
Duchess of Mecklenburg-Strelitz in 1911, she
mentioned,

> my tiresome trousseau of clothes which has meant
> endless trying on .... The fashions are so hideous
> that it has been a great trouble to evolve pretty
> toilettes out of them ...

This was her description of her wardrobe for
the coronation year. Although she had once
enjoyed clothes, her husband had influenced

90. Edward, Prince of Wales 1919; H L Oakley
This silhouette of the Prince of Wales in his army
uniform captured something of the casual, boyish
charm – although he looks about 16 he was 24 –
which made him the most popular member of the
royal family from the Great War until the 1930s.

her public image, with his dislike of 'the fashions which these stupid dress makers will make even when you tell them not to.'[22] Unimaginative, straightforward English gentlemen, of whom George V was typical, disliked fashion; they remained loyal to their tailor, ordered similar styles, similar materials year in and year out, to suit a life in which smart town clothes and country outfits were occasionally leavened by a slightly different style of hat or overcoat. The King was no exception – in this he was much like George

91. Edward, Prince of Wales 1921

At Epsom races in early June the Prince's popularity with all ages and social classes was evident. Although a short, slender man, the formal dresssuit and top hat created the impression that he was much taller.

III – his wardrobe contained rather more uniforms and ceremonial garments than most, but fashion, to him, was an extravagant charade. In absorbing this attitude and acting upon it, Queen Mary evolved a style which was as personal as Queen Victoria's. It is a demonstrable fact that, if three silhouettes of Queens Victoria, Mary and Elizabeth, the Queen Mother, are shown to anyone with the slightest knowledge of English history they can identify them instantly; personal style is not fashionable or unfashionable, it is a statement of individuality. Queen Mary's individual style evolved during the First World War, and modified only in inessentials until her death in 1953. Occasionally she rebelled, urging her lady-in-waiting the Countess of Airlie to shorten her skirts to see how the King reacted. He did not approve

and the Queen's skirts did not rise above the ankle.

The American writer Janet Flanner wrote a long article about Queen Mary in 1938, and in its summary of her life, influence and personal style, it is an unsurpassed essay, not reverential, but not lacking in admiration. Like many non-Britons writing about royalty and ceremonial, she managed to capture the idiosyncracies and strengths of the individual and the role without being caught up with sycophancy or trivialities. Miss Flanner thought Queen Mary:

> looked her best with a diamond crown on her head, wearing dècolletage, loaded with royal jewels ... No longer young and never a beauty, she put beautiful young women around her in the shade. She still has the classic handsome back, the

impressive stately bosom for roped pearls, the tractable curled coiffure of another generation, and the fine old-fashioned skin that companioned them. Above all she has, strengthened by etiquette and softened by her profound personal belief, the grand queenly manner of which she is the last living great example. Her trained court gowns have always been of the richest pale fabrics, shot with

92. **George V, Queen Alexandra, the Dowager Empress of Russia and Queen Mary 1923**
The royal quartet's appearance owed nothing to the fashion changes of the post-1914 period. Dressed for the June wedding of Lady Mary Cambridge, the King wore formal day wear and Queen Mary the characteristic timeless style of dress, loose coat and toque which she adopted a few years earlier. There is no apparent generation gap in style between Queen Mary and her mother-in-law.

*silver or gold; are elaborate in cut; in detail beaded,
embroidered, gusseted, gored, looped, draped, cap-
sleeved; have no connection with any other style
being practised on earth, and are perfect.*[23]

It was a personal grandeur which had been
perfected before the First World War, and won
great admiration from the strict, etiquette-
conscious court in Berlin, during a visit in
1913. An observer of the ceremonies had told
her aunt, 'she never saw anything like your
magnificent Dresses and Diamonds, and your
regal appearance, the Wedding Toilette sur-
passing all!' The last was Indian cloth of gold,
with gold embroidery, worn with a train of
Irish lace lined and bordered in gold.[24] It was
a style of dressing that she still favoured nearly
20 years later, at the four courts of the
1932 season. Other royal ladies wore satin,
georgette, crêpe de Chine, lace, chiffon or
plain brocade; Queen Mary dazzled in 'silver
lamé embroidered with silver and gold
threads'; 'silver tissue scintillated with an all-
over hand-embroidery of cut crystals'; 'pink
and gold British brocade, embroidered all
over with glistening pink and gold paillettes';
and 'Brilliant gold lamé draped with gold net,
magnificently hand-embroidered with fine
diamanté.'[25]

It was both a dated and date-less Ruritanian style of glamour which recalled the brilliance of courts before the First World War
when nearly every country in Europe had a
monarchy. The vast array of jewellery that
the Queen wore on such occasions was a
nostalgic reminder of Queen Alexandra's
individualistic approach to the wearing of
jewels; even the choice of dress and materials
was influenced by the shimmering court and
formal evening dress of the Edwardian period.
By consciously summoning-up a past age of
court fashions Queen Mary emphasized the
importance of tradition and historical continuity, those essential elements if royal ceremonial was to have meaning and purpose.
The idiosyncratic, almost foreign quality of

Queen Mary's appearance impressed Sir
Osbert Sitwell when he visited her at Badmin-
ton during the Second World War. He decided
that she was like a Roumanian in

*the manner in which she smoked cigarettes; her
love of jewels, and the way she wore them; and
the particular film-star glamour that in advanced
age overtook her appearance, and made her, with
the stylisation of her clothes, such an attractive as
well as imposing figure.*[26]

Her day-time clothes, as stylized and notable
as her evening dress, were distinguished,
according to Janet Flanner, by toques 'worn
high on the head like a crown', and her love
of soft colours, such as pale blue, 'even for
tweeds'. Her resistance to change was seen as
an asset:

*She looks like herself, with the elegant eccentrici-
ies – the umbrella or cane, the hydrangea-coloured
town suits, the light lizard slippers, the tip-tilted
toque – of a wealthy white-haired grande dame
who has grown into the mature style she set for
herself too young.*[27]

The Queen had a business-like approach to
her clothes. Like all other objects in the
personal and royal collections in which she
took pride, they were carefully catalogued.
The Royal Archives contain her dress books
for the period 1911–41, which record the
clothing, dressmaker, jewellery and occasion
on which each outfit was worn. Her
dressmakers – principally Reville and Handley Seymour until the late 1930s when Norman Hartnell joined this select band – went to
Buckingham Palace with pre-selected designs
made up in her favourite colours. Janet
Flanner said that she never paid more than
20 guineas for day dresses or 25 guineas for
her 'fifteen annual evening gowns'. Hartnell's
evidence contradicts this; his first commission
was to supply three evening dress designs for
which he suggested a price of 35 guineas each.
He was told that this was 'too little', and that
she wished to pay 45 guineas for each.[28]

Her economies were made in other ways. She knew exactly what happened to her clothes – some were given to relatives who had them re-modelled; one outfit, worn to a family wedding in the 1930s, was given to the London Museum, but recalled for another wedding in the late 1940s before returning, permanently to the Museum. Ceremonial robes were also re-used; the train made for the 1902 coronation when she was Princess of Wales, was worn again for the Delhi Durbar in 1912, for George VI's coronation in 1937, and worn lastly by Queen Elizabeth the Queen Mother in 1953. All of these clothes were impeccably British; none of the Parisian couturiers who catch the eye in the list of warrant-holders to Queen Alexandra were ever found in Queen Mary's lists. Her interest in fashion may have been thwarted by her husband's notions of suitable clothes for a queen-consort, but she never lost her interest in new products; in the 1930s her example of buying British was admired and emulated. Whatever she bought, from plain brown tea-pots to cotton taffeta, became newsworthy, and her patronage instantly boosted sales. By the time of the silver jubilee in 1935, she had become a national institution, a palpable symbol of the grandeur of monarchy. Cecil Beaton, whose great disappointment was that she would never agree to be photographed by him, saw the jubilee procession, and noted:

> *however tiresome and perverse we may be about our Queen's clothes in our more analytical moments there is no one who can give an effect such as she. Any beauty one could mention pales beside her, and to see her today was an unforgettable sight.*[29]

It was during the First World War that Queen Mary became established as a popular public figure, at much the same time that her highly personal style of dress became fixed. Her work on war-aid committees, her visits to hospitals, convalescent homes and factories, and her personal example of domestic entrenchment was much admired. Before the war fashionable

society had been disappointed and mocking about the dullness of court life under George V. Lord Esher had noticed the difference very quickly, 'There is no longer the old atmosphere about the house – that curious electric element which pervaded the surroundings of King Edward. Yet everything is very charming and wholesome and sweet.' Nine months later he added, 'We are back in Victorian times. Everything so peaceful and domestic.' The King, who was a straightforward countryman at heart, accepted that he had to be in London to transact business, but he disliked fashionable social life, preferring to rise and retire early, to shoot and ride, and to see only those people with whom he felt comfortable. The Queen's interest in family history found an outlet in, 'collecting together all sorts of lost treasures, cataloguing and arranging. She has a very keen love of bibelots and of order.' These private pleasures and such exemplary domesticity were appropriate in war-time, even though in London and elsewhere there was a ceaseless, almost frenetic pursuit of pleasure, which gathered momentum in the 1920s, but curiously the monarchy was less popular at the end of the war than at the start. In 1915 Lord Esher had told Queen Mary that, 'after the war thrones might be at a discount, and that the Prince of Wales's popularity might be a great asset,'; a fairly frank request for a livelier, more fashionable and more accessible style of monarchy.[30]

In 1919 a rather subdued attempt at reviving court functions came with the announcement that there would be summer garden parties at Buckingham Palace. Shortly afterwards it was reported that over 75,000 applications had been received – an inevitable concomitant of the fact that, since 1914, there had been no formal court functions. The new style of party was not popular with debutantes, as they shivered 'in muslin and things, blue and green and purple with cold', and even when evening courts were re-introduced in 1922 there were worries about how to fix feathers into bobbed hair, and grumbles about the shorter court train, 'for (the debutantes) complain there won't be enough material in them to make any thing of them afterwards.'[31] The short hair, short dresses and thin fluid materials which were fashionable in the 1920s crept into court dress. This was allowed because of the shortage of materials after the war, and the belief that it would be inappropriate to revive the lavish trains and richly embroidered full-length evening dresses of the period before the war. According to the etiquette books of the 1920s, the new train 'must not extend more than eighteen inches from the heel of the wearer when standing', adding the caveat that 'The instinct of good form renders regulations against very short skirts and aggressively sleeveless bodices superfluous, for any extravagances of transitory fashions are manifestly out of place on an occasion of such dignity.'[32] Feathers had to be white unless someone was in deep mourning, but the colour and length of dress and gloves was left to personal discretion; veils had to be 45 inches, and those delightful fossils of the eighteenth century – lace lappets – could still be worn. Leaving so much to individual choice could, sometimes, lead to recklessness. An 'insufficiently-gowned lady' was once led out of a ballroom at court, 'so that she might repair an unfortunate rent in her gown'.[33]

In the 1920s court entertainments did not include court balls; none had taken place since the war, although dances were occasionally given after state dinners. There were royal dinner parties, afternoon parties and garden parties, which, as described in the etiquette books of the period, sound dull and excessively formal, although one loyal author declared that 'the Throne is the natural centre of social life.' The higher taxation, and swifter, more direct transport by motor car in the post-war period meant that it was no longer so possible or even necessary to take a house in London for the season. The season fragmented into two – the late April/early May to July period in London and 'the little season' just before Christmas. It is questionable whether 'the most important of social functions are any entertainments at the Palace', but etiquette books continued to thrive on the minutiae of the dress and manners required for courts and levees, 'royalty as host and guest', functions such as Ascot, and other events at which royalty might be present. Mrs Massey Lyon's *Etiquette* (1927) runs to 467 pages of text with 40 separate chapter headings.[34] It is doubtful whether she would have agreed with Virginia Woolf's view that 'London Society is a miasma – a mirage... At one and the same time Society is everything and Society is nothing. Society is the most powerful concoction in the world and Society has no existence whatsoever...'.[35] In the 1920s and 1930s this fashionable mirage raced around in motor cars, danced in night-clubs, disappeared to the south of France, week-ended, spent money it could ill afford, and enjoyed the company of its newest and brightest royal star – the Prince of Wales.

He was the best-looking of his family – blond, blue-eyed, rather too short for classical masculine good looks, but lively, amusing and articulate. His sister, Princess Mary, who might have been an inspiration to fashionable young women – she, too, was blonde, had worked with the Red Cross during the war, and learned to type (both thoroughly modern initiatives) – briefly caught the nation's attention with her wedding, in 1922, to Lord Lascelles. This event provided the first, large-scale bout of pageantry since the war, and was the first royal wedding of the modern variety – not held in the cramped privacy of royal chapels at St James's Palace, Windsor Castle or Osborne but in Westminster Abbey – and observed and discussed by the nation. *Vogue* magazine was obsequious about her trousseau, 'Individual Taste Combined with Beauty of Material and Design Result in a Charming Trousseau for the Nation's Bride':

every garment was listed, with the name of the makers – Reville, Handley-Seymour etc. and the Princess was undoubtedly very modern in her choice of silver lamé for her wedding dress.[36] It was a popular wedding, not simply because it brought royal display and ceremonial back into public life, but because the groom was English. The King and Queen had accepted that foreign matches for their children would be unpopular (foreign, in royal circles, usually meant German). Princess Mary's husband, however, was no romantic hero, but a rich, irascible man some 15 years older than his bride. The new style of arranged marriage was impeccably British, but no more sensitive than former European alliances; it is hardly surprising that a fitter at Reville saw the Princess sobbing unconsolably as she tried on items for her 'charming trousseau'. The wedding is now remembered, primarily, because one of the bridesmaids was Lady Elizabeth Bowes-Lyon, who, in the following year, married the Duke of York, later King George VI. This flurry of royal weddings concentrated speculation upon a possible bride for the Prince of Wales, but he continued in his winningly boyish way to remain the most eligible bachelor in the world.

The Prince of Wales was almost certainly the most widely travelled, most photographed, and most admired member of the royal family between the end of the First World War and the beginning of 1936 when his father died. He seemed typical of the young men who had survived that appalling conflict and were determined to disregard the strictures and formality of the older generation. He liked change and novelty, he was energetic and, unlike his parents, he enjoyed the noisy, frantic entertainments and pace of life in the 1920s. He had more than his fair share of charm in a family not noted for it, and on his abdication in 1936 it was observed that he left the royal scene taking the last of the Stuart charm with him. He was the most visible member of his family, undertaking a variety of duties, from

93. **Lady Elizabeth Bowes Lyon (later Duchess of York and Queen Elizabeth) c.1923**
Lady Elizabeth's old-fashioned prettiness is captured in this photograph. Unlike many of her contemporaries, she did not crop her hair, wear dramatic make-up or adopt uncompromisingly androgynous styles of dress.

overseas tours to the essential but more mundane business of laying foundation stones, opening new buildings and visiting industries, thereby giving a momentary gloss of royal glamour to worthy but boring occasions. In addition, his foreign tours impressed contemporary journalists: *The Illustrated London News* wrote, 'Surely there has never been so travelled a Prince as ours, and there never has been such a successful ambassador.'[37] Along with his mother, Queen Mary, he was considered to be one of the best commercial salesmen in the British Empire; everything he bought and, more especially, wore, guaranteed substantial sales. In Janet Flanner's opinion, he was, by virtue of 'what he wore and bought...

94. The Duke and Duchess of York 1926
The image of twentieth-century royalty which most successfully conveys their status is that of the prince in dress uniform bedecked with medals and orders and his princess in shimmering evening dress with an obligatory tiara amongst the jewellery. Conforming to the 1920s style of bandeau, long rope necklace and shapeless beaded dress, the Duchess has added a floating tulle wrap to soften the narrow line.

a special style setter.'[38] The genetic inheritance had skipped a generation and it was he who shared Edward VII's passion for new and different styles of dress. From the day in 1911, aged 17, when he was made, unwillingly, to wear the curious fancy dress which his parents deemed appropriate for his installation as Prince of Wales, he seemed to have decided that once he came of age and had his own establishment, he would dress to please himself.

In ceremonial dress – garter robes, full-dress military uniforms and so forth – he always looked wistfully apologetic, as if he hoped that those who saw such images would forgive him for wearing the fancy dress of his role as heir to the throne. Privately he spent some of his considerable energy on finding suppliers and tailors who were sympathetic to his wish for modernity and originality in dress. In the words of an historian of the 1920s,

When he wore a white waistcoat with a dinner jacket, fashionable society copied him. When he wore a beret so did tens of thousands of other people. Wearing straw hats when they were out of fashion, he brought them into favour again, to the great delight of the people of Luton. He was horseman, golfer, energetic dancer of the Charleston, soldier, sailor, airman, statesman, and the hardest-working commercial traveller in the service of the Empire.'[39]

The sight of him in horizontally striped golfing socks lighting a lamp of remembrance in 1924, an occasion for which his father would almost certainly have worn a uniform, is typical of his relaxed style. He made the double-breasted suit acceptable daytime wear for gentlemen; he wore co-respondent and suede shoes (something his father deplored as the mark of a bounder), even mixing brown suede with a navy suit; he wore jerseys for casual and sporting activities, single-handedly reviving the Fair Isle industry; he adopted shorts and drill trousers for foreign holidays, and constantly searched for new and amusing items to add to his wardrobe. In St Tropez in 1935 he 'went by boat to dine... and acquired a blue and white striped sailor's pullover'.[40] Despite this apparently frivolous vanity, he was capable of great sensitivity, suggesting to his brothers that they briefly stand guard at his father's lying-in-state in 1936 – the three eldest in regimental uniforms, the Duke of Kent in naval uniform. It was a gesture which impressed Queen Mary, for he was her favourite child, but ultimately her greatest disappointment.

He looked and behaved like a cross between Prince Charming and an American film star and was, consequently, able to capture all hearts by seeming to break down social barriers. Unhappily, his very modernity combined with a wilful disregard for matters which did not interest him, made him incapable of fitting in to the nineteenth-century apparatus of monarchy which was his inheritance. He wanted to continue the social changes of the 1920s which had led to the view that:

Our Royal Family, with their simple, kindly ways and unfailing interest in the welfare of every section of the community, have broken down most of the barriers erected by etiquette between the classes, and the gain in friendly feeling has been enormous.[41]

By the mid-1930s, however, the old conservative attitudes were firmly back in position; in 1935 George V, who was resolutely old-fashioned, said that his eldest son, 'has not a single friend who is a gentleman. He does not see any decent society. And he is forty-one.' This view permeated the 'establishment', but King Edward VIII was temperamentally unsuited to a hypocritical strait-jacket of etiquette and protocol. The ceremonial functions of monarchy did not appeal to him;

95. **'The Enterprising Hawker';** *Punch,* **May 1929**
This cartoon exploited the London spectacle of the traffic jam of cars approaching Buckingham Palace for the season's four courts. The proud Mama is dressed in the traditional long evening gown; her daughter preferred the shorter style which had been acceptable since 1922.

he sat glumly through the garden parties which replaced evening courts in 1936, the first time in history when 'debutantes have curtsied to their Sovereign in mackintoshes.'[42]

He was even more bored and stolid than Edward VII in 1902, but he had a great deal more on his mind, primarily the stylish American divorcee, Mrs Simpson, whom he hoped to marry and make queen of England. They would have made an impossibly chic king and queen, a royal version of William Powell and Myrna Loy in *The Thin Man* films which were so popular in the 1930s. The analogy with Hollywood fantasies is apposite, and not just because Mrs Simpson was American; from the 1920s onwards, the public, seeing royalty so regularly on cinema newsreels began to associate the two dream factories of royalty and film stardom. Hollywood also provided a new source of inspiration for fashion, and new ideals of male and female good looks, with the emphasis on professional grooming and personal style. By 1936 Mrs Simpson had, with characteristic American determination, transformed herself from the 'jolly, plain, intelligent, quiet, unpretentious and unprepossessing little woman' who Chips Channon had met at lunch early in 1935, into 'all that is elegant.'[43] She was, in fact, grooming herself for the greatest role of all, with useful injections of princely patronage in the form of expensive new clothes from Paris couturiers, and exquisite gifts of jewellery from the King.

Her bone-thin figure, sleek dark hair and

96. Mrs Ernest Simpson (later Duchess of Windsor) 1931

Despite her later, much publicized, elegant appearance which was based upon a thorough approach to choosing clothes from major couturiers, in June 1931 Mrs Simpson wore borrowed finery for her presentation at court. The Prince of Wales remarked during the court that the lights at Buckingham Palace, 'make all the women look ghastly'.

perfect make-up were ideal for the pared-down elegance of 1930s women's fashions, which required the self-assurance and flawless grooming of the mature woman. *Vogue* began to praise her taste in 1935, describing her wardrobe when she accompanied the Prince on a cruise. She was considered one of the 'best-dressed women' in the south of France that summer, with smart clothes from Paris and London, including a fashionable Schiaparelli 'pouch' dress. She was photographed for *Vogue* wearing a white linen trouser suit designed by Schiaparelli, and soon after George V's death the magazine declared, 'Mrs Ernest Simpson is now the best dressed woman in town.'[44] By November 1936 Cecil Beaton believed that 'Her claim to looks is her dazzling brightness and freshness... (she is) immaculate and as soignée yet fresh as no girl could be.'[45] Such sleekly fashionable perfection of looks and dress was not wholly unknown to the royal family in the 1930s – the Duchess of Kent, formerly Princess Marina of Greece, was elegant and beautiful, but she and her husband were far enough removed from the throne for their cosmopolitan glamour to add spice to rather than detract from the bourgeois domesticity of family life which George V and Queen Mary, and the Duke and Duchess of York and their two daughters had represented for nearly ten years. Mrs Simpson's brittle, foreign glamour seemed just about acceptable for a royal mistress, but perversely both too modern and too Ruritanian for a queen of England. In a film of the period she would have died in the penultimate scene, felled by an incurable illness or fatally injured in a car or aeroplane crash; in reality she was defeated by 'all this graciousness and pageantry (which) were but the glittering tip of an iceberg that extended down into unseen depths I could never plumb, depths filled with an icy menace for such as me.'[46] She and the former King, as Duke and Duchess of Windsor, lived on as the most glamorous socialites in the western world, exquisitely

people around the world, not just in the British Isles, but this new accessibility trivialized as much as it popularized. There seemed, however, to be no obvious antidote to this intrusive form of recording – which in the case of the King and Mrs Simpson, made public property what the royal family considered its private business – except to withdraw back into the castle of tradition, established values and limited access. One certain and immediate way of demonstrating change was to place reliance upon conservative forms of dress, etiquette and ceremonial rituals. Edward VIII and Mrs Simpson had personified modernity, in attitudes and appearance, therefore their successors must stress historical continuity and acceptance of established precedents. It was not especially difficult because the royal household and courtiers, and the 'old nobility' had not adopted the new style. The general public might have felt that they disliked the change in monarch, a situation about which they knew little and were consulted less, but democracy in Great Britain has not, since the seventeenth century, concerned itself with the rights of the citizen in regard to the choice of monarch, or the duties he or she performs. Popular monarchy is a twentieth-century innovation foisted upon the population by a combination of courtiers, politicians and journalists who were unable or unwilling to accept the idea that the alternative to Ruritania need not necessarily be a republic. In December 1936, however, a republic was more than just a spectre, it was a distinct possibility, and the new King and Queen had to prove quickly and conclusively that they were not merely a second-string, second-rate alternative to the only male member of the house of Windsor (as Saxe Coburg Gotha was patriotically re-named in 1917) in the twentieth century to demonstrate the persuasive, charismatic glamour which, since Queen Victoria's reign, has been the preserve of royal women.

97. Edward, Prince of Wales 1932; E X Kapp
The Prince's rather melancholic good looks and innate stylishness are captured in an economic manner in this lithograph.

dressed (they invariably appeared in the lists of the ten best-dressed men and women of the world) but aimless rejects from the exclusive enclave of the British royal family.

It is significant that the life of the Duke and Duchess of Windsor is usually illustrated with photographs, newsreels, film and television. The image of royalty was transformed by these media, made accessible to millions of

It was fortunate that George VI and Queen

Elizabeth were so totally dissimilar to Edward VIII and Mrs Simpson. Comparisons could not be made; a wholly new, or rather different, style was evident. George VI was a taller, slimmer, more reserved version of George V – dutiful, moderately intelligent, an enthusiastic sports man (not just shooting, in the 1920s he played tennis at Wimbledon), and wholly unsympathetic to fashionable society. Like his father he wore clothes to suit his public role rather than enjoyed them for their own sake; it is very apparent that since Edward VIII was shipped into exile in 1936 no man in the British royal family has either wanted or dared to show the same interest in clothes. The new Queen was also not noted for her fashion sense. When *Vogue* wrote about her in coronation year, 1937, they declared,

She is not a 'fashionable' woman in the usual sense of the word. Yet her clothes superbly fulfil the two fundamental canons of good dressing. They fit her personality like a glove; and they are brilliantly suited to her way of life.

Damned with faint praise? Probably not; *Vogue* was undoubtedly hedging its bets like everyone else, waiting to see what the new Queen would do to erase the memory of Mrs Simpson's chic, and to eclipse the idiosyncratic splendour of Queen Mary. To a certain extent

98. **Edward, Prince of Wales, mid-1930s**
A glimpse of the 'successful ambassador' and 'special style setter' – the public image of the Prince in the 1920s and early 1930s. His lightweight double-breasted suits with wide trousers, co-respondent shoes and jaunty straw hat were widely copied.

Queen Elizabeth was initially overshadowed by her formidable mother-in-law and her elegant sister-in-law, the Duchess of Kent. The latter was possibly more of a challenge than the former; Queen Mary was elderly, a national institution who could be respected and depended upon for sound advice and willing support rather than contemporary competitive stylishness. In the same edition of *Vogue* that had described the Queen as 'not a "fashionable" woman', the Duchess of Kent was compared to Queen Alexandra:

> There is the same classic purity of line, the same air of aloof elegance: the same charming vague rather wry smile: the same coiffure is topped by an identical hat... Women scan the papers for the Duchess' confirmation of fashion's newest trends.

The Duchess's trousseau had been designed in 1934 by the French trained Anglo-Irishman Captain Molyneux, and it was so stylish that drawings of it appeared in *Vogue*.[47] Like Queen Alexandra she favoured blue, and one particular shade was called 'Marina blue' in her honour; she was equally idiosyncratic about her hats, wearing a saucer-shaped one for the jubilee procession in 1935 which completely masked her face, an error of royal style that Queen Elizabeth, when Duchess of York, would never have committed.

Photographs and portraits of Queen Elizabeth as a girl and young woman suggest an Edwardian softness and prettiness, totally at variance with the more assertive modern young women who emerged during the First World War and, in the 1920s, were caricatured as 'Bright Young Things'. She never cropped her hair, wore vibrant make-up or adopted the sharp, uncompromising lines of

99. George V and Queen Mary c.1935
The timeless formality of the King's dress coat and Queen Mary's idiosyncratic toque and silk coat are complemented rather than overwhelmed by the ornate theatre carvings and draperies which reduce their companions to ciphers.

1920s dress. If Mrs Simpson was Myrna Loy, the Duchess of York was Mary Pickford, the world's sweetheart – girlish, pretty, satisfyingly feminine, with just a hint of sauciness, but of the old-fashioned Edwardian variety. Very small women are often endowed with doll-like prettiness and an apparent fragility which, if they are combined with charm and relaxed intelligence, win men's hearts more enduringly than almost any other feminine style. As the young Lady Elizabeth Bowes-Lyon and the newly royal Duchess of York, the Queen had these characteristics, so, consequently, until her husband became King, the way in which she dressed was of minor significance.

Her clothes, from the time of her marriage to the Duke of York in 1923 until coronation year, 1937, excited little comment. Family, friends and journalists were so impressed by her not inconsiderable achievement in becoming a well-integrated member of the royal family, devoted and supportive wife to the Duke, and mother of two pretty daughters, that no-one thought it necessary or appropriate to analyse the component parts of her public persona. Her style of dress seemed to be of negligible interest, for it was characteristically English – slightly too fussy, slightly old-fashioned, but unexceptionable within the royal and aristocratic circles within which she moved. There was no model for a young royal duchess's appearance in the 1920s and early 1930s, and not until the Duke of Kent married his tall, elegant Greek princess in 1934, and the Duke of Gloucester married his Scottish bride, Lady Alice Montagu Douglas Scott in 1935, was there any competition. Photographs of the Duchess of York in this transitional period of her life record a smiling, pretty, doll-like woman rather too weighted down by her obvious love of feminine fripperies. She bought her clothes from Reville and Handley Seymour (suppliers to Queen Mary), but there was no indication that these dressmakers attempted or even wished to influence their royal client's taste. Patterns, lace, ruffles, layers and fur trimmings cascaded over the diminutive Duchess, whose small stature was rendered more noticeable by her perverse habit of wearing hats which fore-shortened her and very high-heeled shoes. Only in her simple country tweed suits was it possible to detect something approaching elegance, but the more usual effect was of ladylike but slightly eccentric prettiness. She looked, in fact, like an idealized version of the perfect upper class daughter-in-law: charming, feminine, but completely untouched by the more outré changes which were associated with the fashion industry.

Her physical resemblance to the young

Queen Victoria cannot have gone unnoticed in the royal family. She was a little taller and much prettier, but the lack of inches, incipient plumpness and delight in fluffily decorative clothes was uncannily close to her husband's great grandmother, a fact which was eventually turned to her advantage. To Mrs Simpson she had been 'The Dowdy Duchess' who

dressed 'picturesquely, unfashionably', but to admiring men like Chips Channon she was 'well-bred, kind, gentle ... always charming, always gay, pleasant and smiling ... mildly flirtatious in a very proper romantic old fashioned Valentine sort of way.'[48] Cecil Beaton was impressed by her 'lovely thrush-like eyes and deliciously royal, pink and white skin', and thought, when he saw her in the 1937 coronation procession that she was 'so much lovelier than in any of her photographs.'[49] It was an American, Anne Morrow Lindbergh, who decided that she was like 'an old-fashioned rose, the small full ones, not brilliant in colouring, but very fragrant ...'; while the thoroughly English Lady Diana Cooper thought her 'a spell-binding Queen ... in gloss of satin, a lily and rose in one.'[50] All of these comments, when stripped of their dislike or obsequious hyperbole, focus on the three qualities which were to inspire a memorable partnership between a pretty woman, a talented couturier and ambitious photographer which resulted in a transformation that Hollywood might have envied. The term old-fashioned suggested secure values and the continuance of an historical tradition. Analogies with much-loved flowers and birds indicated her timeless natural beauty which was a welcome antidote to the harsh and unbecoming realities of modernity.

Norman Hartnell's first royal commission was to design the wedding dress for the future Duchess of Gloucester in 1935, and to provide bridesmaids' dresses for her eight attendants, who included the two daughters of the Duchess of York. The commission was suc-

100. **The Silver Jubilee Thanksgiving Service, May 1935, after F O Salisbury**
Church ceremonies for royal weddings, jubilees and national thanksgiving services have provided one of the twentieth century's more public arenas for viewing the 'upper ten thousand'. The magnificence of church vestments, legal robes and military uniforms are softened by the pastel colours and furs of the royal ladies.

101. **George V 1935; F Whiting**

Few twentieth-century portraits of the royal family
are more than bland or saccharine depictions.
Whiting's portrait succeeds because it captured
the quintessential George V – the straightforward
man who loved country pursuits. Riding for pleasure, but to the highest standard, has become a
necessary skill for all senior royals.

cessful and, a few months later, Hartnell was
asked to supply some black dresses for the
Duchess of York after the death of George V.
The Duchess's principal dressmaker was still
Madame Handley Seymour, and Hartnell's
disappointment at not receiving the commission for Queen Elizabeth's coronation dress
in 1937 was softened by the request to dress
the new queen-consort's maids of honour. The
Handley Seymour coronation dress, although
cut on the bias, as was usual with 1930s dresses,
was in every other respect an uninspired and
derivative variant of what Queen Mary wore
in 1911, with the addition of the hanging net
and lace sleeves found on Queen Alexandra's
1902 coronation dress. It was workmanlike,
appropriate but wholly immemorable, and
when photographed it emphasized the

102. **Queen Mary**

The American writer, Janet Flanner, was not alone
in thinking that Queen Mary 'looked her best
with a diamond crown on her head, wearing
décolletage, loaded with royal jewels'. Her glittering lamé or beaded dresses recall the zenith of
European royalty before the 1914–18 war, not the
1920s, 30s and 40s when she evolved into a national
symbol of unswerving strength.

Queen's short, plump stature, giving her a prematurely matronly, middle-aged look, an image dispelled by Sir Gerald Kelly's state portrait of her, which tactfully elongated and narrowed her appearance. Hartnell's dresses for the maids of honour had involved discussions with the King and Queen and study of the Hayter painting of the coronation of Queen Victoria. The late 1930s saw a wave of nostalgia for the early Victorian period, with plays, films and books emphasizing the glamour, achievement and solid values of that period. Hartnell had designed for the stage and actresses, and viewed his clients as distinct personalities who should be enhanced by their dress; consequently he was prepared to take the King's hint that Winterhalter portraits in the royal collection might provide inspiration for the Queen's dresses. The first of these was a 'gleaming silver tissue over (a) hooped *carcasse* of stiffened silver gauze, with a deep *berthe* collar of silver lace encrusted with glittering diamonds', which was worn at a state banquet just before the coronation.[51]

It is generally believed that Hartnell reintroduced the crinoline into fashionable formal day and evening dress, but this was not the case. In the spring of 1937 Cecil Beaton was summoned to photograph the Duke and Duchess of Kent. He was delighted by the Duchess, who 'looked excessively beautiful in a huge brown tulle crinoline, ruched like a Queen Anne window blind, or a lampshade, with old-fashioned jewellery, a bow knot, large drop earrings. She looked like a Winterhalter painting and it was thus that she was photographed'. The results of the session sent Beaton into raptures and he was burbling with pleasure when he took them for his clients to see, 'I think they're incredibly romantic. There are some as nostalgic and summer scented as if Winterhalter had painted your great-aunt Queen Mary.'[52] The Victorian revival, the admiration of Winterhalter's portraits and a return of a modified version of the crinoline was obviously 'in the air' infecting the chic

103. **Edward VIII, 1936**
The formal trappings of kingship – ceremonial military and naval uniforms, rows of medals, stars of various orders and lavish bullion embroidery – made Edward VIII appear uncomfortable, a Peter Pan of royalty, unsuited to such stultifying straitjackets.

Duchess of Kent a little earlier than the King and Queen of England and Norman Hartnell. Although he dressed the Duchess later in her life, at this time Hartnell did not make her clothes, for she was loyal to Molyneux, who made the sleek sheath of creamy gold lamé embroidered with spangles, beads and rhinestones that she wore to the 1937 coronation.

104. The Duke and Duchess of Windsor, 3 June 1937

A wedding photograph of the Duke and Duchess is marred by the absurd screen and draperies against which Cecil Beaton posed them. They are an impossibly chic couple, stylish but tragic. The Duchess's pale blue wedding ensemble, designed by Molyneux, is now in the Costume Institute, the Metropolitan Museum of Art, New York.

105. Queen Elizabeth c.1938; Sir Gerald Kelly

The 'dowdy duchess' after her transformation into the 'Winterhalter queen'. Hartnell's pastiche early-Victorian dresses for the consort of George VI admirably suited her preference for pretty, decorative clothes.

Hartnell was so proud of his increasing circle of royal clients in the late 1930s that it is unlikely that he would have omitted to mention dressing the Duchess of Kent. It must be assumed that what the Duchess's couturiers created for her was seen and admired by the King and Queen and shrewdly perceived to be exactly the type of old-fashioned, romantic style which could transform Queen Elizabeth from a pretty but uninspired dresser into a memorable and enchanting stylist. This does not detract from Hartnell's achievement, it reinforces it, for the difference between the tall, slender, cosmopolitan Duchess of Kent and the tiny, plump, English rose queen-consort was so marked that an attempt to dress the latter in a style which had suited the former so well could have been easily doomed to failure. That it succeeded so brilliantly, so well that the Queen, in popular mythology, is thought to be the woman who single-handedly reintroduced the crinoline into fashionable dress, is due to Hartnell's undoubted skill and ingenuity.

The seal was put upon Hartnell's life-long connection with British royalty after the triumphant state visit to Paris in 1938. The challenge of providing a wardrobe of 'some thirty dresses, grand dresses to be worn from morning to midnight under the most critical eyes in the world' led him to undertake research into the locations for the various events of the visit, the colours worn by the French ceremonial guard and so forth, in order that the Queen might both compliment the French national colours, palaces and orders by including appropriate shades in her dresses, but at the same time be a dazzlingly glamorous focus of attention. Such sensitivity towards host nations and styles of dress and colour schemes and concern for function and climate had occasionally been taken into account by earlier royal dressmakers, but Hartnell set new standards of research, consultation and thoroughness which influenced later royal couturiers. His method was akin to designing for the theatre where the combination of overall effect, tonal values and singling out the principal players is the most important test of a designer's skill. Then, by one of those conjunctions of personal misfortune and creative ingenuity, the Paris wardrobe was transformed. The Queen's mother died, and the court went into mourning, but the state visit was postponed rather than cancelled. The thought of the wardrobe having to be in black or purple horrified Hartnell and, according to his own account he said, 'Is not white a Royal prerogative for mourning, Your Majesty?' The idea met with favour; perhaps some historian close to the royal household remembered that Queens of France had once worn white mourning, therefore rendering it particularly appropriate. It was July and the 'Snow Queen', who was patently not made of ice, captured Parisian hearts with her billowing clouds of white Valenciennes lace, satin, organdie, crêpe and tulle, with silver and gold decoration catching the light in a shimmering, fairy-tale manner. It must have evoked memories of the Empress Eugenie's white court dresses by Worth, although the republican French did not raise this spectre of lost empire, preferring to announce: 'Today

France is a Monarchy again. We have taken the Queen to our hearts. She rules over two nations.'[53] The critical French press went further, with compliments which must have delighted both client and couturier, describing Queen Elizabeth as, 'the best-dressed Queen to visit the world's fashion centre.'[54]

An individual style had been created which, for evening dress and to a lesser extent day clothes, was to be identified with Queen Elizabeth for the next 50 years. It did not impress those with rigidly trained standards of aesthetic symmetry and form. Kenneth Clark, the Surveyor of the King's Pictures, thought that the Queen had no dress sense, and Augustus John, who was summoned to paint her portrait and immortalize one of the Paris crinolines, gave up after a number of sessions, suggesting at the time that he could not succeed because she was not real. The commission, an enlightened one, was suggested by Clark, in whose biography it is hinted that the Queen's discreet flirtatiousness made the King jealous.[55] Curiously, the same story is associated with the John portrait: the artist – a known womanizer – supposedly got on too well with his sitter, and their sessions, punctuated by laughter and an obvious rapport, were ended by an enraged King. The portrait was eventually given to the Queen by John in 1961; it is a wooden piece, contrived and awkward, a poor twentieth-century pastiche of Winterhalter's luxuriously flattering style of portraiture. It was one more stage in the downward spiral of post-Victorian royal portraiture. Lavery had painted George V, Queen Mary and two of their children in 1913, but that group portrait was also without rigour or insight.

Twentieth-century 'society' portraiture has added little of note to the royal collections; the right combination of artist and sitter, with mutual rapport and a desire to extend the traditional format of portraiture has been missing, and royal patrons seem unlikely to rectify this situation. Rows of portraits are

106. The Royal Family 1937

The novelty of a young family at Buckingham Palace, with devoted parents, pretty children and, the modern breed of the corgi dog, captured the imagination of the public. The two princesses were dressed identically although four years separated them; their clothes were in the decorative, feminine tradition which their mother favoured.

commissioned and painted for municipal, regimental and diplomatic purposes, but this process has rarely been used as a sift to find an artist capable of adding works of merit and originality to the royal collection of formal portraits. Instead, the fascination with photography, with its relatively swift processes and selection of images from which a choice might be made, has become the preferred method of depicting royalty. Hartnell's near-contemporary, Cecil Beaton, dignified the couturier's achievements by photographing the Queen, in her Paris wardrobe, inside Buckingham Palace, in its gardens and against the painted back-drops of his own devising. These images were commissioned in the summer of 1939 and, initially, Beaton had similar problems to Augustus John, 'The face looked very dazzling... (but) I was anxious at the lack of definition in it...'.[56] One study, identical in pose to the John portrait, with the Queen wearing the same dress, has a similarly awk-ward banality, but others, because of pose, attitude, and carefully chosen setting, are both witty and glamorous–the transformation was effected.

Evening courts were re-instituted in the summer of 1937, and a new edition of *Dress and Insignia Worn at Court* reaffirmed the traditional forms of dress for men and women. The latter were told that they 'must wear Low Evening Dresses with Court Trains suspended from the shoulders', with all of the usual accessories, but lappets were, at last, omitted. The courts

107. George VI, Queen Elizabeth and the Roosevelts 1939

A supposedly informal visit to Hyde Park, the Roosevelt family home, during a state visit to Canada and America in 1939, provided an amusing anomaly in the etiquette of dress. Queen Elizabeth wore a simple day-dress, the Roosevelt ladies, unused to royalty, wore their best garden-party outfits.

were held until the end of the 1939 season, and the King and Queen also held levees and courts in Edinburgh. The numbers wanting to attend constantly increased, but the number of courts did not; in 1937 'ladies of Scottish domicile' were asked to 'apply to transfer to the Afternoon Drawing Rooms of Holyrood-house'. After the Second World War there was a series of informal courts to accommodate the back-log of presentations, followed by a permanent introduction of afternoon courts

108. Queen Elizabeth and Princess Elizabeth c.1944–45

The Queen, fluffily decorated with furs, flowers and pearls, inspects female troops whilst her elder daughter, minus decorative accessories and dressed in girlish pastels, serves her apprenticeship, in a style of dress more suited to a mature women than a teenage princess.

until their abolition in 1958. At the time, this change, which coincided with the extension in numbers and size of royal garden parties, was hailed as a sign of democracy in action; the deserving would be invited rather than the 'upper ten thousand', but what had actually happened was the removal from all but the most select few – invited to lunches, diplomatic receptions, state banquets and the rare ball – of the opportunity to visit the state rooms of royal residences.

Monarchy and fashionable society, which had come together in Edward VII's reign, and during the brief reign of Edward VIII, separated once more in 1937, and in the last 50 years the monarchy has concentrated on becoming a model for bourgeois, conservative stability. This is disguised to a certain extent by the ceremonial glitter of uniforms and orders, evening dresses and jewellery, but it

was becoming, even in the 1930s, the disguise of a remote and fossilized world in which, throughout the twentieth-century, the most powerful and influential figures have been women. Queen Elizabeth's contribution to this process was of great importance, and the triumvirate of the Queen, Hartnell and Cecil Beaton had a long lasting and profound effect on the royal image. The closely-knit and insulated group of the King, Queen and royal princesses was a source of pride to most English people. The Queen, dressed in 'dusty pink, dusty blue, and dusty lilac' but never green or black, replaced Queen Mary as a symbol of continuity and stability during the Second World War, while her husband and, later, her elder daughter were to be seen in uniform – symbols of total royal commitment to the armed forces.[57] Beaton, whose most successful photographs depended upon establishing a rapport with his subject, did not find George VI a sympathetic personality, and felt he lacked 'mystery or magic'.[58] This hardly mattered to the public who respected the King but were infinitely more interested in the three generations of royal ladies, Queen Mary, Queen Elizabeth and the two princesses. The princesses had been endlessly photographed, from babyhood onwards, by Marcus Adams, Frederick Thurston, Studio Lisa, Karsh of Ottawa, Dorothy Wilding and Beaton – many of these provided informal statements of the harmony of royal family life.

In the 1930s the two most famous children in the world were Princess Elizabeth and Shirley Temple, both blonde, blue-eyed and exquisitely if somewhat fussily dressed. Hollywood 'royalty' in the days of the studio star system and genuine royalty had a great deal more in common than international recognition and considerable influence upon fashions and behaviour. They were both insulated from reality by a 'court' whose role was to protect and safeguard the interests of their 'stars'; they were expected to perform and behave in a manner which was acceptable to

109. Princess Elizabeth
As heir to the throne, but debarred by tradition from being styled Princess of Wales – in her own right – the Princess wore uniform. It suited her admirably, its neat, structured lines emphasizing her narrow waist and minimizing her low-slung Hanoverian bosom.

their public, and they were treated with uncritical obsequiousness for as long as they were perceived to be capable of retaining their great popularity. The wish to be innovative or independent was only granted if this did not upset the status quo, or could be disguised as a response to public demand. The two young 'stars' of the house of Windsor developed from pretty, identically dressed children, whose tweed coats and print dresses and tulle party frocks influenced a generation of children's clothes, into very different young women. Their similar, but not identical frocks and suits in the mid-late 1940s, could not

disguise that Princess Elizabeth was a sturdy, sensible and handsome young woman, or that her sister Princess Margaret was a smoulderingly sensual beauty. When Beaton photographed the latter in 1949, the press compared her to Queen Alexandra; they did not comment on her uncanny resemblance to the young Elizabeth Taylor. It was Princess Margaret who accompanied her mother and the Duchess of Kent to a secret private showing

110. The Duke and Duchess of Windsor c.1955

Regular inclusion of the Windsors in news features and gossip columns suggested a twentieth-century version of the 'king over the water'. Both Duke and Duchess retained their public image as elegant, sophisticated international personalities at variance with the cosy, gentrified image of the British royal family.

111. Queen Elizabeth II and Sir Winston Churchill 1955

The young Queen Elizabeth dressed in the postwar version of Hartnell's Winterhalter style for evening wear – net, tulle and spangled decoration. There is little difference between her choice and the dress worn by the elderly Lady Churchill, only the jewellery is more magnificent. Sir Winston wore knee breeches, which allowed the garter to be correctly a placed around the left knee.

of Dior's 'New Look' collection at the French Embassy in the autumn of 1947, and was delighted to have a Dior ball-gown for her 21st-birthday in 1951. She experimented with her appearance, using make-up and choosing clothes which flattered her petite frame and exquisitely pretty face; she gravitated naturally towards the witty, lively and entertaining world of fashionable society in the late 1940s and 1950s.

112. **Queen Elizabeth II and the Duke of Edinburgh 1966**

One of the few anomalies of late twentieth-century royal dress is that formal wear for the state opening of Parliament is worn during the day time. Flanked by the speaker of the Trinidad Parliament and the President of the Senate in styles of legal dress introduced by the British, the Queen, in slim-fitting, beaded evening dress and the Duke in tropical full-dress uniform, prepare to fulfil the constitutional roles of monarch and consort. The narrower styles of the 1960s made the Queen appear more youthful than the matronly crinolines of the 1950s.

Princess Elizabeth married Prince Philip of Greece in 1947, and was soon concerned with the duties of a naval wife, a mother, and unexpectedly early, in 1952, with the cares of monarchy. She had been the favourite grandchild of Queen Mary – Londoners seeing the two together in the 1930s would call out, 'She's the spit of her granny!' – and had inherited her grandmother's intelligence, sense of duty and her Hanoverian, straight-backed, low-bosomed figure. In uniform she always looked splendid – she was the only female member of her family that it suited admirably; in the simplest of evening dresses, with tiara, ear-rings, necklace and the ribbon of an order she could appear most impressive. In country and riding clothes she looked happy and relaxed, but formal day wear defeated her. Lacking her sister's natural interest in fashion, it was not until the mid-1960s that she found the classic simplicity of line which suited her; however, since that time there have been regular indications that her dress sense is erratic. Her mother's idiosyncratic but wholly successful femininity which found expression in fussy hats, decorative trimmings, floating panels and the soft pastel shades which Queen Alexandra had favoured as half-mourning but which Queen Mary and Queen Elizabeth had turned into a uniform for royal ladies, did not suit her, although she persevered with this style for several years. The Queen's clothes had to be comfortable, visible and functional – hems weighted against gusting winds, rich materials (fine silk or wool) appropriate for travel and climate, and colours complimentary to host nations were the prerequisites. Function and personal style never seem to have married, and the evolution of a coherent royal image defeated even the most accomplished of the Queen's couturiers.

When she became Queen in 1952 the press excitedly hailed a new Elizabethan age, but in fact what they were getting was closer to the style and approach of Queen Victoria and Prince Albert. The Queen, it may be supposed, considers her clothes necessary but troublesome, as did her great-great grand-mother, but brought up in the tradition of Queen Mary and her mother, understands the importance of combining royal splendour with buying British. Hartnell designed her wedding dress in 1947 with its delicately embroidered court train, but although Hardy Amies began to design for her in 1950, the coronation of 1953 was a Hartnell extrava-ganza. The coronation dress, with its embroidery of British and Dominion emblems, was an impressive achievement, a formal interpretation of the ever-popular Winter-halter crinoline style. Hartnell also designed dresses for the Queen Mother, Princess Margaret, the Duchess of Kent, Princess Alexandra, the six maids of honour and the two Ladies of the Bedchamber, and managed an elegantly theatrical harmony for both television and photographic cameras. His one solecism was his mundane re-design of the peeresses' robes, making them into short-sleeved, shawl-collared dressing gowns worn with absurd little fur-edged skull caps. It is a pity that he had not gone with Cecil Beaton to the state opening of Parliament in November 1952, when Beaton had been impressed by the visual spectacle of the peers and their ladies who 'were seen in such extraordinary perspective in their traditional fancy dress that has been developed and tried and improved through the centuries until it is found to be perfect.'[60]

Royal 'fancy dress' was also at its best when it was most traditional in arrangement and inspiration. Princes and royal dukes in army and navy uniform (rarely airforce – princes fly 'planes but they do not join the airforce – it is too modern and perhaps too democratic); queens, princesses and royal duchesses in evening dress – often embroidered, beaded and sequined, with a formidable array of jewellery – present an image of Ruritanian glamour which has little to do with fashion, but a great deal to do with dignity, privilege

and exclusivity. Alongside this, whether it was consciously thought out, or not, the tweedy, aristocratic image of the royal family which attracted so much criticism in the mid to late 1950s, has changed little with the passage of time, but an upwardly mobile population in search of traditional values have emulated the conservative style of the royal family. The comfortable, traditional suits and sensible shirts, shoes and ties of the men are closer to the hearts of the silent majority of successful Englishmen than raffish and ephemeral stylishness. The Queen Mother became an archetype which every middle-class grandmother in the land aspired to; countless wedding photographs of the 1960s and 1970s illustrate humbler versions of her pastel Hartnell outfits and pretty hats, and the same family photographs show the mother of the bride dressed in a cheaper copy of those classic, well cut, flattering, astringently coloured plain coats and matching hats which the Queen wore in the late 1960s and 1970s. The disconcerting amalgam of Ruritanian glamour (by night) and attractive, but not unnervingly elegant day-time clothing answered a need in many of the English who, perversely, require royalty to be grand, but also 'one of us'.

The royal family was a little slow at perceiving this need – for example at Princess Margaret's wedding in 1960, royal ladies wore full-length dresses, a last instance of a day-time 'court style'. Yet with the absorption of three 'commoners' into the royal family in quick succession – Antony Armstrong-Jones in 1960, Katharine Worsley in 1961 when she married the Duke of Kent, and the Hon. Angus Ogilvy, who married Princess Alexan-

113. **Queen Elizabeth II 1970**
Trooping the Colour on the Queen's official birthday in June, is one of the annual events of the summer season. The uniform of scarlet tunic and navy riding skirt is a modern variant of the style worn by Queen Victoria, and suited the Queen admirably. It was no longer worn after June 1986.

dra in 1963 – there seemed to be the possibility of a refreshingly new approach to royalty and its role in modern society. All of the younger royal ladies attracted attention with their looks, wardrobes and lifestyles. Their husbands were ciphers, necessary adjuncts to perfect family life, and this enlarging group and their children began to emulate the numbers of royals found in photographs of Queen Victoria's extended family. Also, without any apparent thought about what was appropriate, all new members of the family took on 'royal duties', and a sense of undue familiarity accelerated as every new building, conference, exhibition, anniversary and similar event was honoured by the presence of a member of the royal family. Magic was replaced by discussion amongst those organizations looking for a royal visitor about whether the individuals concerned were good value – newsworthy, photogenic, interested, charming, well-dressed and so forth – a type of professionalism was consequently being expected from people not trained to provide it. In an era when merit rather than birth was supposed to open doors and confer rewards, an ornamental royal family seemed to pay lip service to the new style, but continued to safeguard its privileged status.

All long-established institutions can, however, appear to change by shifting the focus of attention to new personalities. In the 1970s the two newcomers to the royal round were the Prince of Wales and Princess Anne. Neither of them, on the surface, seemed at all typical of 1970s youth. The prince had grown up in the shadow of his strong-minded and physically tough father, and being a dutiful son and serious-minded young man, settled into a routine of excessively competitive vigour and round of duties which had changed little in content and consequence since the 1920s and 1930s. He had appeared in the best-dressed men list in *The Tailor and Cutter* at the tender age of four, but as an adult both his physique and temperament conspired against him

114. Queen Elizabeth II and Prince Philip at Ascot

One of the major out-door ceremonies each year is Royal Ascot. Racing was fashionable during the Stuart period, but became a ritualized element of the summer season in the nineteenth century. The Queen and Prince Philip wear the smart day clothes which epitomized the height of elegance for middle-class parents at 1970s weddings. Female fashions are as important an element at Ascot as the racing and attract much press attention.

emulating his great-uncle, the Duke of Windsor. In that conservative way, which the nation finds so endearing, no attempt was made when he was a child to have his excessively large ears pinned-back (an operation which American plastic surgeons had perfected years before he needed such attention) and he grew up as the butt of endless cartoons and jokes. He dressed much like his father, wearing predictably safe suits, conven-

tional dinner jackets and uniforms including the uniforms of his preferred sporting pursuits – polo and hunting. Like his grandfather, George VI, he has no mystery or magic, but the mere fact of who he was transformed him, in the 1970s, into the most eligible bachelor in the world. None of his many girlfriends was able to influence his style of dressing, and

115. The Garter Procession at Windsor Castle

The Order of the Garter is one of the oldest and most exclusive orders of chivalry in Europe. The procession, held at Windsor each June attracts many spectators, admitted by ticket only. It is one of the quasi-theatrical pageants which, alongside other royal rituals, is such an asset to the British tourist trade.

in a period of great experimentation and informality in men's clothes he continued to look unashamedly old-fashioned, a testament to the traditional attitudes of English tailoring.

The Prince's only sister, Anne, was a pretty, blond child who grew into a sullen, plump, appallingly dressed teenager. Then, quite suddenly, she underwent a swift metamorphosis into a slim, smartly dressed 18-year-

old. She wore the short skirts which were fashionable in the mid-late 1960s, grew her hair long like other girls of her age, made witty speeches and rode to the highest standard in her chosen sport – the three-day equestrian event. Her brusque competitiveness was at variance with the public's old-fashioned idea of fairy-tale princesses and, although she was grudgingly admired for her unstuffy mod-

ernity – buying underclothes from Marks & Spencer, and much of her wardrobe from Maureen Baker, the chief designer for the ready-to-wear firm of Susan Small – her refusal to be a decorative cypher was not understood until she was in her early thirties. In 1973 when she became engaged to the handsome commoner Mark Phillips, the formal photographs were taken by Norman Par-

kinson. She wore borrowed finery from Zandra Rhodes and Gina Fratini and her make-up was applied by a French beautician. Parkinson's soft focus lens and careful re-touching of the photographs, transformed her, fleetingly, into a beauty. However, her wedding dress by the admirable but non-couture Maureen Baker, and her continued pursuit of success as a rider, indicated that being an ornament to fashionable society and an advertisement for the best of British design, were not to her taste. Her straight-forward, business-like approach to her wardrobe was like that of many young women in the 1970s; clothes had to be attractive, comfortable and practical. The Princess's public image is complemented by, rather than created by, her clothes. Like many of the women in her family she overshadows the men in her immediate circle – her father, her husband, her brothers and her cousins – but by giving the role of a princess modern relevance she is out-of-step with the public's view that female royalty should glamorize the trivial.

By the late 1970s the royal family had, by making itself more accessible through television programmes, interviews, newsreel items, photographs and a seemingly endless number of public appearances, become the best-known family in the world. The Queen's silver jubilee in 1977 was, in many respects, a high point of popularity for this approach. Glamour and discretion, exclusivity and privilege were not totally out-weighed by popular

116. **The Royal Family 1972–74; M Noakes**
Group portraiture of the royal family is a rarity in the late twentieth century. This work, commissioned by the City Corporation, provides major roles for the Queen and the Lord Mayor but reduces the latter's wife and other members of the royal family to 'bit-parts'. The anachronistic dress coats of the men are discreetly elegant, but the fussy details of the female dress have unbalanced the composition.

curiosity about the minutiae of royal life. There had always been books about royalty, but they were often obsequious, perpetuating the notion of a benign but aloof caste. Andrew Duncan's *The Reality of Monarchy*, published in 1970, began the process of analysing the mechanics of royal life and assessing its successes and failures. This approach found favour with the public and more books followed; gossip columns no longer omitted items about royalty, and journalists began to specialize in pursuing certain royals, probing for information about the inevitable Achilles heel. Studies of every trivial and not so trivial facet of royal life were produced. The ever-increasing number of performing royals who are part of the subsidized structure of royal life do nothing to alleviate the devaluation of the magic. The combination of the traditional round of ceremonies and events, in which contemporary royalty, like their Edwardian counterparts, are demonstrably at the apex of the 'upper ten thousand', and the 'pressing the flesh' round of duties which, in the past, were the preserve of local and national politicians and the aristocracy, have become an ornamental treadmill unquestioned by the royal participants and their advisers. The emphasis on the decorative and ceremonial aspects of royal life has produced a tableau in which that most ephemeral and frivolous of the arts – the art of dress – has assumed an importance out of all proportion to its true worth. Royals are increasingly judged by their appearance rather than their achievements, because the substance of achievement has been overtaken by the illusion of visual perfectability.

SIX

The Cinderella Princess

A very nice ordinary girl, with an unusual strength of character, had become a Cinderella princess

By 1978, the year after the Queen's silver jubilee, the style of the post-war monarchy was firmly established. It had eschewed the centuries-old traditional format of present-ation courts and levees and the implicit exclu-sivity, hedged around with regulations for dress and etiquette, in favour of a travelling band of royalty who went out to meet their subjects. It was a twentieth-century variant of the mediaeval and early modern royal progress, which usefully disguised the fact that the ever-larger group of royal players were all, for much of the time, based in London. The idea that royalty, like diplomats, might undertake a three- or five-year 'posting' to various major centres in the British Isles – Edinburgh, York, Manchester, Norwich, Cardiff, Truro – and become thoroughly acquainted with the people, work and prob-lems of a particular area, has never been examined or tested. Modern monarchy is insular and conservative, and consequently

117. Princess Michael of Kent 1980

The Princess wore her wedding dress – of cream silk crêpe de Chine with Chantilly lace decoration, designed by Bellville Sassoon – nearly two years later at an evening engagement. Although her marriage was a civil ceremony in Vienna, and this dress was worn in the evening rather than for the marriage formalities, it is unprecedented for a royal lady to wear her wedding dress after the event.

118. **Charles, Prince of Wales 1980; B Organ**
As a child and an adult, the Prince of Wales was the subject of thousands of formal and informal photographs. His image was of an active, out-door prince; in this portrait he is depicted in the 'uniform' of one of his favourite sports, polo. The feather emblem on his jersey and the union flag are evident clues to his present and future status.

remarkably unprescient about its future role in society. It has deplored the trivialization of its affairs but has shown little willingness to counter criticism by offering innovation or change.

Late twentieth-century popular journalism – the bane of British royalty – likes stories about people not ideas, and is in constant pursuit of new, intriguing personalities whose looks, expenditure and foibles can be praised or reviled. Sophisticated and well advised public figures (amongst whom royalty are rarely to be found) recognize this, and are adept at not providing evidence for such revelations. One of the penalties of great wealth and privilege in the late twentieth-century is that those who have or acquire it must never appear to abuse it. It requires unusual strength of character, intelligence and prescience to develop, from scratch, a public image which combines display of the symbols of wealth and privilege with an unchallenge-able capacity for hard work and tangible achievement.

Cecil Beaton, whose words head this chapter, thought he had observed such a paragon when he photographed Katharine Worsley, who married the Duke of Kent in 1961. He was, of course, marvelling at the transformation which could overtake a com-moner when he or she married into that bastion of wealth, privilege and exclusivity, the British royal family. There was, and is, no training for entrants into this particular form of public life, in which there exists a fairly amateur approach to educating and grooming young royals for the hurly-burly of public favour and disfavour. It was an easier tran-sition in the early 1960s than in the late 1970s and 1980s, but the notion of the prince being able to transform any pretty girl from Cinder-ella into a peerless princess is apposite. Royalty can create modern fairy stories, and the trans-formation scenes connected with female royals in the twentieth century have become part of national mythology. It is one of the few areas of magic that survive, but it is wholly dependent upon personal appearance. Before the invention of photography and the increased pressure upon royalty to be seen beyond the immediate court circles in which they moved, the transformation could be relatively superficial – a wardrobe of fashion-able English clothes, a goodly array of dia-monds and the ministrations of an accompl-ished portrait painter could glamorize even such unpromising material as Princess Caro-line of Brunswick. By the late twentieth cen-tury the process was public and wholly dependent upon the subject for transformation being highly photogenic, having excellent dress sense and being impervious to being discussed like a professional model, actress or film star. The young Duchess of Kent, in the 1960s, managed to avoid most of this, and advised by her undoubtedly elegant mother-in-law Princess Marina of Kent, gradually developed into a discreet, erratically stylish member of British royalty.

The first true Cinderella, of the modern variety, was the young woman who married Prince Michael of Kent in 1978. Beaton lived just long enough to photograph the new Princess Michael in November 1979. He wrote, in a letter to a friend, of 'the girl now safely delivered of a child, who made two marriages... She is quite regal in her manner. Very surprising as a commoner.'[1] Princess Michael was an unexpected addition to the royal family, however distant her husband was from the throne, because not only was she divorced from her first husband but she was also a Roman Catholic. She was tall, blonde, stylish, intelligent and determined, with a rather mysterious past, which entitled her to call herself Baroness Marie Christine von Reibnitz (her parents were Austrian and Bohemian), but all of this, combined with great good looks and considerable directness of manner, fascinated the British public. She had wanted to be a princess, worked assidu-ously to charm and persuade others of her undoubted ability to cope with such a role, and was rewarded by royal acceptance, and a rather subdued wedding. A 'cream silk suit that we made, in a great hurry,' was supplied by Hardy Amies, 'for the civil wedding cer-emony in Vienna in 1978 and [worn] again at the validation service in London in 1983.'[2]

Newly married, the Princess had no intention of settling quietly and slowly into her royal life. Although Prince Michael received no civil list allowance and was not, consequently, on the list of performing royals, she accepted invitations and behaved with considerably more aplomb and charm than many other royals. She was a great success, primarily because she was new, looked so glamorous, was witty and completely without shyness. In the period since she joined the royal family, few of them have dressed so consistently well; she is unmistakably a personage, and understanding her innate disadvantages – her height, rather broad hips and sturdy legs–she has chosen designers and hairdressers with great skill. She defined her needs in 1986, saying, 'I am very keen on femininity, even though I am six foot tall and have large bones.' This self-knowledge and care for detail combined with her lack of inhibition and ability to amuse, suggest a latter-day Duchess of Windsor. Eminently photogenic, the Princess can exclaim, 'I hate royal portraits – so stiff, so boring', or 'I'm extremely lucky in having three tiaras. One I rarely wear because the whole effect is not unlike the Incredible Hulk.' She is not embarrassed by her patronage of foreign designers: 'I have nothing against British clothes, but I am a foreign person and I have a foreign shape... And I don't believe in buying British if British isn't good enough.' Her frank speaking was not always diplomatic, 'English designers are dressmakers charging couture prices. Really, I don't give a toot for fashion. I just want to look nice.'[3] She is loyal to certain British designers, and one of these, Hardy Amies, summed up her approach to dress in his autobiography – 'The Princess has a professional eye for clothes which she chooses with great care.'[4] In August 1987 when *Woman* magazine was drumming up entries for its analysis of best-dressed royals, it described the Princess as 'a shining light in the fashion line-up.' For many she has been relegated to the category of intriguing interlude before the advent of the Princess of Wales, but in terms of fashion sense and natural elegance, and a refreshing directness about the importance of clothes to a female member of the royal family, she is without peer.

Princess Michael was certainly not ordinary, nor was she a girl when she married into the royal family, but her singularity of purpose, her glamour, and her obvious enjoyment of her role and 'duties' would, in any modern, well-run 'family firm' (as the House of Windsor cosily portrays itself) have been recognized and harnessed without regard to precedence, protocol and tradition. It was not, and pressure mounted upon the Prince of Wales to marry and provide the nation with a less strong-minded but equally glamorous princess. The phenomenon of the Princess of Wales is without precedent; there are similarities with Princess Alexandra of Denmark, but these cannot be pursued too far. The conventions surrounding royalty and the privacy accorded to them were different in the nineteenth century, and it should not be forgotten that Princess Alexandra was born royal and understood the restraints and privileges which accompany an arranged marriage to a prince who would become king. Lady Diana Spencer, who married the Prince of Wales in July 1981, was just 20 years old, a pleasant, rather shy and poorly educated member of the English aristocracy. She looked like a grander version of the girl-next-door: nice, straightforward, and young enough to be moulded into a 1980s version of the Queen Mother; she was even lodged with the latter during her engagement, presumably to 'learn the ropes'. Everyone had overlooked the 'unusual strength of character' which allows Beaton's quotation about the Duchess of Kent to fit the Princess of Wales so well. Signs of this character appeared early in the engagement when she wore a hopelessly over-sophisticated, strapless black taffeta evening dress which did nothing to disguise her plumpness and 'generous, somewhat low-slung and thoroughly Windsor' bosom. The archetypal 'Sloane' – the species defined by Ann Barr and Peter York – she quickly abandoned the Sloane uniform of 'ruffled shirts with ribbons

119. **The Princess of Wales 1981; B Organ**

The young woman, transformed from Lady Diana Spencer into a Cinderella princess, is portrayed in a transitional state. The grandeur of the formal setting of Buckingham Palace is in sharp contrast to the informality of her 'Sloane' style of dress, and suggests the royal dilemma of whether it is more essential to dress for the role or to maintain individuality however inappropriate.

at the neck; baggy jumpers with straight skirts or jeans; a touch of ethnic... [and] flat shoes', and forgot the abberrant Harrods suit, the hem of which she is supposed to have re-stitched, and which was worn for the formal announcement of her engagement, and scurried off to *Vogue* to be instructed in the ways of British couture.[5]

Fairy tales and fairy-tale princesses require transformation scenes, and the transformation of Lady Diana Spencer into the Princess of Wales was the most dramatic royal transformation since the 'Dowdy Duchess' became the 'Winterhalter Queen'. However, when the magic wand is waved by a famous fashion

magazine rather than a couturier versed in the ways of royalty and their style of life, the results can be alarming. Fashion magazines are used to tall, bone-thin, highly made-up models to whom dressing up and being photographed is a job. The job of being a princess is somewhat different, although possibly less well defined, but as there are no training schools for princesses, the ideal of a model-princess, a walking advertisement for British fashion design, might have seemed worth encouraging. The plump, shy girl, who was tall, but bent her head and wore flat shoes to disguise the fact that her prince was rather short, became a bone-thin clotheshorse, and a whole new industry was woven around 'Diana watching'.

Being a model is all about personal appearance; it is also a stepping stone into show business – acting in films and on television; consequently, because there did not seem to be a great deal to say about the Princess, except regarding her clothes, her jewels and her celebrity, the media decided that she was a 'royal star'. What she wore was perceived to be more interesting than what she did and books were written about her clothes – *Diana, The Fashion Princess, Diana, A Queen of Fashion, The Princess of Wales Fashion Handbook* – and the media coverage was endless. Royal press officials have become accustomed to supplying details of what clothes will be worn by female members of the royal family on particular tours and engagements and in the Princess's case the telephone can rarely have stopped ringing. The names of her designers – Belville Sassoon, Donald Campbell, Bruce Oldfield, Roland Klein, Catharine Walker, Jasper Conran, Jan Van Velden, Hatchi, Gina Fratini, Murray Arbeid, Victor Edelstein – have become household names, but few women could afford to patronize them; they dress the late twentieth-century 'upper ten thousand'. She also had a very different taste to other members of the family with regard to accessories: memorable tights, shoes, handbags were selected to suit certain clothes, not for comfort or general use. She conformed to tradition only by wearing hats, and by doing so single-handedly gave a useful boost to the declining hat industry in Britain.

The Princess's experimentation with designers, hairstyles, types of hat, and accessories has been observed by an attentive media and public, but she has evolved no distinctive style or select band of preferred designers. The diversity of her clothes seems to fulfil the role of armour or camouflage, distracting attention from the young woman who wears them, much in the way a talented model will enhance the clothes she is hired to project, but without ever being prepared to make a statement of individual personality. In evening dress, wearing an ever-growing collection of jewellery from the royal collection, or presents from tours, she can look quite dazzling, but evening dress conforms to certain rules which are relatively unaffected by changes in fashion, and the undisciplined range of her day-time clothes indicates a desire for novelty at the cost of a style which suits her or is appropriate for her role. Her modernity in some areas has been refreshing – going bare-legged in very hot weather, using small, neat clutch or shoulder bags, appearing throughout her pregnancies without embarrassment in softly flattering coats and dresses (as Princess Anne had also done, a few years earlier) – but the continued wearing of hats is a puzzle, as is her apparent disregard for certain useful conventions – weighted hemlines, lightly padded bras, and gloves – all of which exist to minimize royal discomfort in the face of constant observation.

In February 1984 *Woman's Own* magazine, at the opposite end of the readership spectrum to *Vogue*, told its readers, 'Diana is the lady most of us want to copy,' but what were they suggesting should be copied? An English disregard for elegance and a pursuit of novelty? The press, having vaingloriously claimed to have created the Princess's world-wide appeal, gradually became disenchanted with her. Perhaps they hoped that the pretty girl would develop into a woman who was more than just a living personification of the British fashion industry in all of its good, bad and indifferent moods. In *Family Circle*'s January 1983 edition there was an article entitled, 'How the royals have ridden the recession,' explaining how the Princess of Wales, the Queen and Princess Margaret had items from their wardrobe thriftily re-modelled to extend their public life. Praise of this 'waste not want not' attitude had disappeared by November 1984. *Woman*, pur-porting to debunk the 'myths' about the Princess repeated them – 'Diana is a "shopa-holic". She indulges in spending sprees of up to £1500 a week on clothes.' Interviewed on television about the same topic in 1985, the Princess said,

*At first there were a lot of people to help me (with clothes). It's now really my own choice, I'm afraid you're going to see everything time and time again because it fits, it's comfortable and it still works. Obviously if I'm helping the fashion industry, and helping the British side of things – well, that's marvellous. But I never tried to do that, and I think there's too much emphasis on my clothes.'[6]

120. The Prince and Princess of Wales 1984
The hair-style which launched numerous headlines and a third leader in *The Times* was adopted by the Princess for the State opening of Parliament. Her Gina Fratini dress and the Prince's full dress naval uniform were unexceptional. A softer upswept style would probably have caused less furore, but adverse press comment led to the hasty disappearance of this experiment.

121. The Princess of Wales 1984
Witty tights and clutch handbags are amongst many innovations introduced by the Princess into royal dress. Her fitted coat and simple felt hat look appropriately business-like for a visit to the Police Training Centre at Hendon.

It might have been wiser if she had said: 'I'm fascinated by clothes, I don't spend excessively, but I see one of my major roles as being an ambassador for the British fashion industry for as long as I'm the right age and size to do so.' It would have sounded sensible rather than disingenuous, and the public and the media might have been more understanding than the *News of the World* colour supplement was in June 1987 when it carried a feature called 'Di-saster dresses', drawing attention to expensive outfits in which the Princess had only, as far as they could discover, appeared once. They computed the costs involved and went on to compare her lavishness with the Queen's economy in the reuse of favourite clothes. Memories are short; when the Queen was the Princess's age there were occasions when she wore dresses only once, but newspapers are rather poor at balanced reporting when they want to be uncharitable.

Although royalty is a gilded cage, carrying extraordinary privileges, the potential for criticism has gathered terrifying momentum since the early 1970s. The most absurd issues are inflated into major concerns. In November 1984, for the state opening of Parliament the Princess wore a new, upswept, formal hairstyle with her diamond tiara and creamy silk organdie Gina Fratini dress. It caused a sensation, more press coverage was wasted on this ephemeral matter than on the content of the Queen's speech. The Princess's hairdresser was interviewed, and female reporters tried the new style and canvassed for public opinion; political journalists mentioned it in their columns, and *The Times* carried a third leader on the subject three days later. The press thought that it was 'too old' a style for a young woman; the fashion editor of *The Daily Mail* stated, 'The new look reminded me of her older, elegant relations, Princess Alexandra and Princess Michael of Kent', but as *The Times* noted, 'The general complaint seems to be that the new style makes her look less like the girl-next-door and more like a princess.

122. **The British and Spanish royal families 1986**

Processing through the Waterloo Chamber at Windsor Castle to the State banquet for the King and Queen of Spain, the formal uniform of the men contrast pleasingly with the romantic, bejewelled traditional evening glamour of three generations of British royal ladies. Prince Philip and the Prince of Wales are dressed in the modern version of Windsor uniform – a cutaway evening coat and knee breeches.

But the princess is in fact a princess'. This storm over a hairstyle followed hard on the heels of Canadian criticism of the Queen's appearance during a state visit; the *Toronto Sun* took exception to her make-up, her 'unflattering round necks, long coats and awful hats' and her 'safe and round' hairstyle, claiming that she looked like a grandmother – an undoubted fact. The Queen was sensibly impervious to such remarks; the princess was more sensitive. The new, formal elegance was abandoned and the familiar girlish capriciousness of hairstyle and dress returned, and the popular press continued to praise and criticize her as the mood took them. Such praise is not always very intelligent; suggesting that, 'She's as famous as any film star – ever' as *Woman's Own* did in May 1987, is not likely to assist the public in understanding the role and purpose of modern royalty.

At much the same time as a thoughtful public was beginning to appreciate the hard work, intelligence and commitment of Princess Anne, a royal with whom well-educated career women could sympathize, much in the way that poorly educated girls with no greater ambition than to marry a 'decent' man, have a 'nice' home and children and 'pretty' clothes copied the Princess of Wales, a new royal was taken into the Windsor family fold. If the Prince of Wales is the thoughtful, sensitive traditionalist, marginally modernized by his wife's suggestions about a new hair-cut, stylish shirts and more casual shoes, Prince Andrew is the breezy, good-looking joker who, in the early 1980s, had a taste for unsuitable ladies. Consequently, his choice of a bride – a commoner who worked for a living, with a jolly, gregarious personality but no pretensions to beauty, but from within that circle of aristocrats, country gentry and sports people with which modern royalty surrounds itself, was a surprise to everyone. She was a 'Sloane', like the Princess of Wales had once been, but with a strong, thoroughly developed personality and a wide range of interests, and she was

123 **The Duchess of York 1988**
The Duchess is obviously very proud of her cascade of Titian red hair and wears it loose on formal and informal occasions, but it conjures up, quite irresistibly, the image of a Hollywood starlet rather than a disciplined and hard-working princess.

patently unfashionable. Long titian-coloured hair, freckles and an ample figure endeared her to a nation jaded by the apparent vanity of the Princess of Wales. Another girl-next-door? In royal circles, yes, but in reality, no. She knew about the pressures, the duties, the brick-bats and the praise which accrued to royal women in the 1980s through her long friendship with the Princess of Wales, but the contrast between them in looks, temperament and interests was refreshing. She seemed to have little interest in fashion, and the clothes that she wore for her formal and informal engagement photographs, and for her various public appearances before her wedding in July 1986 were a mixture of dowdy and absurd. She seemed to have little sense of what flattered her, and then, on her wedding day, she surprised everyone by looking traditionally and discreetly royal. The Princess of Wales's wedding dress had been a showy, neo-Victorian design by the Emmanuels, too fussy and flouncy to be classical. Sarah Ferguson also selected a relatively unknown designer – Lindka Cierach – but the simplicity of cut, elegant embroidery and absence of fussiness recalled, with this design, the statuesque good taste and discretion of Princess May of Teck's 1893 dress. It was an auspicious start to a public career.

Then the temptation to experiment overtook the new Duchess of York, and as Frankie McGowan wrote in *The Sunday Mirror* in March 1987,

We are seeing an identity crisis on a grand scale. A toreador outfit for the theatre... a short, tight skirt on an official visit that added five pounds to her knees... (an) unfortunate choice of a figure hugging velvet dress set off by hair that wouldn't have disgraced the average mop...

Letters to *The Daily Express* in the same month wondered 'how Fergie can spend so much on designers and advisers but still look a mess', and equally pertinent, 'Doesn't she realise that she has a more serious role in life – not that of a fashion model?' In May *Woman's Own* called her the 'Dream Duchess' and professed to like everything about her except her clothes,

...whatever she wears publicly never seems quite right. Put her in a simple pair of slacks, woolly jumper and wellies and she looks terrific. But whether in a ballgown or skirt, somehow it never quite works.

The clothes she chose were often awkward and vulgar; a discredit to the designers who sold them to her. If she had been guided tactfully, into a splendidly flattering wedding dress, it was obvious that, properly advised, she was capable of looking stylish on other occasions. The frills, patterns and decoration favoured by the Queen Mother when she was Duchess of York in the 1920s and 1930s, seemed, temporarily, to mesmerize her successor. Fortunately, the new Duchess of York also had the good sense to lose some weight and patronize an established couturier to provide her with a clearly identifiable fashion image.

Her choice was Yves St Laurent, a designer who has always had a reputation for innovative clothes, but has relied upon impeccable cut, colour and discreet patterns to create a flattering modern classicism. The selection of a French designer was controversial, but clever, because the Princess of Wales could never dress at St Laurent and, more importantly, because St Laurent's international reputation is built upon his ability to enhance the appearance of women of all shapes, sizes and ages. There is a long tradition of British royalty buying French clothes, and it would be absurdly chauvinistic for anyone to suggest that this should not continue. Much will depend upon the Duchess's willingness to be highly disciplined about her wardrobe. Like many young British women of her social class she has little inherent dress sense, and without fearless professional advice she is likely to continue to make mistakes about her appearance. This ought not to matter – no-one is remotely interested in her husband's clothes, simply because they are so unexceptionally traditional. However, if the cherished belief that royalty are life-long ambassadors for British prestige is to be maintained, it is essential that they adopt a professional attitude towards their public life–in behaviour, conversation and dress. The fairy story Cinderella was notable for her hard work, sweet nature and discretion; it is a lesson which aspiring Princesses might usefully ponder.

EPILOGUE

'The King is dead. Long live the King.'

At the beginning of this book I suggested that examining the clothing of royalty was not inherently frivolous because the dress of monarchs and their families has, since mediaeval times, been perceived as one of the most telling of visual symbols of power and authority. By emphasising certain elements – the royal fascination with uniforms or specific forms of dress (for chivalric orders, coronations and formal court functions), the need to patronize British goods, and the requirement that those who attended court should behave and dress in a regulated manner – the minute analysis of individual appearance has been subsumed into a wide-ranging investigation of dress as a species of social cement, a statement of historical continuity in which royalty, by example, and their courtiers, by regulation, could play a significant role.

In attempting to draw together these and other important strands, most notably those concerned with the depiction of royalty, and the quasi-theatrical relationship between royalty and their courtiers, it became apparent that changed circumstances, selective modernization and increased public attention have increased the confusion over what might be considered appropriate dress for royalty and their reduced circle. The socially fluid society of the late twentieth century finds the idea of courts, courtiers and formal etiquette increasingly absurd but neither wants nor can formulate an alternative to royalty. It is a source of considerable national pride that Britain excels at antiquated rituals – the state opening of Parliament, the Garter ceremony, the trooping of the colour, thanksgiving services, state funerals and royal weddings. This glittering Ruritanian idyll, which is such a blessing to the tourist industry, and so eminently photogenic, focuses attention on the appearance of royalty to an almost unnatural degree. It is, inevitably, easier to assess the concerns and attitudes of previous generations than those of the present, and by suggesting that there is a growing confusion over role and appearance, I have, consciously, reflected contemporary comment on royal dress which has emphasised the tension between conservative traditionalism and experimental high fashion.

Royal men, with the notable exception of Edward VIII, have managed to camouflage themselves as soldiers, sailors, sportsmen, and classically dressed English gentlemen. Their eccentricities of dress are historically sound, although not without their anachronistic features – the Highland Scottish dress made popular by George IV and The Prince Consort; the modern evening dress version of George III's Windsor uniform; and the bemedalled glamour of unearned high military rank, with its elegantly tailored full dress uniforms. In this century uniform has been worn to signify the formality of an event. The only twentieth-century ceremonial innovation – the installation of the Prince of Wales (Edward VIII and Prince Charles) in the principality – has, on both occasions, resembled a theatrical set-piece, in which the leading participant has been forced into singularly unflattering items of dress. Edward VIII's costume was akin to that of a pantomime princeling, and Prince Charles's gold circlet or tiara was a piece of insensitive modern jewellery design which suggested a ruler in a science fiction film. This uncertainty about how to modernize royal ceremonial dress has been demonstrated, graphically, in the 1980s with the decision of the Queen to abandon riding side-saddle and in uniform to the trooping of the colour parade on her official birthday in June. The sudden transition from the unique elegance of a female monarch in a feminine version of historical uniform reviewing her troops from, quite literally, on high, to the curiosity of a small woman in early old age dressed in a pastel coat and hat, sitting comfortably but somewhat inappropriately in a glorified pony trap, was a telling sign of the lack of thought that is given to image and ritual by contemporary royalty. There is an unsubstantiated, but not improbable, story about the present Queen and her female Prime Minister appearing at a function in identical dresses. This prompted the latter's office to ring the palace to suggest that, in future, they might confer over choice of dress, in order to prevent future embarrassment; this idea met with the response that the Queen does not notice what others wear. This is patently untrue: she has inherited the Hanoverian ability to spot incorrect details of uniform, ribbons and medals. However, the notion that it is impolite, frivolous or not important to care about the dress of others is a curiously short-sighted, and historically unsound response in an era in which the dress of royalty has become divorced from the serious business of government – an example of state prosperity and grandeur – and has become an issue in its own right.

To a certain extent this development was inevitable, given the increased isolation of royalty from any distinct group within society. A court may seem a very old-fashioned institution, but so is monarchy, and whilst the monarch and his or her family continue to rely, quite explicitly, upon the old structure of dignified rituals, privilege and exclusivity, but without the support or camouflage of an identifiable court, they will be the focus of concentrated attention. Public figures can choose one of two paths in regard to dress and personal image: they can be discreet or they can be flamboyant. The former is safe but reassuring. Royalty, by the nature of its oddly fragmented life – wearing the traditional 'fancy dress' of formal state occasions, the 'Sunday best' of its day-time public appearances, and the casual clothes of private life – is caught in the trap of occupational flamboyance. It is a role it shared, early in the century, with a great many other European royal families, and a proportion of the ruling classes. Today this role is shared only by the theatrical profession, in its many branches, consequently, the reviews of new productions, royal or theatrical, invariably discuss dress and appearance.

Earlier innovators of those forms of dress which have survived, virtually unchanged, to the present day, were cultivating a specific image of superior dignity (Garter dress) or relaxed elegance (Windsor uniform) in keeping with the age in which they lived. These styles were a natural extension of royal interest in antiquarianism, portraiture and the potency of visual grandeur or uniqueness; they also reflected a natural desire to compete with developments at foreign courts. Modernity or the pursuit of fashion for its own sake, was eschewed in favour of dignified personal style. George IV and Edward VIII provide examples of how it was possible to care too much about fashion, and not to be taken seriously; conversely both Queen Mary and Queen Elizabeth, the Queen Mother illustrate the success of elegant but stylized conservatism in dress. If this was a moral fable rather than a book on dress, the conclusion would speak for itself – fashion equals frivolity, invites criticism and devalues the magic; stylized grandeur equals dignity, invites respect and promotes historical continuity. That is, of course, too simple an explanation, and the impossibility of drawing together all the disparate strands of this book into a tidy conclusion is not an admission of defeat, it is an affirmation of the quotation given at the beginning of this book. Proust's view is triumphantly upheld as the raison d'etre of royalty – the king is dead, long live the king – whether they are royally born and cognisant of history, or experimental parvenus who sense, if they were not born to it, that they are, for the immediate future, and beyond, splendidly isolated in their idiosyncratic follies of dress and appearance from 'the depths beneath them'.

FOOTNOTES

Prologue

1 N Machiavelli, *The Prince*, Everyman Edition 1958, 127–28.

Chapter 1

1 *Calendar of State Papers Venetian*, III, 659, quoted in F A Mumby, *Elizabeth and Mary Stuart*, London 1914, 180–81.

2 Quoted in H Norris, *Costume and Fashion*, III, *The Tudors, Book II 1547–1603*, J M Dent & Sons Ltd, 1938, 599.

3 A Strickland, *Queen Elizabeth*, London 1870, 309.

4 In the 1590s the Privy Council ordered all portraits which offended the Queen should be found and destroyed. R Strong, *Artists of the Tudor Court, The Portrait Miniature Rediscovered, 1520–1620*, Victoria & Albert Museum 1983, 125.

5 Quoted in N Williams, *All the Queen's Men*, Weidenfeld & Nicolson 1972, 19.

6 Thomas Nashe quoted in Williams, op.cit., 19; John Lyly quoted in C Camden, *The Elizabethan Woman*, London 1952, 235.

7 Quoted in E Jenkins, *Elizabeth and Leicester*, Victor Gollancz Ltd 1961, 241.

8 Quoted in Norris, op.cit., 614.

9 Ibid., 599; quoted in Williams, op.cit., 258.

10 Norris, op.cit., 608–9, 611–12.

11 J Nevinson, *New Year's Gifts to Queen Elizabeth I 1584*, Costume No 9, 1975, 28.

12 J Arnold, *Lost from Her Majesties Back*, Costume Society 1980, 79–80.

13 Quoted in Norris, op.cit., 611.

14 Quoted in R Ashton, *James I by his Contemporaries*, Hutchinson 1969, 12–13.

15 Quoted in E Carleton Williams, *Anne of Denmark*, London 1970, 39.

16 Ashton, op.cit., 13.

17 Quoted in J T Cliffe, *The Puritan Gentry*, Routledge & Kegan Paul 1984, 151; ibid., 54 – the complete quotation summarizes the contemporary confusion over status, dress and piety,

> *Wantonesse in things belonging to the bodie is shewed in costly apparell. Not but there is a diversitie of degrees to be regarded, and everyone may be apparelled as is meete and seemely for their estate; but in no estate or degree may one be so excessive as to forget holinesse and Christian sobrietie.*

18 Ashton, op.cit., 234–35.

19 Quoted in R Strong, *Henry Prince of Wales and England's Lost Renaissance*, Thames & Hudson 1986, 12–13; this important study has illuminated many aspects of royal portraiture and connoisseurship in the early seventeenth century.

20 Quoted in Carleton Williams, op.cit., 114.

21 Ashton, op.cit., 235.

22 N E McClure (Ed.), *The Letters of John Chamberlain*, American Philosophical Society 1939, II, 224, 219.

23 Quoted in Williams, op.cit., 91.

24 Quoted in A F Scott (Ed.), *Every One A Witness*, The Stuart Age, White Lion Publishers 1974, 7.

25 McClure, op.cit., 609.

26. Quoted in P Gregg, *King Charles I*, J M Dent 1981, 246; quoted in C Carlton, *Charles I*, Routledge & Kegan Paul 1983, 130; in January 1623 Chamberlain had noted:

> *some new orders that no man shall come booted*

and spurd into the presence or privie chamber on holy dayes or festivalls, nor likewise into the chappell, where all men must continue uncovered during divine service.

27 Quoted in Gregg, op.cit., 246.

28 Q Bone, *Henrietta Maria, Queen of the Cavaliers*, Peter Owen 1973, pp 31–33.

29 R Strong, *Charles I's Clothes for the Years 1633 to 1635*, Costume vol 19, 1985, 73–89; the relative discretion of Charles' expenditure can be judged against the £4500 spent on his brother's wardrobe over a quarter of a century earlier, in 1608.

30 E Ashmole quoted in A Mansfield, *Ceremonial Costume*, Adam & Charles Black 1980, 58.

31 Quoted in O Millar, *Van Dyck in England*, National Portrait Gallery 1982, 27; Millar's catalogues for Van Dyck and The Age of Charles I, Tate Gallery 1972, have provided much of the information for this brief interpretation of Charles's visual tastes.

32 Inevitably the souvenirs, like fragments of the True Cross, proliferated. The Museum of London has several pairs of gloves which were, supposedly, worn by Charles I on the day of his execution; only one pair has a plausible provenance.

Chapter 2

1. W Bray (Ed.), *Diary of John Evelyn*, London 1879, II, 112.

2 G Scott Thomson, *Life in a Noble Household 1641–1700*, Cape 1937, 83–84.

3 J Welwood quoted in *English Historical Documents 1660–1714*, Eyre and Spottiswoode, 1953, 899.

4 A Fraser, *King Charles II*, Weidenfeld & Nicolson, 1979, 184, 195.

5 Latham & Matthews (Ed.), Pepys Diary, G Bell & Sons Ltd, VIII, 418.

6 D de Marly, Fashionable Suppliers 1660–1700, *The Antiquaries Journal*, LVIII, part II, 1978.

7 Fraser, op.cit., 195–96.

8 Pepys Diary, IV, 400.

9 Ibid., 386–88.

10 An instance of the triumph of etiquette over adversity is demonstrated in Louis XIV's behaviour to James II's Queen, Mary of Modena. After fleeing to France with few personal possessions, early in 1689 Mary prepared to meet the French king. He was informed that she had only the simplest of black silk dresses, so a carriage was sent to her packed with court dress appropriate to her rank so that she might be correctly dressed for their meeting. Cited in C Oman, *Mary of Modena*, Hodder & Stoughton, 1962, 139.

11 Fraser, op.cit., 269; B Bevan, *Charles II's French Mistress*, Robert Hale, 1972, 48.

12 E Ashmole, *The Institution, Laws and Ceremonies of the Most Noble Order of the Garter*, 1672, quoted in A Mansfield, *Ceremonial Dress*, A & C Black, 1980, 59.

13 S Stevenson and D Thomson, *John Michael Wright, The King's Painter*, SNPG, 1982, 80–81; a discussion of the difficulties in dating this portrait does not take into account the style of wig, which reinforces their opinion that this is a portrait of c.1676, not one of the 1660s.

14 Evelyn, op.cit., 304, 437.

15 Pepys, VI, 281; VII 315, 324, 328.

16 Evelyn op.cit., 210–11.

17 Pepys, VII, 372.

18 Evelyn, op.cit., 215.

19 Bevan, op.cit., 87.

20 Fraser, op.cit., 339.

21 Evelyn, op.cit., 256, 259.

22 Pepys, IX, 557. Dining in public, a royal ceremony of considerable antiquity, had been reintroduced by Charles II in August 1667 according to Evelyn; Pepys had observed the ceremony in September 1667. It was not approved of by all European royalties–Peter the Great, Czar of Russia, visited William III at Kensington Palace, but left the King's table complaining 'twas strange he could not eat without being stared at'. Quoted in H and B van der Zee, *William and Mary*, Macmillan, 1973, 435.

23 Fraser, op.cit., 207; Evelyn, op.cit., 145.

24 Evelyn, op.cit., 229.

25 Pepys, IX, 557.

26 Bevan, op.cit., 48, Evelyn, op.cit., 209; Pepys VII, 162.

27 Bevan, op.cit., 36–37.

28 Evelyn, op.cit., 232, 304, 436–37.

29 Van der Zee, op.cit., 53.

20 S B Baxter, *William II*, Longmans, 1966, 44–45, 48.

31 J S Clarke, *Life of James II*, London 1816, I, 388.

32 Baxter, op.cit., 299.

33 Quoted in E Sheppard, *Memorials of St James's Palace*, London 1894, I, 75.

34 M Ashley, *James II*, J M Dent & Sons Ltd, 1977, 130.

35 Oman, op.cit., 242.

36 Van der Zee, op.cit., 143; Baxter, op.cit., 131.

37 Baxter, op.cit., 131, 171.

38 Van der Zee, op.cit., 158.

39 Van der Zee, op.cit., 265. Princess Anne, William III's sister-in-law, dressed in orange, as did her ladies, to indicate their loyalties. Cited in E Gregg, *Queen Anne*, Routledge & Kegan Paul, 1980, 68.

40 Ibid., 27.

41 E Hamilton, *William's Mary*, Hamish Hamilton 1972, 208.

42 Ibid., 211–12. The English belief that appearance and expenditure must accord with rank was affronted by Bentinck, William's most influential Dutch courtier at this date. He was so frugal in both habits and dress that the Spanish envoy thought he must be a servant. Cited in Van der Zee, op.cit., 287.

43 A Strickland, *Lives of the Queens of England*, London 1852, VII, 198.

44 Van der Zee, op.cit., 349, 380; Hamilton, op.cit., 283–88, 323.

45 Van der Zee, op.cit., 411, 433, 442.

46 Ibid., 466–67, 478, 483. In November 1702, however, conscious of the English admiration for William's military achievements, Anne was 'Habited in Purple Cloth, as being in Mourning for the late King William the third of glorious Memory' for a victory service at St Paul's Cathedral. Cited in Sheppard, op.cit., p 233.

47 Gregg, op.cit., 152.

48 Sarah, Duchess of Marlborough, *Private Correspondence II*, 119–25, quoted in *English Historical Documents* 1660–1714, 907–8.

49 J Swift, *The Journal to Stella*, H Williams

(ed.), OUP, 1948, 328, 522.

50 Quoted in Sheppard, op.cit., 81.

51 Swift, op.cit., 456–57.

52 Gregg, op.cit., 354; quoted in Sheppard, op.cit., 81–82.

53 Gregg, op.cit., 154; Sheppard, op.cit., 235.

54 Gregg, op.cit., 231; quoted in J M Beattie, *The English Court in the Reign of George I*, CUP, 1967, 208; Gregg, op.cit., 351.

55 H Paget Toynbee (Ed.), *The Letters of Horace Walpole*, London, 1903. IV, 409.

56 Gregg, op.cit., 337.

57 A Boyer quoted in *English Historical Documents*, op. cit., 937.

58 Beattie, op.cit., 106–9, 18–19, 50–51, 158, 207, 56. This important study provides a major examination of court organization and protocol, and mentions some details of late Stuart practice as well as that of the early Hanoverian period.

59 Ibid, 220, 57, 54–55, 64; R Hatton, *George I, Elector and King*, Thames & Hudson, 1978, 142–43.

60 Lord Hervey, quoted in Beattie, op.cit., 262; ibid., 137.

61 J C Risk, *The History of The Order of the Bath*, Spink, 1972, 10ff.

62 Walpole, quoted in Sheppard, op.cit., 87.

63 Beattie, op.cit., 13, 262–63, 264ff.

64 Ibid., 265ff.

65 D Defoe, *A Tour through Great Britain*, London, 1727, I, 357; Beattie, op.cit., 12–13.

66 Quoted in Beattie, op.cit., 162.

67 W Matthews (Ed.), *The Diary of Dudley Ryder 1715–16*, London 1939, 56, 62, 66, 76–77, 221, 356.

68 M van Muyden (Ed.), C de Saussure, *A Foreign View of England in the Reigns of George I and George II*, London, 1902, 112–13.

69 Sarah Osborn, quoted in Beattie, op.cit., 207.

70 Quoted in Beattie, op.cit., 206.

71 Lady Llanover (Ed.), *Autobiography and Correspondence of Mary Granville, Mrs Delany*, London, 1861–2, I, 99, 191.

72 *Memoirs... of Sir Robert Walpole*, 1798, quoted in Sheppard, op.cit., 95.

73 Delany, op.cit., I, 175, 178–179.

74 Quoted in R L Arkell, *Caroline of Ansbach*, OUP, 1939, 149, 241–44.

75 J H Plumb and H Weldon, *Royal Heritage*, Book Club Associates, 1980, 157.

76 Quoted in G Scott Thomson, *The Russells in Bloomsbury*, Jonathan Cape 1940, 272.

77 Delany, op.cit., I, 193, 437.

78 *The Gentleman's Magazine*, VI, April 1736, 231.

79 Arkell, op.cit., 296; Sheppard, op.cit., 223.

80. Sheppard, op.cit., 187.

81 A Buck, *Dress in Eighteenth Century England*, Batsford, 1979, 15, 89; Arkell, op.cit., 238–39; Buck, op.cit., 33.

82 Beattie, op.cit., 207.

83 N Rothstein, '*God Bless This Choye*', Costume 11, 1977, 69; Arkell, op.cit., 238.

84 Delany, op.cit., I, 138, 436.

85 *Magazine a la Mode*, 1777, 4.

86 De Saussure, op.cit.

87 Walpole Letters, op.cit., I, 303–4.

88 M Hodgart (Ed.), *Horace Walpole, Memoirs and Portraits*, Batsford 1963, 9.

89 Arkell, op.cit., 270.

90 Walpole Letters, op.cit., II, 200; I, 183, 181.

91 Delany, op.cit., II, 28.

92 Walpole Letters, II, 371.

93 Ibid., 249, 307.

94 Ibid., III, 38.

95 Ibid., 244–45, 101, 88; IV, 58, 163.

96 Ibid., IV, 436, 230, 317, 393.

Chapter 3

1 Walpole Letters, op.cit., V, 23.

2 C Williams, (Ed.), *Sophie in London 1786*, Jonathan Cape, 1933, 200.

3 George III's Letters, quoted in J Brooke, *George III*, Constable, 1972, 287.

4 Quoted in Brooke, op.cit., 278.

5 *The Lady's Magazine*, 1788.

6 Lord Glenbervie, quoted in N Waugh, *The Cut of Men's Clothes 1600–1900*, Faber, 1964, 110.

7 *The Annual Register*, 1795.

8 Sheppard, op.cit., 256.

9 Brooke, op.cit., 288; R S Walker (Ed.), *James Beattie's London Diary 1773*, Aberdeen, The University Press, 1946, 62, 75.

10 Walpole Letters, op.cit., XV, 35.

11 Brooke, op.cit., 113.

12 Sheppard, op.cit., 256.

13 A Adburgham, *Shopping In Style*, Thames and Hudson, 1979, 82.

14 Brooke, op.cit., 286; O F Morshead, *The Windsor Uniform*, Connoisseur, April 1935.

15 Brooke, op.cit., 294.

16 Ibid., 313.

17 Ibid., 295.

18 F A Pottle (Ed.), *Boswell's London Journal 1762–63*, Futura 1982, 144.

19 Beattie's Diary, op.cit., 53–54, 58, 62, 56–57, 65–66.

20 Walpole Letters, op.cit., V, 73.

21 Ibid., 81, 105.

22 Brooke, op.cit., 82–83.

23 Walpole Letters, op.cit., V, 107.

24 Ibid., 106.

25 Walpole Memoirs, op.cit., 119.

26 *The Lady's Magazine*, 1792.

27 Sheppard, op.cit., 246.

28 Walpole Letters, op.cit., V, 185.

29 *Magazine à la Mode*, 1777, 4.

30 Quoted in N Waugh, *The Cut of Women's Clothes 1600–1930*, Faber, 1968, 123.

31 Quoted in Buck, op.cit., 183–84.

32 Earl of Bessborough (Ed.), *Extracts from the Correspondence of Georgiana, Duchess of Devonshire*, John Murray, 1955, 46, 213.

33 Quoted in R Bayne-Powell, *Eighteenth Century London*, John Murray 1937, 60, 182.

34 Quoted in Brooke, op.cit., 216.

35 Quoted in Sheppard, op.cit., 96–97.

36 W van Lennep (Ed.), S Siddons, *Reminiscences 1773–1785*, Cambridge, Mass., 1942, 21.

37 Quoted in J Rees, *Jane Austen, Woman and Writer*, Robert Hale & Co. Ltd, 1976, 127.

38 Quoted in Brooke, op.cit., 301.

39 A Aspinall (Ed.), *Correspondence of George, Prince of Wales 1770–1812*, Cassell, 1963, I, 35.

40 Quoted in Mansfield, op.cit., 111.

41 Quoted in Bayne-Powell, op.cit., 182.

42 PRO, LC5/LC6.

43 L Simond, *Journal of a Tour and Residence in Great Britain*, Edinburgh 1817, I, 208.

44 R Rush, *Narrative of a Residence at the Court of London*, London 1833, 104.

45 Brook, op.cit., 264; C Hibbert, *George IV 1762–1811*, Longman, 1972, 2.

46 Brooke, op.cit., 264, 265.

47 Sheppard, op.cit., 223–24.

48 Quoted in Hibbert, 20–21.

49 Georgiana, Dss of Devonshire, op.cit., 289.

50 Quoted in Hibbert, op.cit., 36; Georgiana, Dss of Devonshire, op.cit., 57.

51 *The Lady's Magazine,* 1788; quoted in Hibbert, op.cit., 112.

52 A Aspinall (Ed.), *The Letters of Princess Charlotte 1811–1817,* Home & Van Thal, 1949, 10, 242.

53 *The Annual Register,* 1817, 100.

54 *Diary of Mrs Arbuthnot,* quoted in O Morshead, Court Dress Collection Archive, (typescript notes), Kensington Palace.

55 Hibbert, op.cit., 124–25.

56 Ibid, 140, 144–45.

57 Georgiana, Dss of Devonshire, op.cit., 216.

58 Quoted in Hibbert, op.cit., 225, 218.

59 Hibbert, op.cit., 127, 174–77, 144; II, 278, I, 242.

60 Aspinall, op.cit., 23–24.

61 Quoted in Hibbert, op.cit., II, 48.

62 Aspinall, op.cit., 108–9; 2–3, 19, 153, 231, 253.

63 Hibbert, op.cit., 190–91; 233.

64 Hibbert, 191–92; Z Halls, *Coronation Costume and Accessories 1685–1953;* HMSO, 1973, 12–13, 47–48.

65 Hibbert, op.cit., 249, 252.

66 Hibbert, op.cit.

67 E M Butler (Ed.), *A Regency Visitor, The Letters of Prince Pückler-Muskau,* Collins 1957, 18–19.

68 Georgiana, Dss of Devonshire, op.cit., 167, 169.

69 PRO LC5/8. Correspondence Book of R Chester 1812–1833.

70 Pückler-Muskau, op.cit., 308.

71 *The London Gazette,* 1820.

72 Pückler-Muskau, op.cit., 321.

73 A Fairfax-Lucy (Ed), *Mistress of Charlecote, The Memoirs of Mary Elizabeth Lucy,* Victor Gollancz, 1985, 37–39.

74 Hibbert, op.cit., 343; Pückler-Muskau, op.cit., 334.

75 The auction was conducted by Mr Phillips at the Bond Street sale rooms on 15, 16 and 17 December 1830; items described are taken from the catalogue of the second and third days (MOL 38.294/1).

76 Quoted in A Adburgham, *Silver Fork Society 1814–1840,* Constable 1983, p 155.

77 Pückler-Muskau, op.cit., 338–39.

78 *Mrs Gore's Women As They Are,* 1830, quoted in Adburgham, op.cit., 156.

79 Sheppard, op.cit., 104.

80 Ibid., 227.

81. *The London Gazette,* May 1834.

82 Pückler-Muskau, op.cit., 341.

83 Anon, *Hints on Etiquette,* 1834, Turnstile Press Ltd, 1947, 31.

84 J Gore (Ed.), *Creevey's Life and Times,* John Murray, 1934, 340–41.

85 PRO LC6/2; *The Court & Country Companion,* London, 1835, 138.

Chapter 4

1 R Fulford (Ed.), *Dearest Child, Letters between Queen Victoria and the Princess Royal 1858–61,* Evans Brothers Ltd, 1964, 50.

2 Quoted in C Woodham-Smith, *Queen Victoria,* Hamish Hamilton, 1972, 107.

3 M Ginsburg, *The Young Queen and Her Clothes,* Costume Society Spring Conference 1969, 43.

4 Woodham-Smith, op.cit., 102, 104, 107, 114, 130, 148, 149; E Longford, *Victoria RI,* Pan, 1964, 63.

5 Longford, op.cit. 94–95, 107–8, 111, 115; Woodham-Smith, op.cit., 150, 186.

6 Woodham-Smith, op.cit., 187, 189, 194, 345; D Bennett, *King Without a Crown,* Heinemann, 1977, 32; L Strachey, *Queen Victoria,* Chatto and Windus, 1931, 98.

7 Woodham-Smith, op.cit., 332–33, 395.

8 Strachey, op.cit., 40.

9 Longford, op.cit., 313, 320.

10 Ginsburg, op.cit., 44.

11 Woodham-Smith, op.cit., 296–97.

12 Ibid., 349.

13 Longford, op.cit., 182; Bennett, op.cit., 281; Ginsburg, op.cit., 42–43.

14 Fairfax-Lucy, op.cit., 77–78.

15 S Menkes, *The Royal Jewels,* Grafton Books, 1985, 1–25.

16 Ginsburg, op.cit., 44.

17 Woodham-Smith, op.cit., 249.

18 R Crossman (Ed.), W Bagehot, *The English Constitution,* The Fontana Library, 1966, 85–86, 92, 94–95.

19 Anon, *The Habits of Good Society,* London, 1859, 375.

20 E Ransome, (Ed.), *The Terrific Kemble*, Hamish Hamilton, 1978, 168–70.

21 Sheppard, op.cit., 228.

22 Fairfax-Lucy, op.cit., 91–92.

23 Punch, 2 June 1855, 226.

24 PRO, LC3/6. *Levees & Drawing-Rooms 1858–1874.*

25 *The Ladies Cabinet*, December, 1838.

26 *Habits of Good Society*, 184–85.

27 Sheppard, op.cit., 228.

28 Fawcett, op.cit., 173.

29 Sheppard, op.cit., 228.

30 *Habits of Good Society*, 146.

31 Strachey, op.cit., 180.

32 Bennett, op.cit., 324–25.

33 Strachey, op.cit., 179.

34 Longford, op.cit., 386; B S-J Nevill, *Life at the Court of Queen Victoria*, Webb and Bower 1984, 42–43.

35 Strachey, op.cit., 199.

36 HH Princess Marie Louise, *My Memories of Six Reigns*, Evans Brothers Ltd, 1956, 140.

37 Anon, *The Private Life of the Queen*, 1897, reprinted Gresham Books 1979, 68–69; c.f. Strachey, op.cit., 254.

38 C Kinloch Cooke, *A Memoir of HRH Princess Mary Adelaide, Duchess of Teck*, London 1900, II, 107.

39 Nevill, op.cit., 39.

40 S A Tooley, *The Life of Queen Alexandra*, London, 1902, 3.

41 G Battiscombe, *Queen Alexandra*, Constable, 1969, 102, 44.

42 Tooley, op.cit., 23–24, 30, 33; Battiscombe, op.cit., 49.

43 Tooley, op.cit., 41; Sheppard, op.cit., 260.

44 Battiscombe, op.cit., 52.

45 Tooley, op.cit., 44–45.

46 Fairfax-Lucy, op.cit., 131.

47 Tooley, op.cit., 52, 62.

48 Battiscombe, op.cit., 101, 106.

49 J Pope-Hennessey, *Queen Mary*, George Allen & Unwin, 1959, 134; D de Marly, *Worth*, Batsford, 1980, 144, 137.

50 Tooley, op.cit., 111, 136.

51 Nevill, op.cit., 166, 173.

52 Tooley, op.cit., 160–61.

53 Battiscombe, op.cit., 54.

55 Strachey, op.cit., 235.

55 Longford, op.cit., 473.

56 L Davidoff, *The Best Circles*, Croom Helm, 1973, 61.

57 Lady Violet Greville, *The Gentlewoman in Society*, London, 1892, 112–14.

58 L H Armstrong, *Letters to a Bride*, London, 1896, 215–16. Lady Colin Campbell, *Etiquette of Good Society*, London, 1893, 204–5.

59 Nevill, op.cit., 45.

60 Kinloch Cooke, op.cit., 267–79.

61 Pope-Hennessey, op.cit., 134–35; S A Tooley, *The Royal Family by Pen and Camera*, London, 1907, 1.

62 Pope-Hennessey, op.cit., 169, 170.

63 Longford, op.cit., 643.

64 Pope–Hennessey, op.cit., 264–65, 271, 283, 287.

65 Battiscombe, op.cit., 199.

Chapter 5

1 Nevill, op.cit., 167.

2 Bagehot, op.cit., 100.

3 M V Brett (Ed.), *Journals and Letters of Reginald, Viscount Esher*, London, 1934, I, 274.

4 Ibid., I 296–97, 276, 305, 413, 331, 327; II, 65.

5 A Gernsheim, *Victorian and Edwardian Fashion*, Dover Publications, New York, 1981, 90.

6 Esher, op.cit., I, 318; II, 460.

7 HH Princess Marie Louise, op.cit., 173–74.

8 Esher, op.cit., I, 284, 309, 357–58.

9 Ibid., I, 298, 405.

10 Tooley, *The Royal Family . . .*, 77.

11 Halls, op. cit., 53–54.

12 D Bennett, *Margot*, Victor Gollancz 1984, 182, 191.

13 Esher, op.cit., II, 222.

14 Lady Cynthia Asquith, *Diaries 1915–18*, Hutchinson, 1968, 131.

15 I B McKellar, *The Edwardian Age*, Blackie and Son Ltd, 1980, 6–11.

16 Esher, op.cit., I, 305–7. Lord Esher's deeply ingrained snobbery received an altogether appropriate come-uppance when his son, the Hon. Maurice Brett, married the actress Zena Dare. Esher had the temerity to ask the King for advice on whether it would be necessary for a gentleman to resign from his regiment if he married an actress. Royalty thought it improbable if both parties were of good reputation; the marriage took place, and the regiment asked Brett to resign.

17 Sheppard, op.cit., 217.

18 Quoted in C Hibbert, *Edward VII*, Allen Lane, 1976, 206.

19 Quoted in M Pringle, *Dance Little Ladies*, Orbis, 1977, 15.

20 Quoted in H Vickers, *Cecil Beaton*, Weidenfeld & Nicolson, 1985, 52.

21 Asquith, op.cit., 21, 11.

22 Pope–Hennessey, op.cit., 415, 430–31.

23 J Flanner, *Queen Mary* in *Decade 1931–1941*, Hamish Hamilton, 1941, 191–92.

24 Pope–Hennessey, op.cit., 481.

25 F B Fawcett (Ed.), *Their Majesties' Courts*, Grayson and Grayson, 1932, 27, 71, 117, 161.

26 A Edwards, *Matriarch*, Hodder & Stoughton, 1984, 389.

27 Flanner, op.cit., 192–93.

28 N Hartnell, *Silver and Gold*, Evans Brothers Ltd, 1955, 92.

29 Vickers, op.cit., 183.

30 Esher, op.cit., III (1938), 15, 49, 37, 266.

31 Pringle, op.cit., 17.

32 Mrs Massey Lyon, *Etiquette*, Cassell & Co Ltd, 1927, 30–31.

33 E M Lang, *British Women in the Twentieth Century*, T Werner Laurie Ltd, 1929, 199.

34 Massey Lyon, op.cit., 21ff; Lady Troubridge, *The Book of Etiquette*, Associate Book Buyers Company, 1926, 139ff.

35 Quoted in Davidoff, op.cit., 37.

36 G Howell, *In Vogue*, Allen Lane, 1975, 42.

37 Quoted in J Montgomery, *The Twenties*, George Allen & Unwin Ltd, 1957, 237.

38 Flanner, op.cit., 189.

39 Montgomery, op.cit., 239–40.

40 Howell, op.cit., 103.

41 Lang, op.cit., 199.

42 P Mortimer, *Queen Elizabeth*, Penguin, 1987, 128.

43 J Pearson, *The Ultimate Family*, Michael Joseph, 1986, 76; Vickers op.cit., 193.

44 Howell, op.cit., 103.

45 Vickers, op.cit., 194.

46 Duchess of Windsor, *The Heart Has Its Reasons*, Michael Joseph, 1956, 216.

47 Howell, op.cit., 112, 137.

48 M Thornton, *Royal Feud*, Michael Joseph, 1985, 2, 41, 71

49 Vickers, op.cit., 196, 198.

50 Edwards, op.cit., 328; Thornton, op.cit., 141.

51 Hartnell, op.cit., 89–94.

52 Vickers, op.cit., 197.

53 Hartnell, op.cit., 95–98.

54 Thornton, op.cit., 181.

55 Mortimer, op.cit., 164.

56 Vickers, op.cit., 226.

57 Hartnell, op.cit., 101.

58 Vickers, op.cit., 268.

59 Hartnell, op.cit., 123–27.

60 Vickers, op.cit., 358.

Chapter 6

1 Vickers, op.cit., 582.

2 H Amies, *Still Here*, Weidenfeld & Nicolson, 1984, 153.

3 Quotations from *The Times*, March 1986; *Life*, November, 1986; *Woman*, September, 1985; *Good Housekeeping*, November, 1986.

4 Amies, op.cit., 153.

5 A Barr & P York, *The Official Sloane Ranger Handbook*, Ebury Press, 1982, 20–21.

6 Quoted in *Woman's Own*, November, 1985.

SELECT BIBLIOGRAPHY

This does not include all works referred to in the footnotes, but is a guide to some of the many publications which discuss aspects of royal and court life.

Anon. *The Royal Warrant Holders Who's Who*, London, 1921.

Mrs Armytage, *Old Court Customs and Modern Court Rule*, London, 1883.

S Beddoe and P Byrde, *Norman Hartnell*, Brighton & Bath Museums, 1985.

O Bland, *The Royal Way of Death*, Constable, 1986.

A Buck, *Dress in Eighteenth Century England*, B T Batsford Ltd, 1979.
Victorian Costume, Ruth Bean, 1984.

G Butazzi, *Fasti della Burocrazia*, Sagep Editrice, Genoa, 1984.

P Byrde, *The Male Image*, Batsford, 1979.

V Cumming, *The Trousseau of Princess Elizabeth Stuart*, Collectanea Londiniensis, Museum of London, 1978.
Royal Attributes, The Dress of Two Royal Cousins 1542–1587, The Royal Stuart Society, 1984.

L Davidoff, *The Best Circles*, Croom Helm, 1973.

R Dutton, *English Court Life*, B T Batsford Ltd, 1963.

D Edgar, *Palace*, W H Allen, 1983.

A Edwards, *The Queen's Clothes*, Express/Elm Tree Books, 1977.

E Ewing, *Women in Uniform*, B T Batsford Ltd, 1975.

C Fox and A Ribeiro, *Masquerade*, Museum of London, 1983.

C Fox, *Londoners*, Thames & Hudson, 1986.

R Gibson, *The Masque of Beauty*, National Portrait Gallery (undated).

M Ginsburg, *An Introduction to Fashion Illustration*, The Compton Press & Pitman Publishing Ltd, 1980.

C C Greville, *Journals of the Reigns of George IV, William IV and Queen Victoria*, London, 1885.

T Grove (Ed.), *The Queen Observed*, Pavilion/Michael Joseph, 1986.

C Hesketh, *Tartans*, Octopus, 1972.

C Hibbert, *The Court at Windsor*, Longmans, 1964.
Edward VII, Allen Lane, 1976.

T Hughes, *English Domestic Needlework*, Abbey Fine Arts, 1961.

J Kerslake, *Early Georgian Portraits in the National Portrait Gallery 1714–1760*, HMSO, 1978.

V Knight, *The Works of Art of the Corporation of London*, Woodhead-Faulkner, 1987.

R Lacey, *Majesty*, Hutchinson, 1977.

M Levey, *Painting at Court*, New York University Press, 1971. *A Royal Subject, Portraits of Queen Charlotte*, National Gallery, 1977.

Lady Lytton, *Court Diary 1895–1899*, Rupert Hart-Davis, 1961.

E Longford (Ed.), *Louisa Lady in Waiting*, Jonathan Cape, 1979.

J Maas, *'This Brilliant Year'*, Royal Academy, 1977.

C McDowell, *A Hundred Years of Royal Style*, Muller, Blond & White, 1985.

V Mallet (Ed.), *Life with Queen Victoria*, John Murray, 1968.

D de Marly, *Worth, Father of Haute Couture*, Elm Tree Books, 1980.

H Maxwell, *Sixty Years a Queen*, London, 1897.

S Menkes, *The Royal Jewels*, Grafton, 1985.

O Millar, *Pictures in the Royal Collection: Tudor, Stuart and Early Georgian*, Phaidon, 1963.
Sir Peter Lely, National Portrait Gallery, 1978.
The Queen's Pictures, Chancellor Press, 1977.

H Montgomery-Massingberd (Ed.), *Burke's Guide to the British Monarchy*, Burke's Peerage, 1977.

R Ormond, *Early Victorian Portraits*, HMSO, 1973.

D Piper, *Catalogue of Seventeenth Century Portraits in the National Portrait Gallery 1625–1714*, Cambridge University Press, 1963.

Pss Victoria of Prussia, *My Memoirs*, London, 1929.

P Pullar, *Gilded Butterflies*, Hamish Hamilton, 1978.

A Ribeiro, *Dress in Eighteenth Century Europe 1715–1789*, Batsford, 1984.
Dress and Morality, Batsford, 1986.

M Rogers, *The Queen Mother*, National Portrait Gallery, 1980.
William Dobson, National Portrait Gallery, 1983.
Elizabeth II, National Portrait Gallery, 1986.

K Rose, *Kings, Queens and Courtiers*, Weidenfeld & Nicolson, 1985.

R Strong, *Tudor and Jacobean Portraits*, HMSO, 1969.

S Stevenson and H Bennett, *Van Dyck in Check Trousers*, Scottish National Portrait Gallery, 1978.

S Stevenson and D Thomson, *John Michael Wright, The King's Painter*, Scottish National Portrait Gallery, 1982.

W J Thoms, *The Book of the Court*, London, 1838.

E S Turner, *The Court of St James's*, Michael Joseph, 1959.

R Walker, *Regency Portraits*, National Portrait Gallery, 1985.

D Watkin, *The Royal Interiors of Regency England*, J M Dent & Sons, 1984.

T H White, *The Age of Scandal*, Penguin, 1966.

K K Yung, *National Portrait Gallery Complete Illustrated Catalogue*, National Portrait Gallery, 1981.

The British Royal Family

Name	Title	Lifetime	Relationship	Succession
Henry VIII	King	1491–1547	Son of Henry VII	1509
Elizabeth I	Queen	1533–1603	Second daughter of Henry VIII	1558
James I of England and VI of Scotland	King	1566–1625	Son of Mary, Queen of Scots	1603
Princess Anne of Denmark	Queen Consort	1574–1619	Married James I 1589	
Charles I	King	1600–1649	Son of James I	1625
Princess Henrietta Maria of France	Queen Consort	1609–1669	Married Charles I 1625	
Charles II	King	1630–1685	Son of Charles I	1660
James II	King	1633–1701	Second son of Charles I	1685
Princess Mary of Modena	Queen Consort	1658–1718	Married James II 1660	
William III	King	1650–1702	Grandson of Charles I, son of Princess Mary Stuart and Prince Willem II of Orange Nassau; married to Mary II 1677	1688
Mary II	Queen	1662–1694	Daughter of James II; married to William III	1688
Anne	Queen	1665–1714	Daughter of James II	1702
George of Denmark		1653–1708	Married Anne 1683	
George I	King	1660–1727	Great-grandson of James I	1714
George II	King	1683–1760	Son of George I	1727
Caroline of Anspach	Queen Consort	1683–1737	Married George II 1705	
Frederick	Prince of Wales	1707–1751	Son of George II	
Augusta of Saxe-Gotha	Princess of Wales	1719–1772	Married Frederick 1736	
George III	King	1738–1820	Grandson of George II	1760
Princess Charlotte of Mecklenburg-Strelitz	Queen Consort	1744–1818	Married George III 1761	
George IV	Prince Regent, later King	1762–1830	Son of George III	1820
Caroline of Brunswick	Queen Consort	1768–1821	Married George IV 1795	
Princess Caroline of Wales		1796–1817	Daughter of George IV	
Prince Leopold of Saxe-Coburg Saalfeld	later King of the Belgians	1790–1865	Married to Caroline 1816	
William IV	King	1765–1837	Third son of George III	1830

Name	Title	Lifetime	Relationship	Succession
Victoria	Queen	1819–1901	Daughter of Edward, Duke of Kent, son of George III	1837
Prince Albert of Saxe-Coburg-Gotha	Prince Consort	1819–1861	Married Victoria 1840	
Edward VII	King	1841–1910	Son of Victoria	1901
Princess Alexandra of Denmark	Queen Consort	1844–1925	Married Edward VII 1863	
George V	King	1865–1936	Son of Edward VII	1910
Princess Mary (May) of Teck	Queen Consort	1867–1953	Married George V 1893	
Edward VIII	King, later Duke of Windsor	1894–1972	Son of George V (abdicated in December)	1936
Wallis Warfield, Mrs Ernest Simpson	Duchess of Windsor	1896–1986	Married Duke of Windsor 1937	
George VI	King	1895–1952	Second son of George V	1936
Lady Elizabeth Bowes Lyon	Queen Consort, later the Queen Mother	1900–	Married George VI 1923	
Elizabeth II	Queen	1926–	Daughter of George VI	1952
Prince Philip of Greece	Duke of Edinburgh	1921–	Married Elizabeth II 1947	
Charles	Prince of Wales	1948–	Son of Elizabeth II	
Lady Diana Spencer	Princess of Wales	1961–	Married Charles 1981	
Anne	Princess Royal	1950–	Daughter of Elizabeth II	
Captain Mark Philips		1948–	Married Anne 1973	
Andrew	Duke of York	1960–	Second son of Elizabeth II	
Sarah Ferguson	Duchess of York	1959–	Married Andrew 1986	
Edward	Prince	1964–	Third son of Elizabeth II	
Margaret	Princess	1930–	Second daughter of George VI	
Edward	Duke of Kent	1935–	Grandson of George V	
Katharine Worsley	Duchess of Kent	1933–	Married Edward 1961	
Alexandra	Princess of Kent	1936–	Granddaughter of George V	
Michael	Prince of Kent	1942–	Grandson of George V	
Baroness Marie Christine von Reibwitz	Princess Michael of Kent	1945–	Married Michael 1978	

INDEX

Note: Numbers in *italics* refer to pages on which illustrations appear.